PILGRIM
THEOLOGY

". . . when a thing obscure in itself defeats our capacity, and nothing else in Scripture comes to our help, it is not safe for humans to presume they can pronounce on it."

St. Augustine

"A Christian's business is not to talk grandly about dogmas, but to be always doing arduous and great things in fellowship with God."

Ulrich Zwingli

"Be attentive; be intelligent; be reasonable; be responsible."

Fr. Bernard Lonergan

PILGRIM THEOLOGY

TAKING THE PATH OF SPIRITUAL DISCOVERY

MICHAEL BAUMAN

Summit Ministries
Manitou Springs, Colorado

Request for information should be addressed to:
Summit Press
PO Box 207
Manitou Springs, CO 80829

Library of Congress Cataloging-in-Publication Data

Bauman, Michael.
    Pilgrim theology : taking the path of theological discovery /
Michael Bauman.
        p. cm.
    Includes bibliographical references.
    ISBN 0-936-16339-9
    1. Theology. 2. Hermeneutics. 3. Ethics. I. Title.

    2007928114   CIP

Edited by Leonard G. Goss, Tom Raabe, Vicki Lewis, and David Noebel
Cover design by Pamela Poll

Printed in the United States of America

For

ED SCHUPBACH
FAMILY, FRIEND AND FELLOW PILGRIM

Contents

Contents

ACKNOWLEDGMENTS

I am happy to acknowledge the kindness of Dr. Ronald Youngblood, editor of the *Journal of the Evangelical Theological Society*, for graciously allowing me to reprint here, in chapters four, eight, and eleven, modified versions of articles that appeared first in his pages. I am grateful as well to George Klein and William Sailer for permitting me to reprint in chapters three and twelve altered versions of articles published in the *Criswell Theological Review* and the *Evangelical Journal* respectively. I want to thank the editors of *Faculty Dialogue* for permission to reprint a slightly modified version of chapter 16. I am especially grateful to Angus MacDonald of the *St. Croix Review* for permission to reprint here modified versions of chapter nine and the epilogue, texts that appeared first in his excellent publication.

More times than I can remember, my ideas have been challenged, refined, or confirmed by Robert Umidi, Ferris McDaniel, Larry Dixon, and Edward Scherlacher, colleagues during my tenure at Northeastern Bible College, where much of this volume was conceived and written. Each of them is a compelling example that the best way to go through life is as a broad-minded evangelical.

M. B.

PREFACE TO THE SECOND EDITION

Nearly 15 years have past since this volume first appeared. In that time I have benefited from the help and advice of many fine friends and scholars, but none more so than from Michael Williams and John Reist in Theology, Francis Beckwith and J. P. Moreland in Philosophy and Ethics, Donald Williams in English Literature, Charles Van Eaton in Economics, Ed Schupbach in spiritual formation, Chuck Edwards in ministry, and Paul Henderson in Education. I am indebted to David Noebel in more ways than I can remember. Without his kindness and support this new edition would not be possible.

M. B.

INTRODUCTION

"Could you really persuade us if we did not listen?" he asked.
"There is no way," said Glaucon.

PLATO
The Republic

Christian theology is an activity for those *en route*, and it should be conducted so as to aid those who study it and practice it to travel more efficiently and effectively toward truth. Theology ought to be, in other words, both a statement of present belief and an explorer's compass for further intellectual navigation. "Ought," however, is not "is." Our beliefs often function as a barrier to learning, not a bridge. For many of us, I dare say, our theology works more like the burden on the back of Bunyan's pilgrim than it does a guide or stimulus. What ought to serve as an impetus to further theological discovery serves often as an impediment. That is because bad ideas have bad consequences. The bad consequence in view here results from our functional disability (or unwillingness) to distinguish our own theology from Scripture. Though we often advance them and cling to them as if they were, our beliefs are not the Bible; they are our (often) debatable extrapolations from it. Like it or not, our beliefs sometimes say as much about us as they do about Scripture. Our "ologies" and our "isms" represent and embody both the Bible *and* our present understanding of it. Insofar as they do the former, I offer no objection and no advice. Insofar as they do the latter — and they sometimes do it to a startling degree — I believe we must maintain them in something of a provisional status. They can be, and sometimes should be, questioned, even overturned. As Christian theologians, we are seekers after truth, not merely its custodians. Those who think of themselves primarily in the "guardian of truth" mode are not at all likely to recognize error in

11

their beliefs because their beliefs are no longer subjected to penetrating scrutiny, if ever they were. The beliefs of such theologians serve merely as the presuppositions from which those theologians dogmatize rather than the provisional answers to questions that may need to be carefully reevaluated. Sheltered from critical analysis, those ideas can, and do, block the path to wisdom and to the discovery of further theological truth. Sadly, this procedural neglect results in massive theological blindspots.

I say "sadly" because pedagogy imitates biology, and from biology we know that we reproduce after our own kind. Quite predictably, theological genetics virtually guarantees that when bad theologians plant the seed of bad theologizing, the harvest can only be more bad theologians. That situation would be sufficiently regrettable were it not made worse by the widespread practice of theological incest — the practice whereby graduates from Faithful Christian College go to Faithful Theological Seminary for graduate training so that they can come back to Faithful Christian College to teach students whom they then will advise to go for further study at Faithful Theological Seminary. And, if all this can happen without leaving campus (as it sometimes does), all the better.

Whether they know it or not, whether they believe it or not, students who enroll for their first semester at Faithful Christian College often are in great intellectual and spiritual danger. Unless something quite unforeseen and unpredictable occurs (and, thank God, it sometimes does), they will be indoctrinated, not educated, having mistaken entrenchment in theological bigotry for mental and spiritual readiness to serve a fallen world.

In an effort to short-circuit that unfortunate chain of events, and in an effort to teach theological students (and perhaps even their teachers) how to construct a theological method suitable for a life-long intellectual pilgrimage, I intend to explain and to exemplify the crucial difference between a Pilgrim Theology and a Fortress Theology.

Although these chapters are arranged in much the same way (and sequence) as chapters in a Systematic Theology, this book most assuredly is not a Systematic Theology. It is a Pilgrim Theology. I say that without apology. Systematic Theology, at least the defective way it too often is conducted, is the very thing I oppose. But one should not hastily assume that any theology that stands in opposition to the current state of Systematic Theology must itself be, for that very reason, unsystematic. If you read carefully enough, you will discover a linkage that unifies chapters that might, at first glance, seem unrelated. That unity is methodological and procedural. Therein lies my point. I aim to define and illustrate a common-sense procedure of theological integrity and to identify some of the conclusions to which it leads.

I intend this book to serve, along with books like Helmut Thielicke's *Little Exercise for Young Theologians*, as a preface or as a companion to the study of Christian doctrine. But, whereas a book like Thielicke's is designed to introduce young theologians to themselves and to the spiritual dangers that attach to the academic study of belief, this book is designed to help them learn how to theologize and (what is the same thing) how to recognize nonsense in all its forms and how to oppose it. I consider this attempt successful only insofar as it opens the door to truth, to beauty, and to goodness. These three are, as it were, the vestibule, or the portals, to the Divine Precincts. He who finds them finds More.

Not all theologians find them.

The risk in such failure is both real and great.

Though I am not sure that the erosion of theological certainty itself actually precipitated the unfortunate and premature demise of Christian thinkers like E. J. Carnell or H. P. Van Dusen, I am sure it can. Ambiguity is no friend to confidence and to certitude, states of mind without which some people — theologians included — can be undone. Ambiguity and confusion engender despair, and despair is a potent and formidable threat. That is the danger of studying doctrine: to some (though not perhaps to the two good men named above), the particular brand of systematic theology to which they subscribe becomes their very lifeline, a rope without which they might be set adrift and drown.

For that reason, because this small book is a vigorously articulated challenge to what I recognize as the prevailing fortress mentality in evangelical theological studies, to some it might seem unsafe. It might also seem unduly aggressive. I believe it is neither. This book does not attack confidence and certitude; it simply insists that they must not be misplaced. It argues that certitude (how sure we feel about something) should not outstrip certainty (how sure or secure the thing it-self is in which we trust). In other words, this book insists that we should not put more confidence in any system of thoughts than it can readily sustain.

In that light, I have made this book a summons to theological dynamism, not theological settlement. Some of the things we cling to so tenaciously are not theological lifelines; they are just soggy ropes floating on the flood. Those who cling to them might drown, if they are not drowning already. And, as any lifeguard knows, a drowning man must sometimes be subdued. That is why some ideas (and, indirectly, those who hold them) might seem too roughly handled in these pages. But, I plead compassion and concern for my fellow theological travellers as my defense. *Not* to have worked energetically, even aggressively, would have been unsafe: better a bruise than lungs full of water. Or, to alter the image for a moment, if the house is burn-ing or the ship is sinking, you do not whisper "Fire" or "Mayday;" you shout them.

That I have employed plain language and pointed arguments in this book will be obvious. What I have left out of it will not. Subduing the violent throes of a drowning man is not the same as a bare-knuck-led, two-fisted assault. With one exception, I deliberately have soft-ened every criticism I make about any theologian by refusing to name names, even though to have done otherwise would have been easy. My intention throughout has been to expose errors and dangers, not colleagues, churches, or schools.

Because the rising tide of confusion swirling around us makes the temptation to seize every apparent lifeline a strong one, and be-cause that temptation arises not only very often but very early in the theological enterprise, I have written this book so as to forestall young theologians grasping at things not securely tied to the shore of reality. I well remember how the world appeared to me, as perhaps it does to all the theologically uninitiated: black or white, yes or no, up or down, good or bad, true or false. I also believed that these polarities could be easily and quickly ascertained. Sometimes they can; but not always, and perhaps not often.

Young students of doctrine also need to know that some of the best theological lifelines no longer appear clean or inviting. Quite the contrary; the best theological lifelines are sometimes heavily befouled, not because they are faulty and unsafe, but because they are secure and because large numbers of those who lived before us and who found themselves awash in a whirling torrent of uncertainty, buffeted against the rocks of error and spinning and bobbing in the eddies of theological controversy and confusion, have seized those ropes and clung to them with all the strength their muddy hands could muster. Occasionally our ancestors left those ropes behind them in as good a condition as when they found them. Usually, however, they did not. Human fallenness almost always leaves its mark. Even theology itself (to borrow a line from Gerard Manley Hopkins) wears man's smudge and shares man's smell. In that sense, the smudges and smells of tradition and experience can serve as a guide and an endorsement. They sometimes indicate well tested ways of keeping your head above water. They also expose the erroneous assumption that what looks clean and inviting must be good and that what looks soiled and tattered must not.

But some lifelines, very good ones I am convinced, have rarely been tried. Still others, overused and severely weakened, are ready to break. To examples of each I intend to point.

Such lessons are important and ought to be learned early. That is why I have kept the budding scholar in view throughout. This book is written for those about to embark on a journey of theological discovery. If some of what I have said proves to be of value to the seasoned theological traveller as well, all the better. The Church rarely prospers more than when its teachers are teachable.

That, at any rate, is the burden and purpose of this book — the benefit of the Church through the wise nurture of its theologians, young and old. Accordingly, while these essays are aggressive, they endorse informed tolerance, whenever they can. Or, to put the case differently, this book is an advertisement on behalf of the marketplace of theological ideas. In that marketplace, ideas are subjected to intense scrutiny and sometimes to withering critique. In that process, some notions prove their worth, others are roundly defeated. For still other ideas the verdict is not yet in. With regard to them — and they are legion — this book is a call to informed pluralism, not relativism.

"[What] we often mean by "education" is nothing more than some supposedly acceptable indoctrination."

RICHARD MITCHELL
The Gift of Fire

"If you are on the wrong road, progress means doing an about-turn and walking back to the right road; and in that case the man who turns back soonest is the most progressive."

C. S. LEWIS
Mere Christianity

"The basic choice is the same: to think or not to think."

NATHANIEL BRANDEN
"Social Metaphysics"

THEOLOGICAL METHOD

"You all know," said the Guide, "that security is mortals' greatest enemy."

C. S. LEWIS

"The sure traveller
Though he alight sometimes still goeth on."

GEORGE HERBERT

". . . the pilgrim must be headed back from the side paths into
which he is constantly wandering."

GEORGE MACDONALD

"I learned to go right, even when I went astray."

FRANCIS BEAUMONT

"No matter where one goes, it often looks as if a great many theologians
lack the courage to travel the road of theology to the end."

HENDRIKUS BERKHOF

"Systematization is always the enemy of true theology."

KARL BARTH

Fortress Theology
and the Mirage of Paradox

I doubt that theology,[1] as God sees it, entails unresolvable paradox.[2] That is another way of saying that any theology that sees it or includes it is mistaken. If God does not see theological endeavor as innately or irremediably paradoxical, that is because it is not. Paradox is not a phenomenon natural to theology. Theological paradox is a mirage. When we see it — or think we do — we may be assured that somewhere along the theological path we have taken at least one wrong turn. Things theological begin to look like things paradoxical only because we have led ourselves into a hall of mirrors.

We have a very good excuse for our distorted perceptions: we ourselves are distorted. When a theologian tells me that certain theological propositions appear paradoxical to us because we operate with a fallen intellect, that theologian is right. In that light, the theologian, not theology itself, leads us into the cul-de-sac. And, the theologian had better get us out, or at least try.

Therefore, I admire those theologians who, once they reach a dead end, back up the bus and try another route. That theologian may find himself in a dead end once again, or he may find the one route that leads out of the maze. That route does exist. God, at any rate, seems to have found it. While it may be that we never will, we ought to continue to try. Some theologians, however, being either unable or unwilling to pursue their quarry any further, become entrenched in paradox. They learn to tolerate unremedied paradox when unremedied paradox should be shunned. Perhaps they do so because to them the prospect of going back (perhaps even to the beginning) is too unsettling and too daunting. Rather than striking out in a new direction, or rather than pioneering through uncharted territories in search of the doctrinal Northwest Passage,[3] they hunker down and plant settlements in comfortable valleys, having decided at last that they will never reach the sea, or even continue to try. They have forgotten that, in this case, it is better to travel hopefully and never to arrive than to settle prematurely. To that extent, then, their theological settlements are a failure of nerve. Fatigue and uncertainty have made it seem more desirable to plant roots than to look around one more doctrinal bend or to climb up and peer over one more theological hill. The spirit of pioneering thus gives way to the spirit of dogmatism.

Once a pioneer becomes a settler, he starts to build fences. Fences are soon replaced by walls and walls by forts. The pilgrimage has become a settlement, and those within the walls become suspicious of those without. Outsiders think differently, talk differently, act differently. To justify their suspicions, settlement theologians begin to think that they *belong* in doctrinal fortresses. They develop what I call the "Ebenezer doctrine." "Was it not the map of God — our Bibles — that led us here?" they ask. In one sense, of course, they are right. The Bible did, in fact, lead them this far. But not the Bible only. Their misreading of it is what led them into the valley of paradox. Their lack of strength and their insecurity led them to settle there and to build a fort. In despair of ever finding their way to the sea, and discouraged by the prospect of going back, they traded their theological tents for creedal tenements and their doctrinal backpacks for dogmatic bungalows. Travelling mercies were exchanged for staying mercies. That is because Fortress Theologians interpret the intellectual security they have erected for themselves as the blessing of God. The perceived blessing of God becomes to them the perceived will of God. "Hitherto the Lord has led us" becomes not only their reason for staying, but also for fighting. They become the victims of a beseiged mentality nurtured on autointoxication. Those who settle elsewhere, or those who do not settle at all, are perceived to militate against the truth of God. They must be stopped, the fortress dwellers believe. If the settlers had their way, none of us would reach the golden sea. Only there, on that distant shore, should we plant our flag, with an entire continent of theological exploration behind us and the ocean of infinity throwing waves at our feet. Only after we've seen the sun setting beyond a watery horizon, only after we've awaken to the smell of salt air and the sight and sound of sea otters playing on wet rocks, can we cease our theological quest. Lewis and Clark did not gain fame for quitting in St. Louis. Columbus did not turn back at the Canary Islands. Theologians who settle in the valley of paradox do not deserve acclaim.

Nor ought they to be dogmatic. Any theology that lives comfortably with paradox cannot be labelled "the whole counsel of God." Those that advertise their systems in this way — I could cite examples — give evidence by doing so that they are settlers now, and pioneers no longer.[4]

I believe such theological premature closure is due not only to the emotional weaknesses to which we theologians are subject as fallen people, but also to the systems of thought we adopt. Before I say anything else, I want to say that although I am aware that every theological traveller must proceed according to some method, or some system, I am wary of systems. They are necessary for controlled navigation. In that way they are good. But, theological systems also tend not to accommodate the unexpected, the exceptional, and the untimely — things that can be crucial to our continued theological progress. That is, rather than facing an odd fact in all its rigid wildness, they domesticate it; they tame it; they shave it down and plant it foursquare in the middle of their mental settlement. By assimilating an odd and unruly fact in this deplorable fashion, these systems have made that fact something other than itself. Theologically speaking, one of the worst possible things that *could* happen *has* happened: the road signs have been changed to fit the route as it exists in the head of the traveller, rather than vice versa. Mental maps ought to be shaped by the landscape, not the other way round. By such "faith," some systematicians have been saying to this mountain, "Be thou removed, and be thou tossed into the sea," and it has been done, all by divine promise, they flatter themselves to think. But, such a topographical rearrangement of the theological terrain was not included in the divine intention that we should have dominion over the earth and subdue it. We ought to abandon our theological earth movers, get out our compasses once again, and rediscover magnetic north.

Fortress Theologians are dangerous because they are trying to do the inadvisable, if not the impossible. They are trying to reduce the multifarious complexities of God and his universe to the truncated confines of their own mental paradigm,[5] despite the fact that the world and its Architect resolutely resist that sort of reduction. Fortress Theologians want to be map makers before they have truly been explorers. Nevertheless, exploration *precedes* cartography. Cartographers need to know the lay of the land before they try to reduce it to scale for drawing. In the same way, exegesis precedes Systematics. In that light, Fortress Theologians offer a pre-fabricated structure in which to place one's theological beliefs, but they offer no viable method whereby one could actually *do* good theology. Their pedagogy says that about them. So long as they reduce training in doctrine to indoctrination they shall remain, and continue to produce, Fortress Theologians who are unable to extend the frontiers of theological truth. In the meantime, theological endeavor suffers because we do not need more or stronger doctrinal fortresses; we need more viable theological procedures.

Put another way, I fear the theological system that has a life and mind of its own. No theological system ought to be allowed to do the work of exegesis, for example. But they do. Hard data are not explained, just explained away. Rather than the theologian having a theology, the theology has him.[6] Such systems, rather than being supple and pliable, become omnivorous. They do not take the shape of the data's mold into which they ought to fit. Rather, in what looks like a feeding frenzy of cognitive dissonance, they devour every uncomfortable bit of external opposition. They beat them, grind them, and soften them until they are sufficiently palatable, and then they eat them.[7] Theological systems, if they are not kept perpetually humble, will become incurably expansionistic. Theological systems, if not held in check, if not continually made receptive and teachable, will become imperialistic. They will colonize every fact, compatible or not, that presents itself.[8] Left uncontrolled, they operate like cancer.

The surest sign that a theology is out of control occurs when that theological system itself becomes the theological method, which is the hallmark of Fortress Theology. In such cases, that system usurps many prerogatives not rightly its own. That system not only colonizes biblical exegesis, it becomes its own measure of truth. What does not fit cannot be fact. If it does not fit and Fortress Theologians want it to fit, they make it fit. I say it fearfully: the worst thing about such theological methods is that they are almost always implemented unwittingly. Few theologians, if any, would either admit to the practice or endorse it. Most theologians, however, if not all, do it — me included. When we do so we fail. We must not allow our theology to be turned into a hermeneutic. We have things exactly backwards when we make external reality subject to our own particular brand of theology.

In that light, I have not tried to produce a systematic theology as much as I have tried to employ a useful method for theologizing, a method that keeps its eyes and ears open, a method that is, so far as I can keep it so, more suitable for the theological traveller than the theological settler. That method encompasses several elements.

First, I like the intense biblicism of John Milton. When he compiled his *De doctrina christiana*, he did so by making frequent recourse to the actual words of Scripture. Milton was offended by the theologians he had read who filled their books with their own ideas and crowded their Scripture references out into the margins or down into the footnotes.[9] His own text, he was determined, would be comprised far more largely from the Bible itself. He employed this tactic because he was averse to incorporating any of the "sophistical subtleties" he thought had disfigured theology for many centuries. Insofar as he was able, he tried to ensure that his Christian doctrine was "drawn from the sacred scriptures alone."[10] While I do not believe that he succeeded, I am, nevertheless, impressed by his attempt. As massively biblicistic as Calvin's *Institutes* is, Milton's *De doctrina christiana* is more so. Calvin, for example, made a recognizable allusion to the Bible more than 5,000 times in his systematic theology. In his own somewhat smaller work, Milton reverted to Scripture more than 9,000 times. (One begins to be staggered by Milton's biblicism even more when one recalls that his book was given its final form in his period of blindness.)

To say that I admire Milton's attempt to be biblical is not to say that I subscribe either to his views or to his misguided brand of biblicism. Unlike Milton, I do not believe in Arianism, materialism, mortalism, or polygamy — positions he thought the Bible upheld. To a great extent, Milton's attempt failed because his biblicism was sometimes of a superficial sort. He was the champion proof-texter. Being truly biblical entails much more than lining up 800 Bible verses back-to-back, as Milton does when he tries to prove that the Son is not God. On that count, I number myself among Milton's detractors. Unlike some of his detractors, however, I can feel the weight of his arguments and appreciate the grand, even heroic, scale of his effort. I have learned to learn from Milton, even when he is wrong, because even when he is mistaken, he is often brilliant. Put succinctly, after reading Milton I am heartened and I am humbled. I, too, want to be true to the revelation of God in Scripture, but I know I am liable to error. Error prone as I am, I know that I must not build theological fortresses on ground that, upon divine inspection, proves to be shifting sand. However well I try to prop it up, a fortress built there will crumble. But biblical I must try to be.

Second, I like the methodological skepticism of Descartes. By bringing all things before the bar of private judgment and doubt, Descartes was unintentionally acknowledging that while truth is singular, error is multiform. It is far easier to be wrong than right, and there are far more ways to be it. In other words, while many paths lead into the woods, only one leads through them. That being so, our first response to any alleged road sign must not be to race wildly or unthinkingly to where we imagine it points, but to ask ourselves why we ought to follow this alleged marker at all. We ought to begin, as a matter of course, by being skeptical because, as Vance Havner once said, "It's better to believe a few things for certain than a whole lot of things that ain't so."

Wisdom dictates that taking no turn at all is often better than taking the wrong one. Making sure of one's marching orders is better than sleep walking. Some theologians take this advice too far, however, and rather than being careful about where they go and to whom they listen, stop travelling altogether and set up a fort. About them I have already spoken. Here I simply say that it is better to move circumspectly than precipitously and that we ought to choose our counsellors and advisers carefully. Not every well intentioned hand is actually a helping hand, though perhaps it is meant to be. Of course, I want to be open to help from whatever quarter it comes,[11] but I want to do so in full recognition of the fact that to be skeptical is better than to be gullible. Faith must not be confused with an uncritical mind or method. In this regard, philosophy (whether Descartes' or someone else's) can be an exceedingly useful tool. But, like all such evaluative mechanisms, it must be handled with care.

Regarding its usefulness for the Pilgrim Theologian, I want simultaneously to endorse philosophy and to identify its danger. Philosophy, doubtless, is one of the theologian's most serviceable tools, as well as one of his most seductive detours. It can help to establish the truth or validity of some of our beliefs, or it can serve to expose the errors of our adversaries. It can, in short, serve as a point of contact, or means of contact, between the believer and the unbeliever. But, though philosophy *can be*, it is not always (or even regularly) a preparation for faith. That is because while human beings are capable of reason, they are rarely reasonable. What goes by the name of reason is often not reason at all. What we misidentify as reason is occasionally the source of some of our most blinding error. That danger notwithstanding, however, right reason (as distinguished from reason falsely so called) is an indispensable means of searching for truth, even though on its own it is probably unable to escape incompleteness even when it does escape error.

Put differently, while I believe that right reason leads to truth, I believe it must be employed — like all the tools of the Pilgrim Theologian — carefully, consistently, and in something of a negative or skeptical manner. In order to minimize its misuse, philosophy should be employed in two ways. The first, and perhaps best, use to which we can put philosophy is that use to which Socrates often put it: skeptical debunking. Philosophy can disabuse us and our opponents of intellectual hubris and baseless self-assurance because it can strip away error. In so doing, it can render its practitioners more teachable by exposing them as unenlightened. Philosophy's second use is both less painful and more positive. While it may be, on its own, unable to supply us with much of the raw data we need for proper theologizing, philosophy is often unsurpassed in analyzing and organizing the data we have gleaned elsewhere and in other ways. Thus, with right reason as our pedagogue, we can acquire both the skeptical humility and the necessary powers of analysis that teach us to listen carefully to the truth before we venture to speak loudly on its behalf.

But, before I proceed to my final point, I must add this important proviso, one that separates the methodological skepticism I endorse from the rampant skepticism that I do not.[12] Methodological skepticism must be informed by, and tempered by, objectivism, the common sense belief and practice that the working relationship between mind and senses is fundamentally valid and reliable. That is, while much of what I hear identified as truth may be mislabeled, the normal function and interaction of mind and senses remain foundational to knowledge and to insight. Mind and senses are our window on the world. By them we come to know extra-mental reality, which is itself the umpire concerning the truth or error of our beliefs and assertions. The basic dependability of mind and senses (when they function normally) cannot be denied without self-contradiction and epistemological collapse.[13] To deny the fundamental reliability of mind and senses is self-stultifying: such a denial can be based only upon the workings of one's mind and senses, the very validity of which the denier has rejected. The epistemology I here advocate, it seems to me, underlies the apostle John's declaration to his readers that he was simply telling them about that which he himself had seen with his own eyes, heard with his own ears, and handled with his own hands concerning the Word of Life (1 John 1:1,3).

The philosophical and procedural prerequisite for any method of *knowing* is that it be as fully objective as possible. This does not exclude subjectivity, which, when practiced properly, entails bringing one's own powers of mind and soul to bear upon the study of the object in view. But it does mean that, so far as it can be, the nature of the object itself is permitted to be the controlling factor in all study, not the desires and presuppositions of the investigator. Right and wrong, true and false, all are determined by the nature of the object under examination. They are what they are; they are not necessarily what we say they are, much less what we would like them to be. Our task is not to invent right and wrong, or true and false, de novo — that has already been done. Our task is to discover them where they already are. We are discoverers and explorers, not inventors. Because such objects exist outside us, because these objects are what they are quite independent of anything we might say about them (in fact, quite independent of whether we even existed at all in order to say anything about them), because there is, in other words, an objective reality susceptible to careful analysis and to meticulous scrutiny, (processes able to yield genuine knowledge about the world in which we live), rampant skepticism is out of court.

But that is not all. Rampant skepticism is also inappropriate because, as H. H. Farmer, correctly observed,

> "behind all our discovery of religious truth, prior to it, explaining it, causing it, is God's intention to make His truth known to us, God's personal, purposeful, revealing energy in our lives. . . [W]e entirely misconceive religion if we do not understand that it is essentially a communion, a conversation between children and their father, in which the Father's will and desire to impart are greater than, and prior to, the children's will and desire to question and receive.[14]

"The peculiarity of all vital religious discovery," he continues, "is that it has always in it, not only this sense of you finding something, but also of something finding *you* — of an activity on the other side, as it were, a deliberate will probing into your life."[15] Unlike nature, God is not merely passive to our investigations. There is in theology, though not in natural science, an intentional unveiling by the object under scrutiny. In short, the process of theological knowing entails both the work of the mind, on the one hand, and God's active desire to be known, on the other. Rampant skepticism is out of court because God can and does, so to speak, get His point across. We must never forget "the urgency of spiritual matters . . . *to God*."[16]

In short, a time comes when we must doubt our doubts.

Third, I like the theological tolerance of Erasmus. Like him, I prefer those who define things too little to those who define them too much. I do this not because I am opposed to mental restraints. I am not. I am opposed only to those restraints imposed by some of reality's self-proclaimed but deluded proponents. I know those proponents are, like me, subject both to delusions of grandeur and to the temptation to dogmatize where confident assertion is sometimes neither possible nor right. A thinker like Erasmus understands quite well that the certainties and essentials in theology are few and that the uncertainties and peripherals are many, as unsettled as that might make us feel. Erasmus preferred to find comfort where it could be gotten to manufacturing his own artificial substitutes because he knew that synthetic comfort shelters a theologian not from the cold only, but also from reality. We do better to look at things as they are and not to flinch than to pull our blankets up over our heads. Theologians like Erasmus realize that the restoration of theology is best accomplished by a humble Christian heart searching for truth in a land of theological peace, not by interminable intercamp warfare. Theological exploration is a difficult, even dicey, matter at best, one that we must not complicate by shooting at other explorers. Giving aid and comfort and modest advice to fellow travellers is one thing; to treat them like the enemy is another. This is not to say we have no enemies. We do. A lot of us just don't know who they are, and we begin to shoot at anything that moves. We have forgotten, apparently, that not only does our enemy move, but so also do our fellow travellers. They could hardly be on a pilgrimage to truth otherwise.

In short, we ought to be biblical, skeptical, objective, and tolerant. That is, while we have the record of the very revelation of God in our hands, we must remember it will always be interpreted and applied by our own fallible minds. It is infallible and indefectible; we are not. We try to walk and talk according to our Bibles — and we should. But, we are lame and lisping. To such guides as we have proven ourselves to be, the best response is to be skeptical about what we hear advanced as truth and open-minded and loving toward those who advance it. We ought to listen carefully to what we are told and to evaluate it according to the best workings of our mind and senses.[17] But, in so doing, we ought never to lose our love and appreciation for those whose words and ideas we so carefully scrutinize. That, after all, is what we expect from them.

In other words, I eschew paradox and I advocate a skeptical and tolerant biblicism, one that wrestles with problems until they are solved and that does not quit. And why not? "The field is so spacious that . . . if I should spend all my pilgrimage in this walk, my time would end before my way."

END NOTES

1 In this context, by "theology" I mean knowledge of God and its attendant implications.

2 The astute reader will soon discern that this sentence is the theological foundation upon which the argument of this chapter is based. For reasons I will explain later, I have tried to state this proposition in a mildly Cartesian manner, one that proceeds carefully according to the strictures of methodological doubt and non-contradiction. As I have stated it here, I believe this proposition is theologically necessary. That is, I do not see how or why one would affirm its inverse and continue to theologize. I also must point out that I do not believe that the resolution of theological paradox is possible only for Omniscience. To untie difficult doctrinal knots, one need not know everything, one need only know truly and sufficiently. Insight is required, not omniscience. The possession of a finite mind does not, of itself, necessitate the presence of unresolvable paradox. Though such resolutions might be quite difficult to find, and quite time consuming as well, they can, I believe, be identified, and if not here, then hereafter, when we know more things, but not all. In other words, we require more hard work, more perseverance, clearer thinking, and more data to extricate ourselves from our theological dilemmas, not all possible knowledge.

Concerning the definition of paradox, G. C. Berkouwer, *A Half Century of Theology* (Grand Rapids: Wm. B. Eerdmans Pub. Co., 1977, p. 150), writes: "a little time in modern discussions of paradox reveals a wide variation in understanding of what paradox is. Indeed, we can speak of widespread confusion." When *I* speak of paradox, therefore, the reader should understand that I speak of actual logical contradiction. I give no place here to the idea of "apparent contradiction," which I consider a dangerous self-deception and an intellectual no-man's land. When two or more ideas *appear* contradictory they must be considered to *be* contradictory until they are shown not to be. That is, things are to be thought of as what they seem to be unless and until it can be shown that the appearances are genuinely misleading. "Apparent contradiction" and "unresolved paradox" too often are euphemisms for the authentic contradictions we are unwilling to face because, were they acknowledged as genuine, would show that we are wrong. In theology, as in other disciplines, we must beware of every euphemism.

Put differently, I consider the category of "apparent contradiction" often baseless and useless, at best, and downright misleading and deceptive, at worst.. Ideas can be labeled "apparent contradiction" (and not "actual contradiction") only if we can, in fact, reconcile or harmonize them. If we *could* do that, however, they would no longer *appear* contradictory.

In some readers' minds, the question might arise, does not Paul himself hunker down in, even glory in, unresolved paradox in passages like Romans 11:33ff? No, he does not. Paul's point is not that God's ways are paradoxical or that somehow they are utterly inexplicable — he has just spent three chapters explaining them. His point is that God's ways are not fully known by us, but, based upon what we do know of them, are worthy of our praise nevertheless. Furthermore, we must not confuse Paul's theological conclusions or his piety, both of which are present in the passage before us, with his sometimes unreconstructed rabbinic methodology. The former are authoritative, the latter is not. What he teaches, I believe. How he arrives at *some* of his conclusions, I reject. That contemplation of the ways of God ought to end in praise, as Paul's does here, I heartily endorse. That paradox ought to be part and parcel of our theological method cannot be justified by reference to this passage any more than allusions to Gal. 4:22ff can either justify or require us to interpret both testaments allegorically. The inspiration of Scripture should not be construed to mean that the Biblical writers' theological *methods* are always normative.

One final word about the Cartesian doubt alluded to at the beginning of this note. Descartes was an inconsistent doubter. He doubted himself back to virtual bedrock, and in that he did right. But what he built upon that rock was largely unserviceable because he stopped doubting the full trustworthiness of his own conclusions and built a great and faulty intellectual superstructure as a result.

3 The great advantage enjoyed by those of us who seek the doctrinal Northwest Passage compared to those hardy pioneers who sought the water route to the Pacific is that the goal of our quest actually exists. Their goal did not. In stalking *our* prey, we are not hunting unicorns.

4 While I stand firmly against any theological position that enshrines a paradox (and then pietizes this error by reminding us that we walk by faith and not by sight), I am equally opposed to any attempt to resolve it improperly. For example, some theologians label the relationship between divine sovereignty, on the one hand, and human responsibility and freedom, on the other, a paradox. All too often, they attempt to resolve this difficulty by means of an exegetical sleight of hand. Some of the Calvinists and Arminians I have

seen in action identify those Biblical passages that affirm their position as the more clear and more foundational passages and they label those that militate against their view as the unclear or "problem" passages. They then explain away the "difficult" data in light of the favorable data. Rather than explaining away half of the Biblical witness of an issue, they ought to let the Bible say what it says fully and strongly on both sides of the issue and then develop a theology that allows *both* sides to be fully true. That is, they ought to acknowledge that the Bible is, in some way, both Calvinistic and Arminian. They ought to acknowledge that divine sovereignty and human freedom are not mutually exclusive concepts (If they were mutually exclusive, and if the Bible taught both, the the Bible would not be inerrant.) and that this issue does not reduce to an either/or option.

Inspiration is perhaps a useful parallel issue here. We say that the Bible is the Word of God in the words of men. That means that while we say that David wrote Psalm 51, we do not say that God did not. It is true to say both that David wrote the text in question and that God did. The options are not mutually exclusive. The same conclusion applies to the relationship between divine sovereignty and human responsibility. To say that God was active in the salvation of a sinner is not to say that the sinner must therefore be passive. That sinners are active agents in their own destiny is not a denigration or denial of grace.

5 As Gilbert Highet observes, *Man's Unconquerable Mind* (New York: Columbia University Press, 1954, p. 57): "The aim of those who try to control thought is always the same, and they always work on the same principle. They find one single explanation of the world, one system of thought and action that will (they believe) cover everything; and then they try to impose that on all thinking people." Edward Carnell identifies the distortive dangers that attach to excessive systematization thus: "Whenever a systematic theologian becomes too systematic, he ends up falsifying some aspect of revelation" *Christian Commitment: An Apologetic* (New York: Macmillan, 1957, p. 285).

6 My language here is not gender specific and should not be read as such. I speak here not of the theologian's sex. I am well aware that women can be theologians too, and that they are equally subject to this theological failing. I do not exclude them. I employ the masculine pronoun throughout this text according to its traditional usage. Nothing chauvinistic is implied or communicated. Furthermore, as I will argue in chapter twelve, one must not misconstrue grammatical gender or intentionally generic language as gender spe-

31

cific. They are not. Grammatical gender must not be identified with sex. One does not make a chauvinist statement when referring to a theologian generically as "he" anymore than when one characterizes a nation, a ship, or liberty as "she." As a literary critic and an author, I hasten to add also that I deplore the use of the ungainly "he/she" device. Our language is a clumsy enough vehicle already without burdening it further simply to satisfy the demands of a linguistic special interest group intent on misreading someone else's words and attributing to that author a sexist content and intent he disavows.

7 For a critique of unfairly manipulating data as an immunization strategy designed to ward off an opponent's objections, see Wolfhart Pannenberg, *Theology and the Philosophy of Science* (Philadelphia: Westminster Press, 1976, pp. 56-58). The same point is made by Helmut Thielicke, *African Diary: My Search for Understanding* (Waco: Word, 1974, p. 31): "One cannot dispute with ideologues because their thinking does not deal with questions of truth, but rather with an interest that must be defended, come what may."

8 The same could be said of almost every intellectual system in almost every intellectual discipline, if left to its own.

9 John Milton, *Complete Prose Works of John Milton* (8 vols), Gen. Ed. Don M. Wolfe, New Haven: Yale University Press, 1953-1982, vol. 6, p. 122.

10 Ibid., p. 125.

11 I think here of Ben Jonson's astute observation that no man is so foolish but that he may not sometimes give good counsel. Nor is any man so wise but that he may easily err if he will refuse all counsel but his own.

12 In opposition to such rampant skepticism, C. S. Lewis, *Christian Reflections* (Grand Rapids: William B. Eerdmans, 1967), pp. 60-61, writes:

". . . the view in question is just the view that human thought is *not* true, not a reflection of reality. And this view is itself a thought. In other words, we are asking 'Is the thought that no thoughts are true, itself true?' If we answer Yes, we contradict ourselves. For if all thoughts are untrue, then this thought is untrue.

There is therefore no question of a total scepticism about human thought. We are always prevented from accepting total scepticism because it can be formulated only by making a tacit exception in favour of the thought we are thinking at the moment — just as the man who warns the newcomer 'Don't trust anyone in this office' always expects you to trust him at that moment . . . However small the class, *some* class of thoughts must be regarded not as mere facts about the way human brains work, but as true insights, as the reflection of reality in human consciousness."

13 See Ayn Rand, "Kant Versus Sullivan," in *Philosophy: Who Needs it* (Indianapolis: The Bobbs-Merrill Company, 1982) and Ayn Rand, *Introduction to Objectivist Epistemology* (New York: New American Library, 1966/1967). The hermeneutical equivalent of this epistemology is (unintentionally) set out in C. S. Lewis, *An Experiment in Criticism* (Cambridge: Cambridge University Press, 1961/1979).

14 Herbert H Farmer, *Things Not Seen: Studies in the Christian Interpretation of Life* London: Nisbet & Co. Ltd., 1927/1948, pp. 35, 36.

15 Ibid., pp. 37, 38.

16 Ibid., p. 45.

17 As Owen Barfield explains, *Speaker's Meaning* (Middletown: Wesleyan University Press, 1967, pp. 99-100):

". . . it may be that I shall have to abandon my inescapable conclusions, go back to the beginning, and set about finding out where I went wrong. But before I go to those lengths I shall want to examine very carefully exactly what it is my informant *has* established; and, when I have done that, I shall want to use my own judgment, not his, in deciding whether it is in fact incompatible with my own conclusion. This is likely to involve distinguishing rather ruthlessly between the observed facts and the theories erected on them . . . I shall want to examine the theories themselves *as* theories."

"It is ordained in the eternal constitution of things that men of intemperate minds cannot be free; their passions forge their fetters."

EDMUND BURKE

"The ignorance of the unlettered takes no scrutiny to establish. What we need to plumb is the ignorance of the educated and the anti-intellectualism of the intellectual."

JACQUES BARZUN

"We forget that every age has carried with it great loads of information, most of it false or tautological, yet deemed indispensable at the time."

JACQUES BARZUN

". . . progress, that is, radical progress not just hardware improvements — progress involving change — does come about only when we question (and because we question) our fundamental assumptions."

OWEN BARFIELD

". . . because he is intelligent the Christian, of all men, has to learn to discover with agonizing clarity what is conceivable by him about God."

KARL BARTH

Peer Pressure, Confessionalism, and the Corruption of Judgment: Why Theologians Can't Think Straight

I. Peer Pressure: The Unacknowledged Legislation of Theology

Some things we never outgrow: a passion for deep-dish pizza, a quiet love for the mountains of Colorado, and our boyhood addiction to baseball. Unlike these things, however, some of the things that remain with us are not so unremittingly pleasant or beneficial. (Not that being a Phillies fan has been unremittingly pleasant or done me much good.) Peer pressure, for example, is not merely an adolescent phenomenon. Few of us, if any, ever outgrow it. Theologians and their students, pastors and their congregations, all are subject to its subtle, but relentless, influences.[1]

If you have never considered it before, consider it now. The demand characteristics of the theological classroom exert psychological, academic, and social pressure on students to conform to the viewpoint espoused by their instructors. Very few students would submit the same research paper to Professor A, if he were teaching Systematic Theology, that they would to Professor B, if she were teaching it. Their research topics likely would change; the conclusions they reached likely would change; the language in which their conclusions were presented likely would change; and the methods whereby those conclusions were arrived at likely would change. By this I do not mean to say that such a student is merely contextualizing his theology — he is not. He is changing it, at least on the surface. He does so because he is aware of his instructor's beliefs, passions, methods, and idiosyncrasies, and (perhaps knowingly, perhaps not) alters his efforts and conclusions accordingly. Pragmatically, he is no fool. Intellectually, the case is different.

If memory serves, and if personal experience is a useful guide on this point, I dare say that many professors' objectivity skills are seriously defective. They seem never to have learned to distinguish between ideas they dissent from, on the one hand, and faulty or fallacious ideas, on the other. Only the foolish, the arrogant, or the unteachable assume no difference exists between the two. Such "teachers" have failed to come to grips with the possible (perhaps probable) divergence existing between the positions they themselves hold and the truth. In short, they lack perceptivity and humility. Or, to turn it around, they seem never to have learned to distinguish between good thought and their own thoughts. That failure, because it inevitably leads to inflated grades for the theological conformists in their classrooms and to deflated grades for all others, serves only to extend the professor's own intellectual thralldom onto his students. Those students are justifiably wary both of asking new questions and of answering the old ones in a new (and perhaps better) way. Thus, while the theological party line prospers, theological progress and true education flounder. And more's the pity. Professors ought to be scrupulously honest, not perpetrators of pedagogically insidious pressures that prevent or pervert real learning or discovery. In that light, Jaroslav Pelikan was exactly right:

> Few tyrannies are more insidious than that of a teacher who is interested in disciples rather than pupils, who seeks to be imitated rather than transcended, and who is so sure of the correctness of his ideas that he can evaluate all his students on the basis of their obedience to his opinions rather than on the basis of their judgment and maturity. The history of Christian theology has not lacked for such teachers, who have compounded the tyranny by identifying their notions with the word of God and thus equating their authority with the sovereignty of God . . . no intellectual community can afford to relent in its vigil against the tyranny of the pedagogue.[2]

To forestall this classroom travesty, a theology instructor must be "prepared to give the highest marks to the telling, felicitous and well-documented exposition of views he dissents from or even abominates."[3]

The academic study of theology should have the effect of opening the mind to truth and of gaining skills in recognizing and acquiring it. Theological study should illuminate the student by purging the student of unjustifiable prejudices and of ideas received uncritically. We do not teach, study, or publish in order merely to confirm our theological prejudices, but to expose them to scrutiny and, if exposed as fallacious, to reject them and to find a more suitable set of ideas. We must remember that the enemy is not merely error and our adherence to it, it is also truth held for all the wrong reasons (or for no reason whatsoever) and arrived at all the wrong ways. Teachers who have not learned *that* have not yet learned to learn; nor can they teach their students to learn.

Put differently, Christian scholarship has an obligation to truth, that is, to God. Only by the careful pursuit and acquisition of truth can we begin to execute our calling faithfully and effectively. Theologians and their students must shun the naive ferocity of those who hold to opinions that cannot stand up to careful scrutiny. Do not mistake their vicious passion for intellectual virtue or courage. It is not. It is the anguished outrage of those who have been unfaithful to their commission as apostles for truth, a commission that requires fidelity to things as they are, not to things as we would like them to be. Like Nero, those theologians spend their time fiddling with the evidence while the real world, and its questions and concerns, burns down around them. But, they themselves do not worry because they believe their asbestos dogmatism will protect them, even if it does not protect the world. In truth, however, it will protect neither. That is because Christian theologizing is, or ought to be, a "reality game." The morality of scholarship demands a willingness to face the truth, even when it says that some of our most cherished beliefs are raw fiction. Without courage to face the truth and the freedom to do so, neither Christian scholars nor the students they instruct will ever stand in the vanguard of academic pursuit. They lack the intellectual virtue and wherewithal to do so.

But, the pressure now existing in some theological classrooms makes any very positive outcome unlikely. Nor is the situation even as conducive to education as I have painted it. Many other pressures are exerted equally as apt to undermine effective theological navigation. Students, for example, are motivated not only by fear of failure or grade deflation to adopt their teacher's views, they are also under an even more subtle pressure (because it is a more pleasant one) to adopt uncritically the views of a professor they like or respect, for no other reason than they are his. Popularity and affection pave the way for indoctrination at least as effectively as the unarticulated threat of failure.

Popularity, of course, is a two-edged sword. It cuts both students and teachers. Most teachers are not above saying and believing what will make them popular with students — and deans. Perhaps such professors are unaware of their intellectual capitulation; perhaps they are not. My impression, however, is that the practice of pragmatic accommodation is far more widespread than its recognition. Nor is the pressure exerted on theological instructors in this fashion either subtle or weak. It often is quite powerful. It often is quite overt.

Theological and administrative power is like most other sorts of power: it can be, and often is, misused. The deans who exert this pressure, and who often are responsible for the hiring of new faculty, are themselves under pressure. They are susceptible to the exertions of the faculty already on board and to the exertions of the board of governors (and *they*, in many cases, are the ones who ratify the statements of faith[4]). In that light, theological students ought to realize this about their professors: they were not born with the jobs they now have; they had to get them. All too often that getting was the result of an intellectually dangerous process whereby the dean who hired the new faculty member was struggling to keep his superiors happy, as well as to keep his view of God and the world intact and to spread it, if possible, by means of his faculty. This, of course, is not hard to do, for he will find no shortage of "anxious young instructors who sniff the air to find which way the wind is blowing and nervously nuzzle up to the power centers."[5] These erudite sniffers are nervous because they know the power and pervasive presence of theological bigotry. They know that unless they dot their "i's" and cross their "t's" just the right way, they will never work. Thus, the economic pressures of supporting a wife and family, and of paying off seminary and graduate school tuition debts, intensifies the pressure upon them for theological conformity. They begin to ask themselves if, after all, there might not be some way to sign a statement of faith that, were there no pressure to do so, they would find at least partially objectionable. This usually is done (I am not making this up. I've seen it and heard it.) by employing a hermeneutic for reading statements of faith they would properly castigate should their students employ it for reading the Bible. That method permits them to see if the words of the doctrinal statement can be stretched far enough to accommodate their own private preexisting beliefs (without anyone in authority knowing it). The surprising outcome of this humiliating theological prostitution is that it continues to be perpetrated in the classroom by that same (now employed) theologian. He, in effect, forces his students through the same process he endured. Rather than teaching his young charges the virtue of intellectual honesty and the need to combat nonsense in all its forms, he merely imposes upon them the same pressures under which he crumbled. In truth, he can do nothing else. You can take no one any further than you yourself have travelled, and this theologian seems never to have learned how to pursue truth or how to live it. Sadly, teachers reproduce after their own kind, and his kind have failed in the primary activity of discovering truth — the very thing to which he committed himself when he chose an academic career.

I say this because I know of no better way to guard budding theologians from the ravages of intellectual pressure than to warn them that they must not assume uncritically that their theology professors are *theologians*, not if being a theologian means knowing how to theologize, and not if knowing how to theologize means knowing how to find truth and how to live it.

Professors and systems like those I have described above have transformed institutions of higher education into institutions of higher indoctrination. In that light, some "theologians'" ideas are not ideas at all; they are merely the unexamined recitation of statements and viewpoints they received at the hands of those who indoctrinated them, or else the intellectual capitulations and doctrinal sleight of hand they had to perform in order to get a job. But real theologizing is more than accumulating quotations and opinions from the thinkers in one's own tradition, more than indoctrination, and more than mental gymnastics. Theologizing is faith and understanding coming to grips with reality in order to produce a Christian mind (and character) that knows the truth about things, and, because it knows the truth about things, is liberated from the shackles of error and sham. Seekers of truth are not parrots who mimic other people's words; they are pioneers who are equipped to find truth, and who do find it, wherever it can be found.[6]

The sad fact remains, however, that young theologians are right to believe that if they write with candor, imagination, or creativity about certain theological realities many doors will close to them. They will not be able to make a living. They will not be allowed to participate in the life and activities of various important institutions and professional societies. Participation in new research and in publication programs will be denied them. Influential people will be alienated, and the opinion that a particular young theologian is unsound and unsafe will be disseminated quickly, widely, and slanderously — all under the pretense that evangelical scholarship is objective, reflective, and teachable. Pressure is exerted either to accommodate (i.e., to dissemble) or to leave: "We'll have none of *that* kind of thinking around here!" they are told. Those who agree, and those who can and do accommodate, become the teachers of the next generation; and they perpetuate this sinister tyranny on those who follow. Those who do not accommodate are excluded and are believed to be the enemy. The danger to truth and to integrity can hardly be greater. In theology, as in politics, there are dictatorships it is our sacred duty to oppose, if not overthrow.

We must not succumb to the temptation to treat theological truth as our own school's private property, something we dispense in our classrooms along with our syllabi and lecture notes. But that is exactly what happens in a large number of theological classrooms all across the nation. And, if you are a theological student, this might be happening to you (even now, as you read *this* book). Think about it: different syllabi, different lecture notes, different theologies all are being distributed with equal confidence to students everywhere, and those students readily and uncritically accept them as truth, when it must be the case that on some very significant issues most of them are dead wrong. Truth, I am convinced, is *one* thing, and not many others. Where these theologies differ, they cannot all be true. Luckily for us, of course, the other guy's views that are wrong. It just distresses me that he thinks that about *us*. Won't he ever learn?

Won't you?

II. PILGRIM THEOLOGY AND CONFESSIONALISM

To assume that we already have most of the important theological answers is intellectually hazardous. We may not even have most of the important theological questions. Nor should we blithely assume that all that is yet to be disclosed or discovered will be either consistent with what we now believe or else wrong. But, that is precisely the effect produced by our misuse of statements of faith. If you are a Fortress Theologian and not a Pilgrim Theologian, you will treat your tradition's confession as if it were the wall or boundary around truth: whatever lies outside the walls, or whatever cannot be smuggled somehow into the castle precincts must be, for that very reason, untrue. The problem here is not that theologians are confessional, but that they treat their confessions as if they were impregnable and unassailable truth rather than well-established, but still provisional, working hypotheses for further theologizing. The difference here is between "confessional" and "confessionalism." The former is an academic virtue, the latter is not. Confessions of faith are a means of identification; they state what it is we believe and they identify us as a cohesive group. Of course we think that what we believe is *true*, otherwise we would not believe it. But, our confessions should not be construed either as absolute truth or as absolutely true. They probably contain, like many other humanly devised statements on difficult subjects, an admixture of truth and error. Precisely because we are so intensely committed to our beliefs, and precisely because we perceive the consequences of believing and disbelieving *in our way* to be so momentous, we, of all people, might be the least able to see if, or where, our confessions are faulty. This inability to acknowledge the blindspots in one's own theology is not a problem reserved only for theologians of other traditions. That problem, sad to say, we all share. While confessional theology cannot, indeed should not, be banished, it should be exercised with humility and teachableness. We are the hunters of truth, after all, not merely its custodians.

For a useful Pilgrim Theology, wisdom dictates that we must not prescribe, beforehand, the direction the path of knowledge will take. After all, something might conceivably contradict our theology without contradicting Christianity. It is insupportably arrogant to assume the two are identical. My thoughts about God are not to be confused with God. Neither are yours. Remember, the facts themselves might contradict your understanding of the facts; they will not contradict the God of all facthood.

How else can a theologian grow except by making sure his commitment to his confessional tradition does not close the door to further knowledge? The theologian must remain in a position to determine if some of the discoveries he has made need to be unmade; and he must be willing to do so if that is what truth demands. The scholar who can do that is indeed a scholar because he is still a true learner. Therefore, if your most precious mental reconstructions of reality are overturned, if your intellectual house of cards collapses into rubble all around you, rejoice and be exceedingly glad, for you have been mugged by truth. As a theologian, nothing better can happen to you. That undeception, though momentarily grievous, is a necessary rite of passage. By it you have been changed by reality. So were all the greatest theologians before you.

Thus, to be a Pilgrim Theologian, one who is a path finder and a pioneer, you must permeate all your theological endeavors with scholarly virtue. The first condition of scholarship *of any kind* is an unqualified respect for evidence. That evidence, at this moment, tells us that we ought to maintain an appropriate humility about our alleged familiarity with the Divine Mind and to moderate our certitude accordingly. Until we do, we probably cannot travel any further. Our cherished views, even those we ostensibly derive from Scripture, must not be advanced in such a way as to preclude an increase in knowledge. We periodically must subject our theological procedures and conclusions to the refining fires of fresh analysis and criticism. Any Christian scholar or Christian school not willing or not able to do so is unworthy of the name. As Helmut Thielicke declared, "I detest the defeatism of the 'orthodoxy' which fortifies itself in the closet of seemingly unshakeable but unrealistic formulas. I am proud of the freedom of a Christian who may dare heresy to gain the truth. The freedom to which the gospel calls us also includes the freedom of bold and venturesome thought. God will not despair of us when we err."[7] Thus, while academic freedom has its dangers, none loom so large as its abandonment. Although Martin Luther thought Copernicus a fool, a judgment Luther based on his own pious, well-intentioned, but mistaken, reading of the Bible, Copernicus, not Luther, undeceived us.[8]

But, this does not mean that the *truth* ever changes, only that our understanding of it can change and perhaps should. Our statements of faith should be open to examination and to revision. We who subscribe to them should be teachable (though never gullible). Who knows how many Copernican revolutions still await us? We must be sure to allow ourselves the wisdom and vantage point necessary to welcome them when they come, not merely to react in disgust or horror because they upset a whole cart load of ideas that, while they are dear to us, are (like Luther's) flatly wrong. We must reject any attitude or approach that renders our beliefs unfalsifiable in the future. After all, the final chapter on Christian intellection has not been written, and we must not allow ourselves to close the book of knowledge before it is. Premature closure is a mental vice. Repent of, and arm yourself against, sins of the intellect.

III. PILGRIM PROCEDURE: CONFESSIONALISM AND THE PURSUIT OF TRUTH

So much for warnings and negation. I now must explain the Pilgrim Theologian's rules for handling and implementing statements of faith and theological confessions properly. I mention but three.

A. The Monkey-momma Rule

Statements of faith should be used the way baby monkeys use their mothers: as a base from which to explore. Whether it stretches out its right hand to grab a banana, a branch, a leaf, or even another monkey, the baby monkey clings to its mother with its left. New items are brought back to the safety of mother for investigation, use, and enjoyment. That is how monkeys learn and grow. Eventually, monkeys leave their mothers, and well they should. Any monkey that clings to its mother's neck its whole life is a freakish and unnatural example of arrested development. In the same way, any theologian who has not, or does not, outgrow at least some aspects of his statement of faith (perhaps even major aspects of it) is perhaps languishing in a state of arrested development. No one hits upon the whole truth and nothing but the truth on the very first try. Thus, you must use your statement of faith as a vehicle for further exploration and understanding, and not simply as a way to reconfirm how great your "mother" is. Confessional statements are an excellent point of departure for learning; they are not its limits. You must use your statement of faith as a short summary of the present state of your tradition's theological understanding or knowledge, not as an unscaleable wall around doctrinal truth, or as an indication that whatever lie within its precincts is not to be questioned and cannot be overturned.

B. The Courage and Candor Rule

If an institutionally favored position is seen to be a minority viewpoint when it is set against the backdrop of the entire theological endeavor of modern scholarship (or indeed against the backdrop of modern culture at large), a competent theologian will acknowledge that fact to his students and give good reasons both as to why he believes as he does and why others do not. In doing the latter, he should never indulge in ad hominem attacks, as if all dissenters were benighted, prejudiced, or willfully blind. Nor should he use theological dissenters as evidence that "the natural man cannot understand spiritual things because they are foolishness to him." After all, some things *seem* foolish simply because they are. Not all of those (perhaps not even many of those) who dissent from an institutionally favored belief are uneducated, unreasonable, or unfair. They might, in fact, be quite amiable and quite brilliant. Students should know *that* about the enemy. Students should learn to treat theological dissenters with respect, not with pity or disdain. They should learn from their instructors that humility, not arrogance, is the proper response to the undeniable existence of theological pluralism, and that one must not mistake narrow mindedness for single mindedness. As Allan Bloom has taught us,

"Freedom of the mind requires not only, or not even especially, the absence of legal constraints but the presence of alternative thoughts. The most successful tyranny is not the one that uses force to assure uniformity but the one that removes the awareness of other possibilities, that makes it seem inconceivable that other ways are viable, that removes the sense that there is an outside."[9]

Young theologians must be taught to study their opponent's ideas carefully so that they can feel the weight of the dissenting arguments and feel the force of their opponent's strongest punch. What cannot stand up to the best barrage of analytical dissent deserves to fall. When students are taught to study all sides of a case (and not simply to hear about them from a biased lecturer who never studied them first hand for himself), they actually increase the number of their teachers. Those who reject our views can be useful and insightful guides to *our* theology because they (perhaps) can see some things about it better than we ourselves can see. We ought to remember that he who knows only his own side of the case probably knows little even of that. An intensely parochial or theologically repressive atmosphere will obscure, perhaps even obliterate, the opportunity for fruitful theological investigation — a paradoxical situation in what is designed to be the very arena for advanced religious study. We need to capitalize on our theological diversity, not eliminate it by prior doctrinal fiat. These disagreements ought to be carried out in a spirit of honesty, not in inter-confessional sniping, committeeizing, or inquisitorial kangaroo courts. Without a spirit of teachable camaraderie nothing useful will be gained from these everlasting and acrimonious debates over issues we think are important but might not be.

Both by his academic methods and his life, a theologian should display the courage to let the chips fall where they may. The demands of truth and the good of his theological students (Those two things are the same.) should be always before him. In no other way will the theologian's students learn the difference between Christian dogma and dogmatism. In no other way will they learn to learn. They must be encouraged to shake down their false gods and their intellectual idols and to winnow and to sift the impurities in their own beliefs and practices. Not to allow this is tantamount to irreligion.

Among the outsiders, our reputation for such sifting is very poor. While researching for my book on one of John Milton's theological heresies, I met (and later became friends with) Maurice Kelley, surely the best student of Milton's theology in our century. We had not spoken together for two minutes before Kelley asked me if I were a Christian. When I said I was, he replied that, in that case, he did not think I would be able to handle this issue fairly or properly. He said so because he had butted heads with Christian scholars for forty years over this very point in Milton's theology, and they invariably proved to be careless and uncharitable. They were unwilling to recognize that *Paradise Lost*, perhaps our language's greatest religious poem, was the product of a heretical mind. And not only had they employed every academic subterfuge imaginable in their effort to rehabilitate Milton by winning him back for orthodoxy, but they had continued to abuse Kelley in private conversations and in print all the while. Justifiably, Kelley was skeptical. He had seen us in action and he was not impressed.[10]

We must not shun the truth or shrink from calling things by their real names.[11] In theological scholarship, courage and candor are the definition of excellence.

C. The Precipitous Involvement Rule

This rule is named for what it tries to prevent: doing before you know what you are doing. To prevent this failure, you must move to the cutting edge of your academic discipline. Scholarship at that level requires keeping abreast of developments in your field, not simply "to see what those blasted infidels are up to now," but in order to become, and to remain, well-informed and properly aware of the latest ideas and insights in your academic area, from whatever quarter they emerge. For a teaching or publishing theologian, failure to achieve this widely informed level of competence is an arrogant dereliction of duty. Such "scholars" pose as teachers when they are not even students. Only the neophyte still believes that scholarship flourishes in confessional isolation. No matter how long they wait, those who enter the teaching and preaching arena only narrowly informed do so precipitously. Unless you are very lucky, you will not do well until you know well. Knowing, however, is the one thing a confession-bound teacher or preacher does not do. Precipitous theologians do not realize that the only choice a scholar has is between truth and rest. You cannot have both.

END NOTES

1 Those who object to calling the pressure that instructors exert on their students "peer" pressure because professor and students are not really equals (or peers) are, I believe, condemning themselves. Any teacher who is not a student of his students is, *for that very reason*, not really a teacher. Unless you are a learner, you will not be an instructor.

2 Jaroslav Pelikan, *The Christian Intellectual* (London: Collins, 1966, p. 126). As he further explains on the next page, "It is no tragedy for a teacher to be mistaken. It is a tragedy if he is so afraid of being mistaken that he refuses to take risks, or if he imagines that his offices [or his skills have] endowed him with infallibility." That this indoctrination rarely needs to be *imposed* and that many people actually welcome indoctrination is forcefully explained by Gilbert Highet, *Man's Unconquerable Mind* (New York: Columbia University Press, 1954, pp. 57-59). What happens to those who, like the apostle Paul, resist this mindless indoctrination, Highet explains in the paragraphs that follow those just cited.

3 C. S. Lewis, *An Experiment in Criticism* (Cambridge: Cambridge University Press, 1961, p. 86).

4 We must not confuse administrative power with true theological authority. Some seem to think that because they have the organizational power to generate an institutional statement of faith that they have the divine authority to do so and that dissent from their opinions therefore is dissent from God's. They have no such divine imprimatur.

5 Chad Walsh, *The Literary Legacy of C. S. Lewis* (New York: Harcourt Brace Jovanovich, 1979), p. 119.

6 An interesting example of this parrot phenomenon in evangelical circles is the tendency for some conservative publishing houses to reprint old theological works instead of commissioning new ones. Rather than being on the cutting edge of theological scholarship and investigation, rather than helping to extend the boundaries of knowledge, they are only looking for clean copies of old books that can be photographically reproduced (at little expense). Not that old books are bad. They are not. I own more than 5,000 books myself, al-

most every one of which is used or antiquarian. I *love* old books. But, judging from some publishers' lists, one would get the impression that evangelicals had learned nothing new since the last Puritan died.

7 Helmut Thielicke, *African Diary: My Search for Understanding* (Waco: Word, 1974, p.171).

8 As Luther once said of Copernicus ("who wanted to prove that the earth moves and not the . . . sun"), "So it goes now. Whoever wants to be clever must agree with nothing others esteem. He must do something of his own. This is what this fellow does who wishes to turn the whole of astronomy upside down. Even in these things that are thrown into disorder I believe the Holy Scriptures, for Joshua commanded the sun to stand still and not the earth." *Luther's Works* (Vol. 54): *Table Talk* (Philadelphia: Fortress Press, 1967, pp. 357-358). See also Karl Heim, *Christian Faith and Natural Science* (London: SCM, 1953, p. 13), who says that Luther characterized Copernicanism as "the over-witty notion of a Fool, who would fain turn topsy-turvy the whole Art of Astronomy."

9 Allan Bloom, *The Closing of the American Mind: How Higher Education has Failed Democracy and Impoverished the Souls of Today's Students* (New York: Simon and Schuster, 1987, p. 249).

10 I am pleased to report that he now thinks differently.

11 To do this properly, the language of scholarship should be that of articulate precision. We must be unafraid to show the world (and ourselves) what the truth is, and unwilling to claim a total victory when only half is to be had.

"... theology is a function of the Church."

KARL BARTH

Church Dogmatics I. i

"There is no possibility at all of dogmatics outside the Church."

KARL BARTH

Church Dogmatics I. i

"Dogmatics ... demands Christian faith."

KARL BARTH

Church Dogmatics I. i

Harnack *Redivivus*

To argue, as do theologians like Karl Barth, that Christian theology can be generated, understood or critiqued only from within the Church, or only from the standpoint of faith, seems to entangle one in several logical and methodological difficulties.

First, to limit the proper understanding of theology to the Church is to transform ecclesiology into epistemology and ecclesiastical membership into both a way of knowing and a measure of knowing.[1] In response to such transformations, and in light of the multiplicity of churches with which one is currently confronted, one is compelled to ask the obvious question: "Which Church?" To decide "Which Church?" is to do theology,[2] in general, and ecclesiology, in particular. To decide "Which Church?" entails making complex theological judgments with the most far-reaching consequences. It necessarily includes critiquing and rejecting major portions of, perhaps even the entirety of, various Christian theological traditions, on the one hand, and endorsing major portions of one or more of the various competing ecclesiastical traditions, on the other. To decide "Which Church?" is to do theological analysis of the most profound sort, something the Barthian school of theology insists cannot and should not be done. *But, if one cannot critique Christian theology except from a churchly standpoint, and if assuming a churchly standpoint inescapably requires prior theological critique and commitment, then theology is impossible.*

This view of theology is, in fact, self-stultifying. Its fatal error is to assert an unjustifiable ecclesiastical hegemony over the process of theological knowing, indeed over knowing itself. It does so even though the proper use of the mind in intellectual matters (whether scientific, historical, philosophical, or theological) is not contingent upon one's ecclesiastical commitments. Quite the contrary, such commitments have sometimes hindered the mind's grasp of truth rather than assisting it, as in the Church's various proceedings against right-minded dissidents like Galileo and others. Neither saving faith nor ecclesiastical commitment are required to do Christian theology appropriately any more than one is required to be a Muslim in order to understand Islam or to be a Whig politician in order to understand Edmund Burke. Adherence is not the prerequisite of knowledge or understanding. It is sometimes their worst enemy. Thus, while to theologize from within a historical context or tradition of thought is historically inescapable, to declare that context or that tradition epistemologically or functionally normative and/or necessary is ill-advised.

Furthermore, theologians who claim epistemological hegemony for the Church in theological matters often inconsistently refuse to permit scholars in other disciplines to erect similar iron curtains around their own non-theological academic pursuits. Such churchly theologians continue to write treatises on economics, physical science, public policy, and environmental ethics, as if training in theology were crucial to an understanding of political science and natural science but as if training in political science and natural science were at the same time irrelevant to theology. If an intellectual bridge exists between theology and other disciplines, it is a bridge that carries traffic in both directions. If theology is a ghetto discipline, one cut off from outside intervention, it is also a discipline prohibited from making any forays into the academic life of the world at large. Intellectual isolationism is a two-edged sword. If it cuts outsiders off from theology; it cuts theologians off from all other disciplines.

Second, if by "Church" is meant not a particular ecclesiastical tradition but rather the Church universal, or the body of all believers in all times and all places, then one is arguing that unless or until one is a Christian one cannot properly conduct a reliable theological investigation or critique. Such a position merely transforms personal salvation into a way of knowing. It assumes that one can move only from faith to understanding,[3] but never from understanding to faith. But this will not do. Saving faith is not without its necessary prior theological content. To become a Christian requires one to come to at least some rudimentary conclusions about God, about Christ, and about one's own spiritual status and need. In other words, it requires (correct) theology, which Barth's view says cannot be done apart from the standpoint of saving faith. Adherents to such a view of theology do not seem to realize that their position actually eliminates the *possibility* of saving faith because it asserts that saving faith is the *sine qua non* of theology. The truth, however, is quite the opposite because correct theology of some sort (however primitive and unsophisticated it might be in the case of some new converts) is the *sine qua non* of saving faith.

In truth, neither faith nor ecclesiastical commitment are a means of knowing. By means of their faith and their ecclesiastical attachments many Christians have perpetrated many serious theological errors. That is because the proper functioning of the human mind when it does theology is not fundamentally different from its proper functioning when it does political theory or medical ethics, to name but two other disciplines of thought. The proper use of mind and senses, which does constitute a means of knowing, is not fundamentally altered or suspended in answering theological questions. Nor in answering such questions is it replaced or superseded by conversion or by church affiliation.

Such errors seem to stem from the notion that Christian doctrine is a ghetto discipline, a strictly insider phenomenon, one that not only presupposes the existence of the Church, but which insists that theology can arise only from within the community of faith as it seeks to make sense of, and to give order and structure to, its encounter with God in Christ. But, the mere fact that Christian doctrine is typically a churchly phenomenon and predictably reflects the perspectives common to the community of faith does not mean that theology cannot be done accurately or well outside the Church, however one defines Church, as clearly it must be (by everyone who is to become a convert) and has been (by many of those who, for various reasons, were marginalized by the Church). At times it has been done better from outside the visible Church than from within it, as I believe it was in 1923, when Adolf Harnack (who was, to borrow a phrase from Milton, "church-outed by the prelates") confronted Karl Barth and the new gnosticism of the despisers of scientific theology; or as it is today by Wolfhart Pannenberg, who justifiably complains that his church never really trusted him, indeed (in his words) rejected him.[4]

The notion advanced by some contemporary theologians that Christian doctrine is not primarily concerned with the insights of Jesus of Nazareth, but rather with the insights of the community of faith concerning him, confuses the doctrine of Christians with Christian doctrine, which it is not. True Christian doctrine is the doctrine of Christ. To assert otherwise is to run afoul of Harnack's much maligned (but never refuted) insightful distinction between the religion *of* Christ and the religion *about* Christ. Insofar as these two theologies differ — and they often do — the palm of authority and truth, as well as the function of definitiveness, must be granted to the former, not the latter. In other words, what the modern gnostics identify as the touchstone and definition of Christian theology is better conceived of as the subject matter of the history of Christian thought, which is a very different thing. Historical theology is not systematics. Christ himself, his life, and his teachings constitute the center and definition of true Christian theology, not the various Churches and their sometimes mutually exclusive teachings. Christianity is defined by Christ, not by Christians, whether considered individually or corporately. Thus, it is Christianity — that is, the religion of Christ — to which we must adhere, and not to churchianity — that is, the religion of the various churches — which too often is a weak and truncated substitute.

Put differently, while we must insist that God is christologically defined, we must not extrapolate from that fact something which does not necessarily follow from it, namely that Christian theology is actually the tradition concerning Christ, and that this tradition (or family of traditions) is the inescapably essential controlling model for the genesis and formation of theological constructs. To insist otherwise seems to me to elevate one's own theology (or the theology of the church or tradition to which one belongs) to the level of an incontrovertible universal, which it can never be. Only the theology of Christ himself merits that lofty status, and even that theology, as Harnack noted, comes to us clothed in the verbal and conceptual garments of a specific time and place. As a result, we must hold our own flawed efforts at theologizing less confidently and more provisionally, as well as in less esteem. In short, we must be Pilgrim theologians, not Fortress theologians.

We also must resist the temptation to identify Christ's doctrines too closely and too uncritically with our own. Again, Jesus, his actions, and his teachings, not the history of official and unofficial speculation concerning such things, is what is properly central. The religion of Christ alone constitutes the center of our religion.

Theologians who advocate the position I here oppose seem to be moving from a descriptive historical fact to a normative theological and methodological declaration. They seem to argue that because Christian doctrine is typically done by Christians in a historical Christian context, therefore Christian theology can be done and should be done only by Christians from within the Church, and only from the standpoint of faith. The theology they do in that context, we are told, in order to be good theology, ought to resemble the theology of the theologian's own particular ecclesiastical tradition, against which the theologian's work is to be judged. But from this I dissent because only Christ's theology[5] is normative, not the theology of those who claim to follow him but who cannot and do not agree among themselves as to what He actually taught. Such considerations are fatal to theological imperialism and ecclesiastical positivism of this sort. After all, we live in a world where two opposite assertions cannot both be correct. They might, in fact, both be wrong. In many such cases, I venture to guess, they probably are.

As a result, I have frequently done what Hendrikus Berkhof did: "I never encouraged my students to read Barth during their first academic years," he said, because "we can hardly begin with Barth, [though] eventually we have to make our second start in him, lest our way becomes a deadlock."[6]

55

END NOTES

1 According to Barth, "The Church . . . measures its actions, its talk about God, against its being as the Church," Karl Barth, *Church Dogmatics* I. i (Edinburgh: T. & T. Clark, 1975), p. 4.

2 I use the word "theology" here in a way slightly different from the way it was used in Chapter One. By "theology" I mean human reflection upon God, Christ, self, sin, etc. Such reflection need not be sophisticated and well-informed to be theology, it need only be human thought concerning theological topics. To be *good* theology, of course, it must also be insightful and well-conceived. That is, it must be true.

3 As Hendrikus Berkhof observes, both Schleiermacher and Barth "started with Anselm's motto 'I believe in order to understand,'" Hendrikus Berkhof, "Beginning with Barth," in Donald McKim, *How Karl Barth Changed My Mind* (Grand Rapids: Wm. B. Eerdmans, 1986), p. 25.

4 Michael Bauman, *Roundtable: Conversations with European Theologians* (New Orleans: Insight, 2005), p. 49.

5 Like Jürgen Moltmann, I, too, think of Christ as a theologian. See Bauman, ibid., p. 40.

6 Berkhof, ibid., p. 26.

"He who begins by loving Christianity better than truth will proceed by loving his own sect or church better than Christianity, and end in loving himself better than all."

SAMUEL TAYLOR COLERIDGE

4

Seven Tactical Errors Inerrantists Commit

As some see it, the theological foundation of evangelical unity is the fact that the Bible is an inspired book, inerrant in the autographs. Our commitment to the authority and accuracy of the Bible is a belief we value highly, one we desire to share with those outside our circle, and one concerning which we repeatedly endeavor to convince them. Yet, despite our long term and massive commitment in that direction, despite our meticulous historical, theological, and exegetical treatments of the data, the yield in number of "converts" to our position remains abysmally meager. In fact, if personal impressions can be trusted, it seems that more defections occur in their direction than in ours. Some of these defections we knowingly and willingly support by official decision. Some we do not. Of the former I shall not speak. But why, after we have expended so much effort getting them in the fold — and after getting them there, keeping them there — why do they yet reject us? What's *wrong* with those non-inerrantists?" we ask ourselves. "Can't they recognize truth? Don't they know compelling arguments when they see them?"

Perhaps they do. Perhaps what they see and read from us is not as convincing as we think it is. Perhaps flaws in arguments are like headlights on a dark highway —everyone else's seem brighter and more glaring than our own. That, at least, is the contention of this chapter.

The evangelical view of the Bible's veracity I believe to be sound. Our Fortress Theologian's arguments for it occasionally are not. After a brief disclaimer, to those failings I presently will turn.

First, the disclaimer: if it is not already clear, I must reiterate that I am not challenging the accuracy or authority of Scripture, which is inviolable, but rather, I am questioning our methods of defending and propagating it, which are not. If I find some aspects of our case for inerrancy less than convincing and can explain why, then we might possibly be able to identify, and to correct, some of the tactical lapses in our dealings with non-inerrantists. In the end we might also discover, if we had not already suspected it, that the reason the non-inerrantists refuse to line up with us on this important issue is not because they are stupid, dishonest, narrow-minded, or reprobate. Perhaps we have not yet made the convincing case we think we have. I, for one, believe some of our more commonly repeated arguments are faulty. To date, I have identified what I believe are seven such tactical errors that we evangelicals frequently commit in defending inerrancy.[1]

I. THE SLIPPERY SLOPE ARGUMENT

Because the issue of the Bible's inerrancy appears to some of us to be a watershed issue, we frequently argue that if one takes a stand against full biblical authority, one has stepped onto a slippery slope that very probably will lead to further theological concessions and perhaps even to spiritual shipwreck. Examples from the past of people or institutions and denominations that have slid down that slope are marshalled as evidence for our case. Once the anchor of inerrancy is rejected, we reason, one's theological and spiritual stability is jeopardized. We conclude, therefore, that one ought to hold to scriptural infallibility, for safety's sake.

But, for several reasons, this argument will not do. First, it posits a highly suspect cause and effect relationship between one point of doctrine and a subsequent course of events. Every good historian realizes that the relationship between ideas and events is exceedingly difficult to identify and to analyze. The historical reconstruction this argument proposes could involve as many as three historiographical fallacies: 1) the fallacy of *post hoc, propter hoc*, which assumes that if event B occurred after event A, then event B was caused by event A; 2) the fallacy of *cum hoc, propter hoc*, which misidentifies repeated correlation with causation by assuming that if A and B occur in tandem with a great deal of regularity, then A caused B; and 3) the fallacy of mistaking logical sequence with historical causation by arguing that, because B follows A in a logically causative sequence, when B follows A in a historical sequence a cause/effect relationship can reasonably be assumed. When we employ such faulty arguments we leave ourselves open to harsh and justifiable criticism from the outside. Though it is obviously overstated, we ought to remember Wittgenstein's caveat that belief in the causal nexus is sometimes a superstition.

Historiographical fallacies aside, the debatable cause and effect sequence we have reconstructed from our (arguably biased) selection of the historical and theological data before us, nevertheless, is advanced as confidently as if we actually *knew* the theological and spiritual dynamics at work in the mind or life of any given individual rather than were merely speculating about them. I question whether we know even ourselves[2] so surely as we claim to know others, even vast numbers of others who are, in some cases, long dead, and, in other cases, unknown to us even by name or by sight. We have cause to be far more modest in our generalizations about historical causation and about the psychological factors operative in believing and in changing belief. When we evangelicals are treated so cavalierly and with such insensitive generalization by those who oppose us, we respond with horror and indignation. I think our response to such treatment is warranted. Yet, when we inflict such treatment on others, we are bewildered by the way they cling so tenaciously to their obvious error. Our tactical and procedural unfairness is perhaps one reason they do so.

When we advance the slippery slope argument against our opponents we fail to appreciate how really weak it is unless and until we aim it at ourselves and feel its actual impact. Imagine, if you will, that a non-inerrantist argued, in true slippery slope form, that inerrancy is a dangerous belief that could, and has, led to tragic consequences. "James Jones, Bob Jones, and Jehovah's Witnesses believe in inerrancy," he says. "Once you believe *that* doctrine, you could end up a madman, an obscurantist, or a cultist. By all means, then, avoid it. The lesson of history is clear. Once you give in on this point and become an inerrantist, the camel's nose is in the tent. Who knows where it will lead?" No competent evangelical theologian would be convinced that inerrancy was dangerous, much less to abandon it, on that basis. That theologian would see immediately how repulsive and unfair such a case is. But, of course, when *we* argue that way, we think the case is different. Used in favor of inerrancy, we deceive ourselves into thinking this argument is more compelling than it really is.

The third reason non-inerrantists reject this slippery slope argument is because it is an argument based upon expediency and not truth. It says, when used alone, that one should believe inerrancy because it works rather than because it is true. By using this argument it appears as if we assume that non-inerrantists build their theologies on a utilitarian basis rather than on what they perceive to be a factual one. Our assumption that they are, in effect, theologically dishonest, is highly insulting. Like us, they believe what they believe because they think it true, not because they think it convenient, useful, or safe (concepts that admit of considerable debate themselves). Non-inerrantists, like inerrantists, are interested in truth, not merely pragmatic preference. Moreover, if we argue according to the slippery slope paradigm, we do so probably because we find it convincing. That may imply some very uncomplimentary things about us, our epistemology, and our methods.

The fourth weakness of the slippery slope paradigm is the debatable value judgment inherent in our analysis of the relative desirability of past and present theological conditions. This argument can have force only to those who think the present state of things is worse than the first. Leaving aside the vexed question concerning what constitutes a better or worse theological condition, I know of few non-inerrantist theologians who believe Princeton Seminary was a better place 150 years ago than it is today. The slippery slope argument is absurd to those who think recent trends constitute an advance and not a fall.

In short, the sooner we abandon this approach to the problem of defending inerrancy the better it will be. This argument is inconclusive, uncharitable, and historiographically and philosophically faulty.[3]

II. The Theological Deduction Argument

In our zeal to defend the reliability of the Bible, we often implement arguments based on the theological deductions we draw from certain scriptural texts. This method of argument can entail not only certain exegetical fallacies,[4] it seems to depend upon certain discredited medieval methods of theological formulation. For example, we argue that 1) God inspired the Bible; 2) God does not lie; 3) therefore, the Bible is without error. But this is a faulty argument in at least two ways. First, it is an "apples and oranges" affair. That is, it falsely identifies errors with lies. Mistakes in Scripture, if they existed, would not necessarily be lies. Inaccuracy and moral culpability are not the same. When we detect an error on a student's test or in a student's research paper, we do not think that student is evil or despicable: "A" students are not necessarily more moral than "B" students. When a student tells me something he thinks is true about Zwingli but is not, he is not lying to me. Nor are we to think that either the human or the Divine Author is lying to us if we find an error in the Bible.

The reason we must not draw such blasphemous conclusions is my second point. Such a false identification of scriptural result with the being and character of God is insupportable. Our method fails to distinguish between the intentions of God (which do reflect His nature) and the resultant phenomena in space and time, which may not. We cannot label (or libel) God by means of our perception of the state of the biblical data. For example, we would consider as ridiculous any conclusion that God had but a pedestrian command of Hebrew and Greek because of the occasional grammatical lapses in Scripture. The state of the text is not necessarily a reflection on God. Nor could we conclude that God was poor at math because the Biblical text contains some strange and confusing numerical data. That He permits such things to occur, even employs them for His own ends, is no bad reflection on His character or His abilities. God is not to be thought ambiguous, deceitful, or duplicitous simply because Paul's words occasionally are infuriatingly vague or unclear. Other beings than God have had their way in the matter. Their actions do not necessarily reflect on Him. The book before us is both human and divine. In other words, whether they occurred in the original autographs or in subsequent copies, if errors of fact ever surfaced in the Bible, they would not necessarily be lies from God. Furthermore, it does no good to argue that mathematical errors or grammatical infelicities are inconsequential or else not as important as errors of substance. God's idea of substance might possibly equate with those entertained by twentieth-century American evangelicals. It might not. We have no sure word that grammatical infelicities bother God any less (or any more) than infelicities of number or sequence, for example. We cannot dogmatically assert that Paul's shipwreck of grammar in portions of Galatians is any more or less appealing or appalling to God than the unusual numbers in Kings or Chronicles. It's all guesswork, and the non-inerrantists are not likely to resign their beliefs over *that*.

III. The Christological Argument

In our effort to convince others of the Bible's infallibility, we frequently make appeal to Christ himself. We appeal, on the one hand, to his recorded words and, on the other hand, to our understanding of the incarnation. Jesus, we say, held to the supreme accuracy of Scripture. Furthermore, in the same way that Christ was without sin, the Bible is without error. But these are not telling arguments. First, they repeat the error of labeling mistakes as sins, about which we have previously spoken. Second, even if we demonstrate beyond any possibility of dissent that the words recorded in the Bible are actually the words of Jesus Himself and not those of the evangelists, and that Jesus, when he so spoke, was not accommodating himself to his audience; even if we demonstrate that those words reflect a bibliological view identical to that which we espouse, we have not yet got a case against the non-inerrantists. To those who, like me, maintain a high view of Christ, such an argument is a conclusive one. But, judging from those I studied under in seminary and in graduate school, I dare say that most theologians outside our circle do not hold such a view of Christ. Unless someone already holds an exalted view of the authority of Christ (which, in most instances, is to say that unless someone already holds a high view of the Bible) such an appeal is unconvincing and circular. Apart from an exalted view of Christ, appeal to His words does not constitute proof. Normally, one cannot establish an exalted view of Christ without appeal to the reliability of Scripture, and *that*, in this case, is begging the question. An appeal to Jesus is conclusive only if Jesus is an authoritative teacher of doctrine and only if the Bible gives reliable data about His teachings. Because a number of non-inerrantists believe both these premises are faulty, they reject our conclusion. We do the same to theirs. In other words, unless our opponents already share certain of our theological presuppositions, a mere appeal to Jesus will not settle the issue. Our deft alteration of a bibliological issue into a Christological one ("Don't argue with me, argue with Jesus.") is flatly ineffective.

Much less will an appeal to our understanding of the incarnation resolve the question. We sometimes attempt to justify our belief in the inerrancy of Scripture by drawing an analogy between inspiration and incarnation. We trot out all the comparisons *we* see between the Word becoming flesh and the Word of God coming to us in the words of men. From those comparisons we argue that a sinless Jesus is analogous to an errorless Bible. My point is not that no analogy exists — it might. But I deny that we have any sure idea of what exactly it is. The process of incarnation and its multiform consequences and implications remain a profound mystery to us. How God became a man we do not know. In the same light, the incarnational consciousness is not readily open to investigation by us; nor can it be used as a convincing basis for argumentation. We do not know much about what it was like to be both God and man in ancient Judea. Across this great distance in time, and over this great gap in culture, such a retrieval of knowledge is no longer possible, if ever it was. To combine this vast incarnational mystery with our equally sketchy notions of how we imagine God inspired written words long ago and far away, and then to make from this double guess an argument by analogy for the inerrancy of the Bible is, at least as it concerns its evidential value, an exercise in futility. The inherent tenuousness of argument by analogy aside, such speculations have little, if any, real conclusive force. They arise not from demonstrable fact, but from mere educated guesswork, perhaps even ignorance. This is only dead reckoning. We know not whereof we speak, and the non-inerrantists know that about us on this point. The functional procedures of God on the frontier between the human and the divine in the incarnation may be the same as those on the frontier between the human and the divine in inspiration. Only God knows for sure, and He has not said. In light of that divine silence, non-inerrantists will remain unconvinced by our vociferous declamations. And they should. Silence is much to be preferred over arguments drawn from it.

IV. The Definition of Error Argument

Most of us probably have endured the frustration of arguing theological epistemology with our Roman Catholic and Eastern Orthodox friends. Their assertions of papal or ecclesiastical and conciliar infallibility seem to us to be protected by the wall of a thousand qualifications. They seem to us to be what Erasmus seemed to Luther: a slippery eel only Christ could grab. Their answers sometimes appear to be evasions. We may think we have struck a telling blow only to find that they maintain their views merely by verbal nuance, not by argument.

Non-inerrantists find our definitions of error equally exasperating. To them we seem to employ one sense of the word error in reference to the Bible and another the rest of the day. To them, what we quickly would count wrong on a student's test, we offer reverential adherence to simply because it occurs in the Bible. To non-inerrantists we appear to cheat. We expend prodigious effort justifying a scriptural writer's statement or harmonizing one biblical text with another, but when it comes to a student's paper (or a liberal's monograph) negative judgment is hastily rendered. We seldom hesitate to correct sophomores, liberals, or writers in journals. But, when it comes to the Bible, our opponents believe we are unwilling to call a spade a spade. Until we can establish, *and consistently apply*, a definition for error that holds both inside the Bible and out, we will not convince dissenters to join us.

V. The Bursting Balloon Argument[5]

The fifth tactical failure I recognize is that argument which implies that the authority of the Bible is very much like a balloon. If you put a pin prick in it anywhere it collapses. Except for its power as a scare tactic, this argument is without merit and will not serve to establish the doctrine of biblical inerrancy. I reject it for two reasons. First, while it springs from, and is intended to uphold, our profound reverence for Scripture, it accomplishes the opposite result. It treats the Bible with an almost unparalleled procedural disdain. If the Bible is wrong on this point, we say, it cannot be trusted anywhere. If the Bible is not fully reliable, it cannot be trusted at all. But no book in the world, much less the Bible, should be handled with such extremism or rejected on such radical grounds. None of us would throw our telephone book away if we discovered an error (or even several errors) within it. The phone book has proven its reliability in many instances. Telephone numbers shown to be correct are still correct whether or not the last one you dialed got through to the person you intended. The same holds true for the Bible. Those places in the Bible that truly have been verified by external evidence still remain verified whether or not some portion of Zephaniah is contravened in the future. One error does not undo that fact. When the stakes are so high, as they surely are in terms of our spiritual destiny, premature rejection of any volume that has upheld its credibility as admirably as has the Bible is patently foolish. No non-inerrantist will return to inerrancy (and no inerrantist should continue to maintain it) solely on the strength of that advice.

The second weakness of this argument is, if anything, more dangerous than the first. To reject the Bible so utterly and so contemptuously on the basis of some irreconcilable error (or errors) is not a counsel of wisdom; it is a counsel of despair. Rather than teaching students to commit spiritual suicide, we ought to be teaching them that even if errors did surface, all is not lost — including their souls. No clear thinking theologian would teach that if the sequence of the succession of kings is flawed in some Old Testament narrative, or if Luke's political details cannot be made to harmonize with extra-biblical sources, then Christ is still in his grave, the Bible is junk, and everyone will live and die without hope. Such conclusions are simply detestable. They encourage people to build houses of cards for their souls. They engender misplaced faith by focusing it upon our doctrines about the Bible rather than on the living God behind Scripture, and on Jesus Christ, His only Son. Do not wonder that non-inerrantists find this dangerous and wrong-headed advice less than compelling evidence for biblical inerrancy.[6]

VI. The Expectation Argument

This tactical error is committed when we argue that because scholarly investigations have established the reliability of the Bible in so many previous instances, we may reasonably expect they will continue to do so, in every case. In that light, we may confidently expect (indeed publicly assert) that all the cards will fall our way.

Yet, despite these assured results and our confident predictions, non-inerrantists remain non-inerrantists. They do so because they understand quite clearly that expectation does not constitute proof. The fact that archaeological investigations seem to support some statement in Joshua does not mean that all Jude says is correct. Simply because I believe that the Bible's integrity has been upheld repeatedly by previous investigation, I can neither conclude nor argue that it always will be. It might. It might not. The verdict is still out on that count, and it is that verdict which is at issue. We cannot assume the point to be proven and, on the basis of that assumption, urge people to join our side. All we can conclude from past investigations of particular phenomena is what those past investigations actually have concluded. Such prior analyses are conclusive (if at all) only about previous issues, not those yet to be addressed.

Not only does this argument beg the question by assuming inerrancy for that portion of Scripture where external verification is still lacking, not only is it unfairly disguising expectation as proof or argument, but it fails to note sufficiently the ambiguity of previous investigations. The yield from earlier analyses is not so overwhelmingly compelling as this argument makes it appear. Despite our claims that not a single spadeful of Middle Eastern dirt stands against the Bible, no non-inerrantist shares our opinion that our win-loss record in argument and in investigative analysis is absolutely unblemished. We argue as if it were obvious to all non-inerrantists that we were 36-0. They would say, in a generous mood, that perhaps we were 16-20, and that perhaps we were not even that good. In many cases, the verdict concerning the outcome of an investigation depends in large part upon the person passing judgment. Such verdicts often are far from incontestable. The fact that we continue to evaluate each new case in our favor does not persuade non-inerrantists to become inerrantists. *Their* expectation from the track record is not that the Bible is error free, but that we probably will continue to claim it is. Perhaps they see better than we do that our verdicts on past arguments and investigations, and the expectations we derive from those verdicts, often say as much about us as they do about the Bible.

Theirs do the same.

VII. The Perspectival Argument

The final tactical error arises from what C. S. Lewis identified as "chronological snobbery": the tendency to identify truth with modernity. Because we naturally incline to measure all statements from the past against the yardstick of prevalent current consensus, we are, in effect, identifying truth with our own view, however culturally determined or culturally relative (and hence transitory) it might be. When a Fortress Theologian asserts the truthfulness of the Bible, he usually does so on the assumption that what the Bible teaches is congruent with the fundamentals of his own modern worldview, apparently forgetting that the modern mindset is but one in a series of successive worldviews and that it too will probably be slowly modified, if not abandoned, as were all its predecessors. Thus, insofar as a Fortress Theologian successfully ties the truth of the Bible to prevailing notions, and insofar as those notions will be slowly overturned, the Fortress Theologian has succeeded in *falsifying* Scripture for future generations.

To be specific, the way the fundamental structures of the universe have been perceived through the centuries has altered dramatically and repeatedly. But, because the wheels of time turn imperceptibly in this regard, we tend to forget that the movement of the ages that brought our present view to the fore might well relegate it to the background in succeeding centuries, as it has those that came before, and as it seems to be doing even now. But, our unconscious chronological snobbery tempts us to assume that viewpoints that prevail today are absolute truth and can never be superseded. Our ignorance of our historical conditionedness blinds us to the transitory nature of some of our most cherished beliefs and prevents us from holding them with appropriate humility and teachableness. We vainly imagine that what happened to the greatest thinkers of the past and to their revolutionary insights will never happen to us and to ours. Somehow (though we cannot say how) we presume that we shall escape the fate of the previous greats, upon whose very shoulders we stand.

That is, while the Copernican revolution rightly threw the Church and its prevailing theology into great turmoil, Copernicanism itself has been corrected on some fundamental points. The same holds true for Darwinian evolutionism and Einsteinian relativity, both of which have undergone (and are undergoing) serious modification. We do not know what modifications yet await us and which, if any, of them will endure. Thus, to tie the Bible irretrievably to modern notions that themselves are subject to revision is to undermine for future generations the very text we so desperately seek to defend to ours.

Beware of the subtle arrogance that argues that because the Bible agrees with you and your group, it therefore is without error. If you do not, you too might become the theological buffoon to succeeding generations that the church appears to us to have been in its dealings with Galileo.

Our views are significantly perspectival, and our arguments ought to take that fact into account.

Those are, to me, the seven chief tactical errors we make in our dealings with non-inerrantists. I am persuaded that none of them has merit enough to justify continued use, at least as they relate to our efforts to convince the unconvinced. Exaggerations, question beggings, faulty logic, uncharitable assumptions, and unsubstantiated conclusions can hardly be said to further our cause. Nor do I believe that our case is any more compelling when these arguments are seen together. Let us not delude ourselves into thinking that the juxtaposition of seven flawed arguments constitutes a conclusive case, simply because the arguments are joined. The conjunction of inconclusive arguments constitutes a case that can be questioned, perhaps even refuted, at every point. The non-inerrantists, at least, think so. That is why most of them stopped reading our books long ago. They think them sometimes silly and sometimes offensive, both to reason and to good taste. I used to hold it as a point of pride that in my schooling in evangelical institutions I was required to read the texts written by the other side, while in my schooling at liberal institutions I was not. Being an inerrantist, I did not understand fully why this was so. I thought it was a clear case of liberal obscurantism. I never noticed how glaring my own headlights were. I kept staring only at theirs.

But where to go from here? My advice is twofold. First, we can believe in and argue for the Bible's inerrancy only if the Bible is inerrant. Our focus must be, therefore, on the accuracy and reliability of the Biblical data, not upon our theological deductions about them. All arguments must derive from a careful and honest evaluation of the factual accuracy of the scriptural phenomena. Arguments based upon our theology have been, and will continue to be, unproductive. Conclusions drawn from premises our opponents do not share will leave them unmoved. The case is to be determined by an assessment of the data that is as objective and even-handed as possible. Even *that* may not win them over, as events have shown. It is, nevertheless, our best shot, the only one I'm told they'll listen to patiently.

Second, if we counsel our opponents to be open-minded, teachable, objective, and patient scholars of good will, scholars who can feel the weight of the other side's case, then I believe we ought to insist upon the same qualities in ourselves and our colleagues. We ought also to remember that these academic virtues, like spiritual humility, are exceedingly difficult to attain and, once acquired, are not self-conscious and cannot be flaunted. Any scholar who publicly proclaims his objectivity (or even cherishes it in his own private thoughts) probably lacks that very thing he praises. The best of us has ample reason for modesty and considerable room for improvement. A healthy skepticism (or even agnosticism) on many of the points at issue is not unjustified. This, at least, is what the best among us tell me. That is what helps make them the best. The rest of us have miles to go before we sleep.

END NOTES

1 Because my intention in this chapter is to expose fallacies and not individual theologians, I purposely have avoided naming names or providing bibliographical references for the errors I cite, even though such citations could easily be made. Moreover, many of these apologetic failings are so well known and so widely employed that formal citation would be redundant.

2 The self-knowledge and motivation of some inerrantists, most notably himself, has been poignantly and courageously revealed in Clark Pinnock,

The Scripture Principle (San Francisco: Harper & Row, 1984), p. 58.

3 For further criticism of these and similar historiographical shortcomings, see Colin Brown, *History & Faith: A Personal Exploration* (Grand Rapids: Zondervan, 1987), pp. 40-42.

4 I am thinking here of the common evangelical practice of moving from grammatico-historical exegesis to logico-critical exegesis. The former seeks to determine, as far as possible, what the author of a text intended it to mean. This is done by determining how words were used at a given time and place and how the author in question probably was using them in the text under review. Logico-critical exegesis, by contrast, tries to establish the Bible's teachings by treating an author's statement as a philosophical proposition. It then draws a series or sequence of logical deductions from that reconstituted philosophical proposition in order to establish its theological implications. The failure and/or weaknesses of the latter method are at least fourfold: (1) by deducing implications B, C, D, and E from premise A, the exegete is moving *away from* the Biblical text, not into it; (2) by transforming a statement that might originally have been historical, poetical, theological, or exhortational, into one that is philosophical, the exegete has altered the fundamental nature of the text in question and drawn it through an alien and distortive interpretive grid; (3) by failing to evaluate his conclusions carefully, the exegete often has not adequately distinguished among philosophical conclusions that are (a) necessary, (b) probable, (c) plausible, and (d) possible; (4) by identifying his deductions as Biblical truth, the exegete has forgotten that inspiration and inerrancy relate to the sacred writers and their texts, not to philosophical deductions made from Scripture. The former are reliable; the latter might not be. That is, deductions are glosses, and glosses are fallible. By confusing the two, the reader has obtruded himself upon the text and corrupted the author's meaning with interpretive philosophical deductions. The elaborate rationalistic superstructure that some exegetes erect upon the text must not be treated as if it were the text. The one may sink and the other rise. Logico-critical exegesis, in other words, is usually a gloss upon the text, not an exploration into it.

5 In some respects, the "Bursting Balloon Argument" and the "Slippery Slope Argument" are quite similar. In this chapter I relate the former to our perception of errancy's epistemological and spiritual consequences; I relate the latter to our understanding of its historical consequences.

6 Arguments such as this also make objective analysis *exceedingly* difficult

to achieve. If one believes that spiritual destitution and epistemological chaos inevitably result from a single error in the original autographs of Scripture, one is highly unlikely to be able to recognize such an error or to acknowledge its presence, even if it occurred.

THEOLOGY PROPER, CHRISTOLOGY, SPIRITUALITY

"We see but one aspect of our neighbor, as we see but one side of the moon; in either case there is also a dark half which is unknown to us. We all come down to dinner, but each has a room to himself."

WALTER BAGEHOT
Literary Studies, 1: 134

"The man who believes in his heart that man is an animal will live like an animal. In a certain sense and within certain limits the statement is true, you are what you believe yourself to be."

EMIL BRUNNER
Our Faith, p. 36

"It is the glory of man that even the most abject misery cannot efface the image of God which he bears; under any condition, however ghastly, he is still the vice-regent of God, and his final destiny is the vision of God in Heaven. Man must go on, but unless man believes that he is what the Christian Faith says he is, it is doubtful whether he will have the courage to do so."

ERIC MASCALL
Man: His Origin and Destiny, p. 85

"The dust to which this flesh shall return, it is the ancient dreaming dust of God."

JOHN MELLENCAMP
"Human Wheels"

5

The First Adam and the Second

I. THE FIRST ADAM: WHAT WE WERE MADE

You'd be hard pressed to understand the shape or function of a key if you had never seen a lock; hard pressed to understand a bow if you had never seen or heard a violin. Some things need to be seen together for you to understand them aright. Seen in isolation, they remain a mystery.

Human beings are like that. You cannot understand them, one or all, if you see them alone. You cannot understand a man without a woman, or a woman without a man. You can understand neither women nor men without God. Indeed, you cannot understand even yourself, if you see yourself in isolation. Here's why:

While Genesis explicitly tells us that all the other creatures of God were made "according to their own kind" (Gen 1:20), that language is curiously and significantly missing from the Biblical account of human beginnings. For humans (and for humans only), the Biblical text says that we were made "in the image and likeness of God" (Gen 1: 26), not simply after our own kind. Presumably there is something about us that makes us different from the animals, something about us that makes us in some way God's "kind" — his picture and his partner. Between God and us there exists a reciprocity and kinship not found anywhere else. He relates uniquely to us, and we to Him.

We can, and we did, walk with God in the Garden (just as later he walked with us on the roads of Galilee). Between God and humans is a profound and enduring companionship rooted in likeness, much as there is between one human and all others.

Put differently, because we human beings are the living pictures and partners of God, divine things cannot simply be brushed aside when human beings are the question, as if the Divine were irrelevant or insignificant in our quest for self-knowledge. To know who we are is first to know who He is. According to Genesis, we have the divine as the distinctive and determining influence upon us and within us. In that light, anything we might say about God is somehow related to what we might say about ourselves. In light of the creation account in Scripture, there exist many things we might say about God.

When, in the Bible's very first chapter, God declares his intention to make human beings in his own image ("Let us make man in our image," he said.), the only thing we know about him at that point is that he is a communal, articulate maker. By communal I mean that God is a community ("us"), a Trinity as we learn later: Father, Son and Holy Spirit. By articulate maker I mean that his Word is the creative power behind the universe. He makes worlds with words.

Because we are made in his image, and because he is a communal, articulate maker, we are communal and communicative too. That means that we humans are not complete in isolation. Togetherness, not aloneness, is our natural condition. Togetherness (community and communication) is what God intended for us. He made it a requirement both for our prospering and for our joy. Indeed, the God who made us explicitly declared that "it was not good for Adam to be alone" (Gen 2:18). We are social, communicative beings by divine design, because we are like God, and because He is a communal, articulate maker. From that fact emerges both a theology of society and a theology of politics, if we care to think them through. Biblical anthropology leads to politics and to culture, and it all has it roots in Genesis. In other words, because God made us in his image, and because he is Trinity, we are inescapably social and verbal beings. We need others in order to become ourselves. Without others, we cannot even be born. We are dependent upon others throughout life, and they depend upon us as well. This interdependence is rooted not in our sameness, but in our differences. Even though God made all persons, and even though God made all persons in his image or likeness, he did not make them all the same. Just as no two snowflakes are the same, no two persons are identical either. Not all persons have, or even can have, the same social functions or make the same contributions. While God fitted some persons for spectacular tasks, most are not. But all are needed and all are valuable. When one of us does not become all that he or she could have been and should have been, the world is poorer for it, for we are neither interchangeable nor replaceable. Not all persons have the same duties, privileges and rewards because not all persons have the same God-given capacities. But our natural and God-given differences do not mean that all persons do not have a right to the freedom and respect for which God Himself made them.

When I say that we are like God, I do not wish to give you the wrong impression. *Like* is not the same as *equal to*. We are God's image, not his equal. That is why in God's presence we often feel two very different things at once – comfort and awe. He is our Father, which is comforting; and He is our Maker and King, which sometimes stops us in mid-stride or in mid-thought. In other words, we are like Him, but we are his subjects, his creatures, not his counterparts.

I can say it differently: Among the first questions you must ask yourself about things new or strange to you are these: What is it? Who made it? and Why? In our case, the answer to such questions is: We exist by the will, the work, and the Word of our heavenly Father. He spoke and we were made. Whatever else you might say about us, we are the result of divine command. He spoke; we live. We do not just happen to exist. We come from eternity itself; that is, we come from our eternal Divine Parent. We come from the will, and mind, and Word of God. Our roots go deep into "the everlasting counsels" of our heavenly Father. His eternal counsels define both our role and our destiny. As my friend Michael Williams explains our role and destiny: "The image of God does not make man unique from the created order; but rather unique within the created order . . . Polar bears are creatures of God, but they are not persons. Angelic beings are persons, but they are not called to rule over creation. Only humankind is given this dual relatedness, the calling to mediate the covenant of creation."[1]

The image of God is found more in our relationship to God and the world than in our supposed substance or in the aggregate of our component parts. The image of God is more relational and personal than it is ontological, which is why I have said simply that we are God's pictures and partners. As such, we represent Him to the world He made, and the world He made to Him. In other words, the Biblical description of humanity is representational and relational, not philosophical or ontological. For example, God commanded us "to be fruitful and multiply," to "fill the earth and subdue" it (Gen 1:28). We are to have "dominion" over it. A higher position in this world is inconceivable.[2]

As Genesis also makes clear, God created us not only by his Word, but for his Word. We were made to receive God's Word. We were made to hear Him, to contemplate Him, to respond to Him, to accompany Him, to love him, and to reflect Him. We were made sometimes even to speak for Him, as Adam did when he named all the animals (Gen. 2:19). We were intended for dialogue with God. We are able to respond to God, and He to us. We become fully the persons God intends us to be only when we receive and reflect something from God, namely his Word, whether you think of God's Word as his Son or as his message. We are to receive and to respond to both. We are properly and fully human only so far as God's Word echoes in our hearts and renews and reforms our minds, only to the extent that we resemble his Son, the Word, into whose likeness we are being transformed.

Adam and Eve's intimate fellowship with God indicates that we live with God and for God. Upon our connection to God literally everything concerning us depends. If ever he forgot us, we should cease to be. However often we might forget God, He never forgets us — not for a moment. We are his friends, his companions, his creatures, his likeness, and his image. We are his own living pictures of Himself. I say it reverently, and I say it with amazement, but it seems for all the world like God finds us endlessly fascinating, endlessly troubling and infuriating, and yet suitable for his love. If that is what He thinks of us, it must be so, no matter how we might feel about ourselves from moment to moment or from day to day.

To put the whole matter differently, we are amphibians. We live in (and we were made for) two worlds at once, and our very nature makes it clear. Our physicality ties us to the earth and to the dust from which we were made, while our souls, breathed into us, as it were, by the breath of God Himself (Gen 2:7), tie us to heaven. This world is our home, our bodies say, and heaven is as well, so say our souls. Our dual nature (our amphibian selves) indicates that we have both a vertical relationship to the God above us, and a horizontal relationship to the world around us.

From Genesis we learn that we human beings are dual in another way: Not only are we body and soul, we are (taken as a whole) "male and female" (Gen 1:27). From that amazing and significant fact has sprung much of life's beauty and richness, on the one hand, and much of its treachery and sadness, on the other. That we are male and female is the root of much of our greatest literature, our most beautiful music, and our most haunting and memorable art.

Not only do many of the greatest cultural monuments of our civilization stem from the fact that we our male and female, but the survival of the race itself depends upon it. By the union of male and female immortal souls meant for eternal life with God are brought into existence. What serves to increase the population of this world can, and should, increase the population of the next, which is why Jeremy Taylor, the famous 17th century English theologian, insisted that marriage was the nursery of heaven. Nothing we do confers so much dignity upon us and our actions as when, in human intercourse, God makes our physical union the means of producing an everlasting soul that will know God, serve God, and enjoy God forever. Natural actions sometimes have supernatural consequences. But not all of them are good. Some of the souls thus made will be lost, and perhaps lost forever. Sex can eventually lead to that tragedy too, just as it has led to so much of the world's sordid treachery and to the breaking of billions of hearts and the ruining of countless lives.

From the account of our creation in Genesis, we deduce also that when we fulfill our duty, we are doing what we were made for, doing what leads to our blessing and fulfillment. In rejecting or neglecting our duty, we are turning from God and from our soul's health, our soul's food, indeed from the only thing that can make us content even in slums, even in dungeons, even in the face of death itself.

To put a point on it, God commands us to live lawfully with Him — not for his sake, of course, but for our own. God made us not for his happiness, but for ours. God is complete and needs nothing. We are fallen and need everything. Indeed, one definition of a human being in a fallen world is to be one unending need. What we need is God, as St. Augustine so memorably confessed long ago when he said this to God: "You have made us for yourself, and our hearts are restless until they find their rest in You."

In other words, God is to us what water is for fish, what air is for birds, and what earth is for animals — He is our proper environment, our natural habitat. In Him we are to live, to move, to love, and to have our being (Acts 17:28). We can hardly have a better indication of our nature and of God's intention for us than to know that without Him we can never truly prosper, which is another way of saying that every human pleasure pursued apart from God inevitably leads to frustration, destruction and despair — every one. But that lesson is as old as Ecclesiastes: Without God all is vanity; all is empty; all is tedious, all is worthless and dead. In our all-too-individualistic and selfish age, we forget that the Biblical notion of person means not an autonomous individual, but one who is able to take part in the lives of others, including the life of God Himself, our Maker and Redeemer.

In obeying God you are not doing Him any benefit. In obeying God you are doing the one thing that brings you the greatest joy and the greatest satisfaction, even though we seem to forget that fact continually. As C. S. Lewis once observed, we human beings are far too easily satisfied. We dally endlessly with sex, money, power, and fame while infinite joy is being offered us. Or, as Eric Mascall puts it, when you turn from God and seek your satisfaction in yourself, you not only are sinning, you are distorting your very nature and deforming yourself.[3]

II. THE SECOND ADAM: WHAT WE MADE OF OURSELVES, AND WHAT CHRIST INTENDS TO MAKE OF US

Both for better and for worse, we humans have the freedom to be different from what we were created to be, from what we ought to be. Indeed, we all are different from what we ought to be. We bear about in our very hearts the expansive and enduring inner contradiction about what it means to be a fallen creature in a fallen world. We all are prime examples of the grandeur and the grime of being human, what Pascal called the misery and the majesty of humanity. Nothing human is wholly absent the original glory of our divine creation; and nothing human is wholly devoid of the marks of the fall.

To understand better both sides of that coin, to understand better both what are the marks of the fall and the marks of the glorious destiny which, under the grace of God, still is ours, we have to look at not only the first Adam (which we have done), but also at the Second. To see most fully from what heights we have fallen, and to contemplate the splendid transformation that is our destiny, we need to look at Christ, for nowhere else but in Him are God, grace, and humanity so fully revealed. Everything in Scripture moves toward this pivotal Person, and to what theologians sometimes call "the Christ event" — the Incarnation of Jesus — for in Him God has created (or recreated) a new breed of humans. Christ is the Second Adam. He is the head of a new humanity. What Christ is, we shall someday be (1 John 3:2). In the life and person of Christ, both what we are now and what we shall become are most clearly revealed. In Christ's death we see the depth and reality of our sin, but in his blessed and all-conquering resurrection and ascension, we see our destiny. Despite our sin and guilt, we are bound for glory and bliss. For that astonishing fact, praise God. We shall see Christ as he is, for we shall be like Him. In the shocking and sobering words of 2 Peter 1:4, we sinful, broken, rebellious wretches shall one day become "partakers of the divine nature," just as the Divine Redeemer became, and always will remain, a partaker in human nature. So to Him, the Second Adam, we now must turn.

When God became a man, that man was Jesus of Nazareth. In Him something happened that never happened before or since: What Martin Luther called "Deus absconditus," or the hidden God, the unseen God, became visible and tangible. The very Author of human life came out from hiding, came out from behind the curtain of this world and showed Himself to us both visibly and tangibly. Indeed, in Christ God became so visible and so tangible that Jesus could say with full confidence and with deep meaning that "he who had seen me has seen the Father." He and his Father, he said, were one. He did what he saw his Father do, and He said what he heard his Father say. He is God in flesh, God in human terms. Indeed, He is the one place where we can see God most clearly and fully, which is why, in his first letter, the apostle John so confidently affirmed that his message and his epistle are based upon that which he, John, had seen with his own eyes, heard with his own ears, and had touched with his own hands concerning the Word of Life (1 John 1:1) — Jesus of Nazareth, whom the New Testament calls "the express image of the Father." He is what we were intended to be: the human image and likeness of God.

Jesus of Nazareth is the Rosetta Stone of all things divine and human. He is, so to speak, the cosmic Decoder Ring of all things visible and invisible. For example, Scripture tells us that no one has seen God at any time, except the Son, Who has exegeted, or elucidated, God for us (John 1:18). God is the one we meet revealed in Christ. The word "God" is a Christologically defined term. As Gareth Moore once explained to me, "While there are many descriptions of God, there is no privileged description of God, unless one speaks of the scriptural images. When we do, we realize that God is like Jesus Christ. Thus, if you ask what is God like, the answer is that he is not like anything. But, if you ask who is God like, the answer is he is like Jesus. To understand God, therefore, you must read the Gospels.[4] To know God is to know Christ. It's as plain as that.

But to know Christ is also to know ourselves. Apart from his spotless humanity we don't really know who we are. Without the light shed upon us by the Incarnation, we comprehend neither the unimaginable depths to which we have fallen, every one of us, nor the heights to which we are destined. Without Christ, we don't understand rightly the horrifying depth and breadth of our depravity. Only in light of Christ do we see how poorly we reflect the God who made us. In Christ we see the reality of both our high birth and our low descent. He came to show us ourselves and to remake us in redemption. He came to reconcile us (along with the whole world) to the Father in whose image we are, and in whom our happiness is exclusively found. In the light of Christ's righteousness and truth, we see what lies we have believed and what lies we have become.

To think of ourselves as living, breathing lies is not to be a mere naysayer or a cynic. You are not a cynic simply because you look the ugly facts squarely in the face. Quite the opposite: you are a Pollyanna and a silly coward if you do not. Our real business is to keep an open eye and a clear head, so that we can arm ourselves against the vapid and self-congratulating slogans of our day and against the half–true truisms by which we too often live, if living is the right word for thoughtlessly wandering through life, unresistingly falling for every solicitation to evil and hypocrisy that comes down the pike. We must look the facts in the face. We must see ourselves as we are. There's no sense lying to ourselves when it comes to our soul. It's the truth that sets us free (John 8:32), and the truth about us is that our miseries are of our own making. Our deepest and most enduring afflictions are not outside us, but inside us. Indeed we ourselves are this planet's most enduring and malignant ailment. Our problems are not the fault of our Maker. Both the world and the very selves that we were given were, in God's own words, "very good" (Gen 1:31). But what was all "very good" we have scrambled and spoiled. Our troubles are moral and spiritual at the root. "We are not like an accountant who has got his books wrong through bad arithmetic; we are like the one who has got them wrong because he is out to swindle his employer."[5] We are diseased at the heart. We are defective across all the lines and divisions of life, without exception. We are not wounded; we are dead. We have not stumbled; we have perished. Nothing in us — nothing — is truly good. Indeed, we are dead in soul, lost in spirit, and for that reason alone no amount of injunction, no amount of commandment, no amount of law of any sort, can restore us any more than laws and injunctions can heal the plague or give sight to the blind. We do not need legislation, but grace; we do not need rules, but redemption; we do not need resolve, but resurrection — resurrection of body and soul — resurrection of both halves of our dual nature.

What we can never do for ourselves God has done for us in his own humanity. What He made, He redeemed. He went face-to-face with evil, and He won. In Him was life; in Him was the death of death. Just as our first birth makes us the children of Adam, our second birth makes us heirs of the second Adam — the children of God. What we lost in the Garden of Eden — and more — was regained for us in the Garden of Gethsemane and on Calvary's nearby hill.

Put succinctly, every person reaches his or her own destiny only if he or she becomes again like the God in whose image he or she was created. Because Jesus of Nazareth is Himself the express image of the Father, then the fulfillment of our destiny is reached only in so far as we are like Jesus. We are like Jesus only if we have his mind and character. We have that mind and character only to the extent that we find ourselves naturally doing and saying the sorts of things He said and did, the things He saw his Father say and do. Reflecting the Son is how we reflect the Father.

Think of it this way: God made Him who had no sin to be sin so that we might become (not simply have) the righteousness of God (2 Cor. 5:21). That is our special destiny: we shall become the righteousness of God. Christ became the kind of person we are so that we could become the kind of person we are not. He who was in some ways so different from us identified fully with us, so that we might become more fully and properly identified with Him, and in so doing become more fully and more properly human. Our task now is to reproduce the mind and character of Christ within us, a task that only the Holy Spirit Himself is competent to perform.

To reiterate, we do not see the whole picture of who we are and who we shall become if we see only the death and burial of our Savior. We need to contemplate the resurrection, ascension, and glorification of Christ as well, for in them we see not only our present condition but also our destiny. Because Jesus, as a man, entered into the glory of God, glorification is our destiny, too.[6] In other words, if you want to know what God has in store for his children, you look to Christ. Things happen in Christ that summarize our destiny. In Him a new order is created that transcends even the great blessings we had in Eden. Christ is for us, and where He has gone we will follow. In Him, the absurdity of sin and death are set right forever. That is our destiny.

Part of that destiny is control over nature — dominion — something we were given by God in the Garden both as a gift and a task. Christ's miracles over nature foreshadow our renewed and enhanced powers for our destined dominion. They vividly illustrate the future form taken by our ancient task of subduing the earth. As Hendrikus Berkhof explained, "The miracles of Jesus are a revelation both of his humanity and of the true humanity God intends for all. To dominate nature is a distinct calling and possibility for man . . . But this has never been achieved except in the one true man, Jesus the Christ, in whom this control of nature appears as . . . a promise and a challenge.[7]

Here is the sum of the matter: We are the sons and daughters of Adam, with all the dignity and all the shame that now entails. We also are the brothers, sisters, and joint-heirs of the Second Adam, Who is the first-born of a new race, a new creation. We are, in the end, not only what we were at our beginning (persons in the image and likeness of God) but we are something even more: We are partakers of the divine nature, which is a deep mystery. The details of that mystery are yet unknown to us, but they are hidden safely with God in Christ (Col 3: 3, 4), and will be revealed to all the world when He returns (1 John 3:2), maybe soon.

END NOTES

1 Michael Williams, *For as the Curse is Found* (Phillipsbury, NJ: Presbyterian and Reformed, 2005), 60 (emphasis added).

2 Hendrikus Berkhof, *Man in Transit* (Wheaton, IL: Key Publishers, 1971), 25.

3 Eric Mascall, *Man: His Origin and Destiny* (London, UK: Dacre Press, 1940), 28.

4 Michael Bauman, *Roundtable: Conversations with European Theologians* (New Orleans, LA: Insight, 2005), 103.

5 Mascall, 91.

6 Berkhof, 75.

7 Ibid., 20.

*I should like to acknowledge here the great debt I owe in this essay to both Eric Mascall and to Hendrikus Berkhof, whom I consider the 20th century's greatest under-known theologians. I have purposely centered my remarks on their notions and explanations of theological anthropology. Hardly a paragraph I have written here has not been informed by their work. What has not been acknowledged explicitly in the epigraphs and in the text, I am pleased and proud to acknowledge here. If something I have said in these pages is useful or memorable, thank them, as I do. By sticking closely to their words, their arguments and their ideas, my wish is that their work would become more familiar to American evangelicals, whom I here direct to the originals.

"The Pharisee stood up and prayed about himself: 'God, I thank you that I am not like other men . . ."

LUKE 18:11

"Let us fix our eyes on Jesus, the author and perfector of our faith . . ."

HEB. 12:2

"God never gave a man a thing to do concerning which it were irreverent to ponder how the Son of God would have done it."

GEORGE MACDONALD

"By a Carpenter mankind was made, and only by that Carpenter can mankind be remade."

ERASMUS

6

Imitatio Mundi, Imitatio Christi: The Problem of Misplaced Focus

Our natural distaste for ambiguity sometimes leads us to reduce the complexities of human life to false equations. Even where those reductions are not false, our desire to simplify sometimes compels us to focus on one side of the equation only and not on both. In much evangelical spirituality this misplaced focus has resulted in a Christian life centered almost exclusively on negation. Rather than directing our spiritual energies toward a satisfying and positive imitation of Christ, we reduce our religious practice to little more than an arid *imitatio mundi* in reverse—seeing what the world does and then doing the opposite. We have forgotten, apparently, that we are Christians not primarily by denial or by negation, that is, not by opposing the world, but by affirmation, that is, by accepting and imitating Christ.

Our negative preoccupation with the world has engendered some unfortunate results. Once a Christian defines his lifestyle (or worse, himself) by *opposition* to anything, the essential surrender is already made. Christians who define their calling primarily in terms of opposing secular society (the world), physical desires (the flesh), or evil (the Devil), have already allowed their antagonist to become their operative god. That god, rather than God, absorbs their thoughts, molds their conduct, defines their relationships, and alters their destinies.

Such Christians have fallen into the subtle, but serious, error of mimicking the world in reverse. Rather than positively imitating Christ, they choose to be society's negatives, showing black where it shows white and white where it shows black. But the negative of a snapshot of the Devil is not a portrait of Christ. Those who, in this fashion, allow the world to control their lives will discover, to their great dismay, that the world (even the world turned inside out) is a ruthless taskmaster. In time, they degenerate into mere antitypes of the world. They exile themselves to the chiaroscuro shadowlands of an imaginary black and white universe of their own (and the world's) making. In short, they exchange the multi-dimensional, rainbow richness of genuine Christian existence for the schematic starkness of a checkerboard. They trade being revolutionaries for being merely reactionary.

Jesus will have none of it. His energies are not expended aping Jerusalem in reverse. He does only what He sees the Father do. He says only what He hears the Father say. He knows that being out of step with the Pharisees is not the same as being in step with God.

Proof that we focus our attention on doing what the world does not, rather than on acting like Jesus, is found in the fact that if we actually did some of the very things He did, we would be considered bad Christians. No evangelical minister that I know would escape the censure of his colleagues or his flock if he showed up at a wedding with sixty gallons of fine wine. Even a liter would be unwelcome. To many Christians, it hardly matters that providing such a vast amount of alcoholic refreshment on such a festive occasion was Jesus's first public miracle. He changed water into wine, and we've been busy for 2,000 years trying to change it back into water again. The first thing He did in public is about the last thing we would do. What seems to matter far more to us is the fact that the world celebrates marriages *that* way, and we must be different. Jesus, however, has other concerns. Because he cares more for the dignity of his friends than about his image with the Pharisees, He designs an act of kindness to save his host from embarrassment. We, by contrast, design acts intended to preserve our own image as a separated people. Unhappily, in our passion for separation we have succeeded in separating ourselves not only from the ways of the world, but often from the ways of Christ. And it does no good to object that the example I draw here is an extreme example. That the action even appears extreme is evidence of how far away from a real *imitatio Christi* we have moved.

The *imitatio mundi* in reverse does not produce Christlikeness because it is based on a glaring error in logic. It assumes that only two possibilities exist: if one is not acting like the world, then one must therefore be acting like Christ. If all options reduced to two — one error and/or one correct answer — then, of course, anything that was unlike the world would be true godliness. But the options do not reduce to two. While there is only one Christ from whom we derive our salvation and according to whom we live, the opportunities for deviation and for error are vast and multiform. For example, if each of the thirty students in a mathematics class missed the second question on a test, I could not assume that I, as the 31st student, could answer the question correctly simply by looking at their responses and giving a different one. That method would work only if the question at hand were a true/false question and the other students all chose the same answer and got it wrong. Life in a fallen world, however, is seldom that simple.

While the choice is, in one way, between worldliness and Christlikeness, we must not think that the options are only two. Worldliness is a theme upon which we find countless variations. (Godliness itself also might admit of various forms and degrees — an unsettling prospect for any binary mentality!) Merely because you sing a note other than the one groaned out by your tone-deaf neighbor, you cannot assume your own music is celestial. I've heard too many church choirs to believe that.

For turning people's eyes toward the world and away from God, we theologians must bear some of the blame. By the words we employ to describe Him, we often have shrouded the Deity in an imposing cloud of language. Though they may be theologically precise and doctrinally reliable, it is counterproductive to speak of Jesus *primarily* in terms of the hypostatic union, kenotic theory, and incarnational consciousness. (If you do not understand these words, you realize first hand the truth of what I am saying. If you have not looked them up, you should.) Though useful in some contexts and in some ways, language like this, even when it does not put people off, serves most to make them good theologians rather than good Christians. Those two conditions are not the same. Satan, I imagine, is a fairly keen theologian, but it does him little good because knowing about God does not equate with knowing Him. Of course, knowing about Him must not be despised. I am far from denigrating theology.

Here's the point: when the language of faith causes our brother to stumble, we must repent. We must rend the verbal veil, not simply by new language, but by a new focus. We must do it the way Jesus does: by drawing attention back to Himself and to His character. Let me explain.

Among other things, God is omnipotent, omnipresent, omniscient, impassible, ineffable, and triune. We Christians adhere also to the ideas of divine aseity, infinity, complacency, and immutability. (More words to look up.) While I subscribe to the truth embodied in this litany of attributes, it does not go very far toward repairing within me the ruin wrought by Adam. After hearing a recitation of theological labels like those given above, I still want to make Philip's request: show me the Father. I feel that way because I have a difficult time relating to a series of Greek concepts that are an accurate description of only One Being in all the universe, and an invisible one at that. But, if you tell me that God became a man and then show me the man, I will rejoice. *That* I can relate to.

And that's just what the Bible does. John's gospel, for example, tells us that no one has ever seen God, no one that is, except God's Son, and (thank God) He has exegeted (or expounded) Him for us. This He did not simply by theological disquisition, but also by a righteousness and insight so revolutionary and so unsettling that even some of the most religious people of His day mistook Him for a blaspheming firebrand and led the movement to end His life. As one man among many, He lived the life of God, graphically; so graphically, in fact, that when Philip asked to see the Father all Jesus had to do was point to Himself: "He that has seen me has seen the Father," He said. With those words, Jesus brought the *Deus absconditus* out of hiding by translating Him for us into the language of human life. Jesus is, as Paul tells us, the image of the invisible God. We finally got to see God himself feasting and fasting, rejoicing and crying, praising and castigating, healing and whipping, asking and answering. He has walked our roads, breathed our air, eaten our food, and spoken our language.

In short, we live on a *visited* planet, and because we do, we have a beacon light to guide our battered ships to harbor. Only that Light will bring us to safe haven. Our one secure refuge is not found by locating the garish lights of the world and then steering the other way. That leads us only out to sea again, and we desire to go to the port of peace. That cove of tranquility lies close by the Light that shines in darkness, that one special Light that darkness never overcomes. To that Light I now turn.

But, before I do, I want to make note of the "half-way" solution some Christians adopt as a cure for their misdirected anti-world spirituality. They practice what I call "Paulianity." They act, perhaps unwittingly, as if "Christianity" were a misnomer, as if our religion did not need to center in Christ not simply for faith, but also for practice. Some have let slip the truth that Christ is not merely the Redeemer who saves us, He is the Lord who leads us. Christ is the center and standard of Christian existence. *He*, not Paul, not Peter (or Peter's alleged successors), and certainly not we ourselves, *He* is the standard for the doctrine and practice of the religion that bears His name. None of his disciples is to be greater than, or equal to, the Master.

"Then he isn't safe?" said Lucy. "Safe?" said Mr. Beaver. "Don't you hear what Mrs. Beaver tells you? Who said anything about safe? 'Course he isn't safe. But he's good."

C. S. LEWIS

"There is no historical task which so reveals a man's true self as the writing of a Life of Jesus.*"*

ALBERT SCHWEITZER

". . . the Christ that Harnack sees, looking back through nineteen centuries of Catholic darkness, is only the reflection of a Liberal Protestant face, seen at the bottom of a deep well."

GEORGE TYRRELL

"And Jesus grew constantly in wisdom, in stature, and in favor with God and man."

LUKE 2:52

The Nose of Wax

Do not be deceived. While we must look to Christ as the model for our spirituality rather than imitating the world in reverse, it is not enough simply to look to Christ. We must be sure that when we look at Him we actually see Him as He is. Too often our Bible study degenerates into an exercise in narcissism. Looking into the gospels becomes something like looking into a well: all we see is our own mirrored image. Jesus has become a nose of wax in our hands, and rather than conforming ourselves to his character, we conform Him to ours. We seem to act as if, because God made us in his image, we can return the favor.

Perhaps you have noticed how Christ is made to look like the one doing the preaching, the teaching, or the writing at the moment. In the hands of Thomas à Kempis, for example, Christ is reduced to little more, and little else, than a medieval monk — as if Jesus really was a mystic, a monastic, and a nominalist. But, of course, Jesus is not simply a glorified version of Francis of Assisi or Bernard of Clairvaux. He's not a monk's monk.

And He's not a Protestant.

Not only do we make him a Protestant, but in our hands the Creator also has become an American evangelical dispensationalist from the Bible Belt. Naturally, non-fundamentalists are offended by such obscurantistic clap-trap. Jesus doesn't look like that any more than He looks like the abbot of the monastery at Monte Cassino. He's not the prototype of John Chrysostom, of Innocent III, or of Che Guevara. That is, He's not Eastern Orthodox; He's not Roman Catholic; and He's no model for liberation theology. And, distressing as it may be to some, He's not the Calvin before Calvin or the Arminius before Arminius. He's the Son of God. Regardless of how strenuously we might try to make Him one of us, we will be frustrated. His unique combination of divinity and sinless humanity transcends easy categorization. Trying to cram Jesus into our own ecclesiastical molds is no simple task. It is like stuffing ten pounds of potatoes into a five-pound bag — either the bag bursts or something gets left out.

Nevertheless, people try. Their attempts to make Jesus conform to their expectations (rather than shaping themselves to meet his) are a thinly veiled exercise in self-justification. We all tend to read our own theological and ecclesiastical biases back into the Bible. Rather than being confronted there by Something solid and resilient, Something other than ourselves, we assume the role of modern John the Baptists: we rebaptize Jesus into the modern Presbyterian, Coptic, Mormon, Baptist, or Russian Orthodox fold. It simply won't do, of course. The important thing in Christocentric spirituality is not what we can make of Him, but what He has made of Himself and intends to make of us.

We must strenuously resist the temptation to rearrange the Savior. Christ, even to Christians, seems a little too shocking. We are forced (we think) to play the iconoclast and to knock down (or touch up) the image of the divine character He has left us. But the true sanctity of Jesus is not often like the sanctity of those traditionally called saints. He was holy, but He had no halo. His purity was a blood-and-guts affair that held together, in the grip of his two strong hands, a holy God and a fallen world. That union would not be broken, not even over his dead body. In other words, his brow is no place for our tinsel crowns. His head will not support the paper hats and paint-by-numbers halos of our misdirected and self-glorifying piety. So much the worse for halos. We need the real Jesus, not one of our own making. What good is a potter shaped by clay?

Now, I'm not so foolish (or so arrogant) as to think I can improve upon the multi-dimensional portrait of Christ painted for us in the four gospels. I can't. If I tried, I'd probably be making just one more flawed (and self-glorifying) copy of myself. Jesus, after all, doesn't look like me either. But what I can do I will do, and that is to point out some of the character traits of Christ that are most often overlooked, at least by those who move in the same circles I do.

But, before I do, I need to explain something. I am going to focus on the character of Christ rather than on the specific actions and events that comprise his life. I do so for two reasons. First, the actual events and actions of Christ's life are not reproducible. That is, almost by definition, *those* things can't be done again. Past events are just that — past. Furthermore, none of us is capable of walking on water, raising the dead, calming storms, or withering fig trees on command. Such things are neither possible for us nor required of us. True Christlikeness lies elsewhere. Second, I focus on the character of Christ rather than his actions because his character *gives rise to* his actions, not vice versa. What He does grows out of what He is. Character is foundational. To imitate Christ some other way than in character is not really to imitate Him at all. A superficial mimicking of externals is not sufficient. You must not congratulate yourself simply because, like Jesus, you have been accused of being a wine bibber and a glutton. Facile identification of our ways and his must be avoided. They are not only mistakes, they are misleading. Character is the crux. Christocentric spirituality should never be reduced to mere mimicry.

And what about the character of Christ—what is it like? Is Jesus really the meek and mild house pet Christians have made of Him? Was the Lion of Judah a kitten after all?

God forbid.

More than we are likely ever to imagine, Jesus had a mind and spirit that were completely awake. Little, if anything, went on around Him and went unnoticed. With cheetah-like quickness, with eagle-eyed vision, and with surgeon-like precision, He saw (to borrow a phrase from Wordsworth) "into the life of things." And here, I am not speaking of his omniscience. I refer to the fact that his eyes and mind were always penetratingly open. He never seemed to lapse into the mental and spiritual stupor so typical of us, his followers. He never slid from life back into mere existence. His mental life was an intense interchange between a mind fully awake and a world charged with beauty and fraught with evil. *That* is what seems to have formed his stunning character. He was perceptive, teachable, and shrewd — three qualities we seldom link with spirituality and Christology and usually fail consciously to inculcate either in our children or in ourselves.

The reason Jesus was such a remarkable teacher and could dispense such shocking insights (apparently) instantaneously is twofold. First, like all good teachers, He was always on duty. In the midst of a fallen world, and surrounded by a pervasive human depravity that rendered (and still renders) every human being an unending need, his mind was almost always on the lookout. His spirit was almost always in the watchtower, looking, listening, and learning. The few times He ever closed shop were to rest awhile and to pray awhile with his Heavenly Father, so that He could return to his disciples and to the crowds even better able to discharge the duty that his virtue and love placed upon Him. I do not mean to say that He was always solemn and never cheerful. That is not true. Whole books have been written on the humor of Christ. But, his merriment, as C. S. Lewis once intimated, is of the kind that takes people seriously from the start. His was a merriment that was never flippant or superficial because He was so fully aware of the intrinsic value of each member of the race and of his own responsibility to them as brothers and sisters in need. His humor, when it surfaced, was, in fact, the merriest kind because it was never inappropriate. It was coupled with a determination to see things as they really are, and not to wince. Jesus seems to have understood with perfect clarity that He could never undeceive others if He were mistaken or misinformed Himself. So, he *saw*. Jesus was a good teacher, in short, because He was diligently and appropriately perceptive.

Second, like all good teachers, He was first a good student. Like all good students, He was largely self-taught and He made it a point to learn from whatever was set before Him. Unlikely as it might seem to us, Jesus trained Himself to be the Savior of the world while working next to Joseph in his carpenter shop. Somehow, some way, sweeping up sawdust and finishing off chair legs proved to be suitable preparation for the messianic and cosmic work of redemption. Not that there is anything magical or mystical about the ancient equivalent of either a wood chisel or a crosscut saw, but in the hands of a teachable young man, one who is determined to glean insight from whatever source presents itself, it is enough. Thousands of boys (and girls), in various countries, cultures, and centuries, have grown up working as helpers in their father's carpentry business. For none was it so productive of virtuous character and wisdom as for Jesus. Unlike them, He had eyes to see and ears to hear. He had them, in part, *because* He used them. He is proof that what is used grows strong. We are proof that what is not used weakens and withers. The point here is not what his father's small business made of Jesus, but what Jesus was able to make of Himself by means of carpentry and his own resolute teachableness. He discovered for Himself what He later would teach to others: those who hunger and thirst after an awesome righteousness will find it, even among the saw horses, hammers, and smashed thumbnails of Your Dad's repair shop. Jesus grew to be what He was because He was diligently perceptive and resolutely teachable. He did, after all, *learn* obedience (Heb. 5:8).

He also was shrewd.[1] I say it reverently, and I say it firmly: Jesus knew, and used, every angle. The practical offshoot of this formidable skill was his virtual impregnability. Try as they might, his enemies never caught Him sleeping. They never found Him with his guard down. They would deliver what they had calculated to be a knockout punch, only to find themselves on the ropes, staggering and struggling to remain upright. He was quick on his feet and could bob and weave his way through a barrage of doctrinal jabs and uppercuts that would have left us unconscious. He was a superb theological counter-puncher. He was a virtuoso of verbal combat. This was no accident. He had apparently explored and mapped for Himself every theological, spiritual, and psychological highway and byway. He knew, by the cunning and insight produced from years of perceptive teachableness, precisely which paths were the dead ends and why they were so. He was what He told his followers to be—as wise as serpents and as harmless as doves. He understood quite clearly that a Christian could never avoid inflicting serious harm (on himself or others) without first having developed the piercing insight and the startling perceptivity that instantly and accurately assesses the true nature of any moral dilemma and deftly unties the spiritual knot that mocks less nimble fingers.

With Jesus, this skill is legendary. Leaving aside, for the moment, the question of textual authenticity,[2] I believe the incident of the woman taken in adultery is an excellent case in point.[3]

While Jesus was busy teaching the crowds around the Temple, some of the scribes and Pharisees brought before Him a woman caught in sexual misconduct. They had devised a scheme whereby they might catch Jesus in his own words. "The law," they said to Him, "commands us to put a woman like this to death. What do *you* say?" They had reasoned that if Jesus said to stone the woman He would look horribly unmerciful. He could not sentence her to death with all these people around, perhaps some of them even her friends. And, if Jesus took the other alternative and dismissed her, He would appear to be a renegade law-breaker, one who condones (in the Temple courtyard, no less) what the law does not. Either way, they figured, they'd get Him.

But Jesus, with characteristic aplomb, and perhaps to buy a little time to think or else to underscore the point He was about to make, knelt down and traced something (I don't know what) in the dirt. When the Jews continued to press Him on the point, He deftly drew the issue to a resolution. He kept the law of Moses, extended mercy to the woman, and uncovered the flaw in his opponents' character and motives all in one quiet, but electric, sentence: "Let him who is without sin cast the first stone." It was a shrewd and stunning retort, and as He knelt again to finish writing what He had begun, the point began to sink in. In what I imagine was a profound silence, punctuated only by the sound of rocks falling from guilty hands, his enemies left Him, determined never to try *that* again. Then, with a combination of mercy and rebuke, he turned and dealt with the woman in a fashion that was both gentle and firm. "Who condemns you?" Jesus asked. "No one," she replied. "Neither do I," said Jesus. "Go and sin no more." Thus, in this one brief confrontation between a sinner, her accusers and Jesus, He won her freedom, her loyalty, and her obedience.

I have described Jesus as perceptive, teachable, and shrewd. I believe He was. I do not believe that is *all* He was, but He was at least that. I have not stopped to explain, for example, that Jesus was loving and compassionate. Almost no one reading his book needs to be lectured on that count. We Christians have not forgotten his grace. But we have mislaid the nuts and bolts of his grace and neglected the machinery of his forgiveness and wisdom. His divine love shows up *in the form of* his diligent perceptivity, his resolute teachability, and his train-stopping shrewdness. He invested both the effort and the years needed to ac-quire those characteristics precisely *because* He loved us and because He knew we'd need them. Those of us who claim to be his followers, those of us who desire to have his character, must learn to grow as He grew before we can hope to do as He did and be as He was.

It is precisely here we fail. Not only have we not learned, but we have not even learned to learn. The omni-competence typical of Jesus, and required of us if we ever hope to engage ourselves effectively in the cure of souls (our own and others'), is the harvest of perceptivity, teachableness, and cunning. Unless we sow the seed, we shall never reap the harvest. Spirituality does not progress by neglected means. Jesus's didn't. Neither will ours. We must do more than admire.

That, at any rate, is how Jesus looks to me. I trust it is no self-glo-rifying exercise in narcissism. If what I have said sounds anything like self-portraiture, I trust it is because those things first were in Him, and in me only later, by devoted imitation. Though I fervently believe that what I have said about his character is true, I am willing to admit that what I've said might be mistaken. Correct it if you can. I prefer to be undeceived. But if you try, be careful to point me to Christ, not your own reflection.

END NOTES

1   Many Christians mistakenly believe that to be shrewd is to be sinister or evil. As the following dictionaries establish, it does not: (1) "In early use: cun-ning, artful. Now only in favourable sense: clever or keen-witted in practical affairs; astute or sagacious in action or speech. (The chief current sense.)" — *Oxford English Dictionary*; (2) "Intelligent, discerning, cunning" — *Webster's Dictionary*; and (3) "sharp or wise; sagacious" — *Funk & Wagnall's Dictionary*.

2   The textual question has no bearing on my point. What I am saying about Jesus could be derived from other gospel passages quite as easily. His shrewd-ness is equally evident, for example, in Matt. 22:15ff.

3   I must not fail to direct the reader's attention to Richard Mitchell's en-

lightening analysis of the same incident in his excellent book, *The Gift of Fire*, especially Chapter Four, but also in passing references throughout the remainder of the volume, from which some of my ideas were drawn.

"*Christianity may exist without any speculative Christology, but it never has existed without faith in a living Saviour.*"

JAMES DENNEY

"*[Jesus is] greater than any or all these ways of representing Him; neither the imagination of the Jew nor the philosophical faculty of the Greek can embody Him.*"

JAMES DENNEY

"*The discovery of the pluriformity of models and concepts in the history of Christological thought is itself a liberating experience. It breaks the illusion that the finite structures of our language of dogma and worship actually encompass the reality to which they refer.*"

ROBERT C. WARE

Anatomizing Jesus: The Challenge of Contextualization

I. Words and Concepts: The Pilgrim's Walking Stick

Effective theologizing requires contextualization. That is, those of us whose task is to proclaim the Christian gospel to our contemporaries in as understandable and compelling a fashion as possible, face a two-sided challenge. Looking to the past, so as to avoid mistaking the merely transitory for the perpetually true, we must separate the kernel of Christian revelation from the husk of the incidental ancient trappings in which it was delivered. Looking to the present, we must translate that truth into the most appropriate words and concepts offered us by contemporary receptor languages and cultures. A proclamation that neither rightly identifies the content of the faith nor accurately and attractively packages it for modern consumption (a failure not uncommon in Christian history) is likely to enjoy little success. Appropriate contextualization is essential to discharging faithfully the commission given us for global discipleship.

Because He himself is the personal disclosure of God, Christ is one of the most important foci for contextualization. To misunderstand Him, or to mistranslate Him, is not simply to misunderstand a man from ancient Galilee; it is to misconstrue no less than the Creator Himself. In seeing Christ, we see the Father, because He and the Father are one. But, seeing Him as He is, and seeing Him for all He's worth, *that* is the rub. And, to translate what we have seen into acceptably precise terms and concepts, descriptive concepts that are understandable to those around us, *that* is the task of contextualization.

The four gospel writers accepted that task. They each solved the puzzle before them in a different way. When Matthew, for example, tried to recount (apparently for Jewish eyes and ears) the shocking story of when God became a man, he set his focus largely upon the motif of a King and his kingdom coming in fulfillment of prophecy. John (perhaps to Hellenistic Jews) adopted and then adapted the old Stoic concept of the divine logos, a logos that was both the pattern and the patterning force behind the universe, a logos that has enlightened every man. This he then combined with insights he had drawn from Genesis and elsewhere. Mark and Luke (and Paul, too) chose different emphases yet, all in an effort to understand Christ and to make Him understood. Their varied attempts have produced a more fully-orbed and multi-dimensional portrait of Christ than we would have had otherwise. The Bible — and we ourselves — are richer for it. Had the gospel writers not done so, Christian theology and Christian piety would have been immeasurably impoverished. Put differently, the purpose of the gospel writers was to explicate and to proclaim the significance of Jesus's life and work, not simply to supply a journalistic report of them. The gospel writers are evangelists and theologians, not merely news reporters.

But contextualization, even that done by the Biblical writers, is not an unmitigated blessing. It entails dangers and shortcomings as well as insight and usefulness. Along with the perceptivity and incisiveness native to a given language or culture, one must also accept the attendant limitations. The trick to successful contextualizing is to maximize the former and to minimize the latter as best we can. Because no one language and no one world view (or even the entire world, for that matter) are sufficient to articulate the Deity fully, distortion — at least in the sense of foreshortening — is inevitable, even for the gospel writers. They each have selected as their means of contextualization a method of theological reportage centered around and conducted according to a specific motif, one that was appropriate to their historical and intellectual milieu. That selected motif served to illuminate and to elucidate some (but not all) of the important aspects of God in Christ. The gospel writers brought to light that portion of the significance of the incarnation that was accessible to them from their selected perspective. At the same time, they also eliminated (or passed over) the significance accessible only from other perspectives. They had to do so. Not all vistas can be viewed from one standpoint. Like all other finite texts, those written by Matthew, Mark, Luke, and John are perspectivally limited. That is, while I regard what the gospel writers wrote as true, I recognize that it is not the whole truth. It is but a portion. The half has not been told by means of these four perspectives. Nor can it be, even if they were multiplied tenfold. God in Christ is too vast a horizon to take in, even after many looks. John himself tells us as much (John 20: 30; 21: 25).

To put it differently, while theological contextualizing is a useful and necessary endeavor, its usefulness is of a limited sort, limited by the restrictions native to any given perspective. And, because these insights are communicated to us through the medium of language, the attendant natural limitations of that perspective are amplified by the shortcomings native to language itself. That is, to explain the redemptive action of God in Christ requires the use both of historical and cultural perspectives, on the one hand, and of words and concepts, on the other. This can entangle us in a two-sided ambiguity: the Biblical writers have had to translate the *personal* revelation of God in Christ into *propositional* forms suitable for theological narrative, and we, in turn, must translate the insights yielded by their efforts at contextualization into language and concepts appropriate to our own time and place. Both procedures entail accommodation and loss. Let me explain.

Theologians must always bear in mind that the highest and clearest revelation God ever gave us of himself was as a Person, not as either a proposition or a story. In doing so, He came to us not in grammatical syntax, but in flesh. And while revelation contains words from God and words about God (words that are true), it was only in Christ that God *himself* arrived. Revelation changed from narration and propositions about a person to the person Himself. We cannot comprehend the accommodation required for the infinite Creator to become a finite creature. We can only guess at what (and how much) He had to lay aside to contextualize not only his message, but himself. For *us* to become ancient Galilean infants would require massive accommodation (and truncation). Much of what we are and know would have to be laid aside simply because of our different historical context. To do anything else, or to speak to ancient Jews on *our* terms or in *our* language, would hardly constitute a revelation at all. We simply would fail to make ourselves understood. Obviously, the accommodation required of God to do the same thing is even more profound. We can only guess at what He has chosen to withhold from us in his revelation and why He has done so.

Perhaps few of us take seriously enough Luther's disquieting insight concerning *Deus absconditus*: God hides not only in his revelation but behind it as well. In other words, the revelation of God (yes—even the *revelation* of God!) is partly an ambiguity and a reduction. There is much, very much, we do not know. Humility is the only appropriate response to such a phenomenon, not contentiousness and bickering about such unknown, and unknowable, things as the functional relationship either between the divine *ousia* and the divine energies, on the one hand, or that between deity and humanity in the hypostatic union, on the other hand. Before we hurt anybody else, we ought to realize that our theological reach sometimes exceeds our grasp. We simply do not know much of what we think we know. When God contextualized *himself* (in order to teach us theology proper, anthropology, soteriology, etc.), He did so in a way that included — and transcended — theological propositions and disquisition. He did it in a Person, and that "in-personation" itself was a staggering accommodation.

The four evangelists' reduction of that in-personation to theological narrative was a further accommodation, though, to be sure, a necessary one: how else could we learn about Him except through the witness of others? But, when they (and, as I think, under the direction of God Himself) contextualized that in-personation in a way suitable to their readers, the gospel writers had to leave something out, as the words of John, alluded to above, clearly indicate. Their omissions were necessitated not only by the requirements of a book-length manuscript (or even, as John's hyperbolic statement intimates, the shortage of universal shelf space), but also by the exigencies of human language and thought. Even if all the papyrus and ink of his day were available to John, the end result would be incomplete. Persons (especially infinite persons) do not reduce to words without loss. Persons and propositions share an uncertain exchange rate. Beyond a certain indefinable point, such translations and reductions become an apples and oranges affair. No completely effective common denominator is available when one moves from persons directly into propositions. Again, this does not mean that what the evangelists write is untrue. It is not. It means only that what they write necessarily entails accommodation and loss.

Put differently, the doctrine of the apostles is primary. The personal revelation of God in Christ was set before them in a way that was unique and unrepeatable. Jesus is not present to us in the same way He was present to the apostolic band. He was present before their eyes, in the flesh, in person. To us, He is not. The apostles cannot present the person of Christ to us in the same way He came to them. They must present Him to us in their words, in their writings. The New Testament writers present the story of Christ (Gospels) and a partial explanation of the meaning and implications of that story (epistles). But, one must notice that revelation has taken on a new form in the process: it has been transmuted from a personal disclosure in Christ into a narrative and propositional disclosure in Scripture. Because *persons* are not reducible to propositions, no man, much less a God-man, can be fully or exactly captured in words or ideas, even inspired words or ideas.[1] While inspired words are true, they are not exhaustively so. The truth they contain is not only foundational, it is sometimes inexact and not truly comprehensive. It is also truth that sometimes lacks absolute clarity. Doctrinal differences arise because of the occasionally inescapable inexactitude of scriptural words and their contextual relativity. Doctrinal disagreements emerge when we push for truth and clarity beyond that which the Bible's narratives and explanations supply. Although the Bible is the finest source for theological truth, it is not a repository of exhaustive or unambiguous truth. It comes to us in human language and from various specific human points of view. This is not to say that Scripture has *conflicting* viewpoints. I do not think it does. But this is to say that Scripture is a book of various theologies, not the home of one theology only. Those theologies are complementary and contextual — as ours must be.

Our task, to reiterate, is to translate the gospel writers' privileged insights concerning the divine in-personation into compelling contemporary language and concepts. Translation, however, is an inexact science. Between most languages, for example, many words (and ideas) cannot be made to sustain an exact one-to-one exchange. While most verbs and concrete nouns can yield inter-language equivalents, many abstract concepts and culturally relative thought patterns and modes of expression cannot. Poetry, for example, because its language is typically compressed and symbolic, and because it sometimes requires rhyme, meter, and visual arrangement, is notoriously difficult to translate adequately. Theology is often in the same quandary, for some of the same reasons, compression and symbolism among them.[2]

Therefore, whatever receptor language and concepts we choose, great care should be taken to recognize their inherent limitations. The verbal and conceptual roads we select can (and probably will) open out onto new theological vistas, revealing insights, and truth previously unrecognized and inaccessible. If we follow them relentlessly on to their termini, however, those roads might also lead us down one-way streets to theological dead ends that allow no forward progress and no retreat, as the history of Christian doctrine has shown.

II. The Pilgrimage to Chalcedon

Though they themselves did not think so, the orthodox Church Fathers who composed the first four ecumenical creeds, I believe, travelled down just such a dead end road. When they asserted, against Arius, that the Son of God was truly and fully divine, they did right. But, they did so by means of the Greek words and concepts like "*ousia*" and "*hypostasis*." Having chosen to understand and to defend Christian doctrine from that perspective, they (and, as we shall see, the heretics they subsequently opposed) were committed to a Christology and a Theology proper that were constructed under those and other closely related conceptual rubrics, both for better and for worse. Their endeavor would yield great insight. Also, because God in Christ is not fully contained in or expressed by one family of Greek concepts, their approach would eventually reach a point beyond which theological travel was virtually impossible.

The road from Nicea to Chalcedon contained, as the historical record bears out, a number of turns. When it reached Constantinople, for example, Apollinarius, who perhaps was orthodox by Nicene standards, took one turn while the council itself, in line with the two Gregorys, took another. That is, while Apollinarius accepted the full deity of Christ, he fell short of affirming His full humanity. The council, in opposition to him, rightly affirmed both. To the orthodox, Christ was fully God and fully man. By the time that theological road reached Ephesus, theologians were faced with another fork. Nestorius (the heretic) and Cyril (the champion of orthodoxy), though both considered themselves orthodox by Nicene and Constantinopolitan standards, selected different directions. Nestorius could not affirm that Christ could have a fully divine nature *and* a fully human nature without being a divine person and a human person both. He thought so because he believed that it is of the essence of human nature to be a human person and of the essence of divinity to be a divine person. That is, one could not possess a truly human nature unless one was a truly human person. To Nestorius, human nature and human personhood were inseparable. Because personhood is a necessary part of human nature, to have human nature is to be a human person. God could not take human nature upon himself without taking upon himself a human person at the same time. Divine nature also necessarily entailed divine personhood, Nestorius believed. Furthermore, unless one distinguished carefully between the divine and human natures (and therefore the divine and human persons) in Christ, one would have to affirm the (to Nestorius) unthinkable notion that Mary was the mother of God! Surely, Nestorius argued, one must shun any notion that the eternal God Himself was the offspring of a mere woman.

But, while Nestorius could not affirm the full unipersonality of Christ (that is, the idea that in Christ there were two natures but only one person), Cyril and the orthodox could. To them, Nestorius had too radically separated the two natures in Christ, thereby making of Him something of a "they" and not a "he."

The limitations of the usefulness of the theological route embarked upon at Nicea and followed on to Constantinople and to Ephesus became even more obvious at Chalcedon. Three times the orthodox had successfully opposed and exposed dangerous error. In doing so, they were forced to state with greater and greater clarity and precision just what the great in-personation entailed and what it did not, all from the perspective of those few key Greek concepts and their close relatives. At each juncture they excluded an unfortunate and misguided alternative. By jettisoning those erroneous formulations, the orthodox also were eliminating more and more of the possible turns in that one road, a road that began with only a limited number of possible turns in the first place. By the time they had followed that road to Chalcedon, I believe, the orthodox theologians had used up all the remaining viable possibilities. By Chalcedon, the extent of that Hellenized perspective's usefulness had been largely exhausted. When Eutyches and Leo took their opposing stances, both did so from the position of what they believed to be Nicene, Constantinopolitan, and Ephesian orthodoxy. Both intended to affirm the full deity of the Son (Nicea). Both intended to affirm the full humanity of Christ (Constantinople). Both intended to affirm the unipersonality of Christ (Ephesus). But, when Eutyches took one direction at the fork in the road and attempted to explain all this by saying that the divine and human natures in Christ coalesced into a sort of *tertium quid*, the orthodox were up against a wall. They had reached the end of the road. In order to refute Nestorius they previously had to affirm that Christ's two natures were not separated or divided. In order to refute Eutyches, however, they now needed to maintain that Christ's two natures were not mixed. To them, the divine nature and the human nature were (among other things) simultaneously unmixed yet undivided, inseparable yet distinct.

That position, it seems to me, left them with no genuine or meaningful theological options. Between the concept of separation, on the one hand, and that of inseparateness, on the other, and between the two categories of mixed and unmixed, no real or meaningful middle ground exists. But *right there*, between those all-inclusive concepts, is where the orthodox located the truth. Nestorius had previously claimed the one option (separate natures) and was excluded. Eutyches had claimed the other (mixed natures) with the same result. The orthodox were left to occupy the remaining nonexistent middle ground and simply called it "mystery."

But they did so in the face of the fact that "the biblical mystery is not one that arises amid abstract problems of theoretical knowledge."[3] They should have seen that they had followed the trail down to the trail's end, but that they still were not out of the woods. Their perspective, while eminently useful and insightful, left much yet to be seen. Their resort to mystery was no solution to the dilemma in which they found themselves. While we have the Bible's word for it that the Christian faith entails mysteries, we are not told that the exhaustion of Greek concepts at Chalcedon is or ought to be one of them. While I affirm, with the Chalcedonians, that God became a man, I recognize the real limitations inherent in describing the incarnation primarily in terms like *nature, essence, person,* and *substance.* To their great credit, while they kept to that road, the orthodox were able to prevent the Church at large from falling into the ditch on either side and from taking the wrong turns taken by Arius, Apollinarius, Nestorius, and Eutyches. But, having led the Church safely down that road, the road itself finally ended, because no theological road goes on forever. The actual extent of that good road's usefulness was exhausted (though not recognized). Several erroneous possibilities had been identified and eliminated. But no substantial, meaningful, or (as I believe) definable orthodox position yet remained. The bus had finally pulled into the terminal and it was time to disembark.

Put differently, when the multi-lane highway of christological investigation reached Nicea, the lane in which the Arians were travelling was shut down and all orthodox traffic was merged to the right into the lanes that remained. At Constantinople the Apollinarian lane was lost and all orthodox traffic merged back to the left into the lanes still open. After Ephesus, all orthodox traffic was crowded into the one lane still usable. That lane itself was closed to further traffic once it reached Chalcedon. The road had been a good one and a long one. It took some of the best theological minds in the ancient world more than 125 years to travel it from end to end. Along the way they saw things about God in Christ that probably could not have been seen from any other road. But these things, while useful, were of limited use, and while true, were not the whole truth and were not truth only. Like all perspectives and like all efforts at contextualization, this one necessarily contained foreshortening and truncation.

The subsequent monothelite controversy shows how incapable of theological extension the first four ecumenical affirmations really are, and how continuing to theologize from them leads to insupportable conclusions. Despite the fact that the orthodox affirmed at Ephesus that Christ was only one person, at Constantinople II they were compelled to assert that He had two wills, one divine and one human.[4] They did this in order to avoid sanctioning the Eutychian tendency of the monothelites, who said that the will native to the divine nature and the will native to the human nature coalesced into one will. Having already rejected that sort of reasoning with regard to the two natures of Christ, the orthodox now rejected it again with regard to His wills. They now affirmed with regard to will what they affirmed earlier with regard to nature (but *rejected* with regard to person): Christ had two. They defended this duality of wills by asserting that the will attaches to the nature and not to the person. Christ had two natures and hence two wills, but He was only one person.

But, such a conclusion is untenable because it implies (quite without biblical support) that *natures* will, not persons, and that willing pertains not to persons but to natures, as if a human will and a human nature ever existed without a human person and as if human nature and human person are (and ought to be considered) as distinct in extra-mental reality as they are in some people's thought. The orthodox argued as if it were essential to human nature to be willing but not personal. That is, they proceeded as if it were essential to human nature to have a will and to be willing, but that it is not essential to human nature to be a human person. To affirm that it *is* essential to human nature to be a distinct, discrete human person would be Nestorianism; and would go counter to the Ephesian conclusion. In other words, the orthodox had to reaffirm the earlier unproven (and unprovable) view that a human nature can exist without being a distinct human person and that Christ could take a human nature on Himself without also taking on a human person (what we call the adoptionist heresy). They introduced, and creedally enshrined, what I consider a largely useless concept, one that is in direct opposition to reason and to existence as we know it: human nature in the absence of a human person. Christ, they tell us, took upon himself the former without taking on himself the latter also. How the orthodox could prove that it is essential to human nature and divine nature to have a human and a divine will respectively, but not to be a human person and a divine person is beyond me and, I believe, probably beyond the truth.[5] They then arbitrarily attached the concept of will indissolubly to human nature while excluding that of person. In short, the Christology from above that dominated the earlier centuries ended up in objectionable metaphysical intrigues.[6]

Put differently, Christian theology is our knowledge of God as revealed both historically in Jesus of Nazareth and textually in the ancient documents pertaining to him. Christian theology, the science of grasping the gospel and its manifold implications, is best pursued by means of historical analysis and critical reflection upon the ancient inspired texts, as we contemplate them (so far as possible) on their own terms, and not by means of either metaphysical or subjectivist categories and methods that are alien both to the Old and New Testaments and to religion itself. We meet God, not in metaphysical abstractions (as at Chalcedon) or in subjective encounters (as in Schleiermacher), but in Jesus of Nazareth. Jesus of Nazareth is best and most fully known to us by means of our historical analysis of, and critical reflection upon, inspired texts properly understood. Metaphysics is but one interpretation of this historical and textual revelation; it is but one intellectual dress in which we array it. It is not the dress God himself has given it either in Scripture or in person. Thus, while it may be that historical analysis and critical reflection do not have the final word in Christian theology, they do have (so far as our own mental work goes) the first. That is, the Pilgrim Theologian must be a historian, but not a historicist; he also must be rational, but not a rationalist.

A new road along which to explore God in Christ is now required. A new effort at contextualization is now needed. Not that the old and venerable ones are to be neglected or rejected; but most of what can be seen from them has been seen. We need to explore other paths. We need to learn to break new ground. While no path will lead us all the way up the summit of knowing God in Christ fully, we need to explore those paths for what can be seen from the perspectives they alone afford us.

Do I believe that Christ is fully God and fully man? Yes. Am I a Chalcedonian? Basically. Is there more to Christ than this? By all means.

END NOTES

1   Certainly, however, some aspects regarding God in Christ can be truly captured, but that is not to be confused with the idea that God *Himself* is so captured. We must always beware of identifying God with our words and thoughts about Him.

2   For what I consider the best discussion of the value and the limitations of theological language to date, see Edwyn Bevan's *Symbolism and Belief* and Owen Barfield's *Poetic Diction*.

3   G. C. Berkouwer, *A Half Century of Theology* (Grand Rapids: Wm. B. Eerdmans Pub. Co., 1977), p. 148.

4   In this light, Berkouwer, ibid., p. 234, asks: "Did the decision made at Constantinople (680) — that there were two wills — correspond with the Christ-profile of the New Testament? The New Testament, after all, speaks of Christ's will and the Father's will (as seen in Gethsemane), but never of the two distinct wills operating in Jesus."

5   For a brief and useful discussion of some of the difficulties surrounding the alleged "impersonal" assumption of human nature by Christ, see Berkouwer, ibid., pp. 229 ff.

6   Ibid., p. 236.

HERMENEUTICS

Tis you that say it, not I."

JOHN MILTON
(quoting Electra)

"What could ever be written at all so carefully that it could never be twisted
by an angry opponent into some sinister meaning?"

ERASMUS
(to Jacob Hoogstraten, the Inquisitor)

"If you give me six sentences written by the most innocent of men, I will
find something in them with which to hang him."

CARDINAL RICHELIEU

Shrinking Texts: Hermeneutics Under Freudian Auspices

A good friend of mine, a man who had mentored my dissertation on John Milton, once chided me for dismissing, out of hand, a book of Milton criticism written from a Freudian point of view. This book, as it happens, was written by the mentor of *his* dissertation on Milton. "You must not," my friend said, "reject a book without ever having read it."

That, of course, is perfectly reasonable advice. I accept it enthusiastically and with conviction *as a general principle*. This rule, however, has exceptions. By their very nature, some books do not deserve this courtesy. Books that advocate a flat earth, for example, fall into such a category. So also do books of Freudian criticism. The burden of this chapter is to explain why I believe as I do, and in so doing to debunk Freudian hermeneutics by means of the methods and principles of Pilgrim Theology.

Simply put, I reject Freudian hermeneutics because I reject the Freudian conjectures upon which it is based. These conjectures tell us, for example, that dreams "*mean*," and that they mean symbolically. Kings and queens, Freudians say, represent fathers and mothers. Journeys represent death. Small animals represent brothers and sisters. Landscapes, gardens, fruit, and blossoms represent either the female anatomy or various parts of it. Furthermore, when these images appear in art (verbal or representational), the same exegetical and iconological deductions can be made concerning them.

I disagree.

Every schoolboy knows how easy it is to foist sexual overtones onto almost every sentence one hears in normal conversation, asexual though those sentences might actually be. If we put our minds to it, we can transform countless words and notions into sexual innuendo. When a young wit exercises his ingenuity in this way, and is brash enough (or disrespectful enough) to voice his indiscretions publicly, he usually succeeds only in embarrassing those around him and discrediting himself. We who hear him know that his perverse projections are merely that — projections. They have no real bearing on the original speaker or on that speaker's language, character, or motivations. We hear such indiscreet interjections and dismiss them, (if our standards of morality and of social decorum are not too severely offended) as the immaturity of youth. When he is older, we hope, he will put away childish things.

In some portions of academia, however, such indiscreet interjections are called Freudian hermeneutics and are thought to be scholarship. Freudian interpreters, after all, like some teenage boys, are experts at creating double entendre with *someone else's* words. This, they tell us, is what the writer really meant, whether he knew it or not. When, for example, John Milton employs latently sexual images, Freudian critics say, it is evidence of Milton's "predicate thinking," that distorted form of thinking which confuses two roughly similar objects or actions. Such thinking is said to occur when, for instance, "a tree and a male sex organ are equated in a person's mind because they both share the same physical characteristic of protruding."[1] Thus, "as we read *Paradise Lost*, we should remember the serpent as phallic symbol."[2] The fallacy ("phallusy?") here lies in attributing confusion (i.e., "predicate thinking") to someone else other than the interpreter. I reject any effort to employ adolescent sexual innuendo as a legitimate exegetical device. I do not classify either as literary scholarship or insight the assertion that, because the narrator in *Paradise Lost* is sometimes portrayed in birdlike images, we "should recall that in dream psychology a bird and flying have sensual significance" and that "flying dreams are erection dreams."[3] I stridently dissent when such interpreters tell us that "we cannot help being struck by the sexual overtones of the metaphor of inspiration"[4] employed in *Paradise Lost*. We *can* avoid it, and most of us, I dare say, have done so. Sexual and/or pornographic intrusion, after all, is not a hermeneutical requirement or existential necessity.

What Freudian hermeneutics misconstrues is not simply the nature of the literature under scrutiny, but also its own unsuitability as an exegetical tool. Freudian criticism is not legitimate exegesis and does not illumine the text at hand any more definitively than schoolboy jokes honestly elucidate the character, intention, or meaning of their victims. In the hands of Freudian critics, writers are victims too. That is because Freudian criticism is a mirror, not an eyeglass. It reveals the critic, not the text or the author under examination. Rather than explicating a text, Freudian hermeneutics merely interposes the perverse machinations of the interpreter between the reader and the text and, as a result, genuine understanding is injured, not aided. I reject the idea that we understand Milton's theological epic poem better when we realize the sexual overtones and implications of Satan (the phallic symbol turned toad) whispering disturbing things into Eve's ear ("a symbol of the womb"[5]). To say that such exegesis is hopelessly over-subtle or that it is wildly speculative is not enough; it is schoolboy perversity and chicanery, unworthy of serious scholarly consideration.

In other words, I do not believe that dreams mean, that they mean symbolically, that their unconscious iconography is either universal or interpretable, that their interpreted meaning ought to be understood as extensively sexual, or that their sexuality is of the sort described by Freud. Nor do I believe that these same symbols, and the iconic significance with which Freudians invest them, are appropriate ways of interpreting art, whether textual or visual. We have only the unconvincing assertions of Freudians that they are. What these interpreters fail to understand is that their theories reflect far more on *them* than on the text or author under consideration at the moment. Perversity, like beauty, is often in the eye of the beholder.

I reject as the worst sort of hermeneutical fiction any interpretation of Milton's "Lycidas" (a pastoral elegy dealing with, among other things, the problems of fame, of a corrupt clergy, and of death) that, despite Milton's conscious aims, identifies the rose (line 45), the hyacinth line 106) or the violet (line 145) as parts of the female anatomy. Nor should anything sexual be made of the fact that water is a dominant and recurring theme in the poem. One could hardly expect something very different from a poem occasioned by a college friend's death at sea by drowning. *Any* physical element in which Edward King's death had occurred would likely find prominent and repeated expression throughout Milton's monody. If King had died in fire, *that* element would likely have been employed by Milton in various symbolic and/or ironic ways, none of which necessarily would be indicative of the sexuality of Milton's infancy. Freudian interpreters, nevertheless, in a plethora of audaciously bizarre articles and monographs, would have told us what the fire images unconsciously signify about Milton and his fear of castration.

What Freudian hermeneutics fails to appreciate sufficiently is that things like flowers and water are common and time honored images in pastoral poetry. As elements of pastoral convention, the nature and use of such things was determined long before Milton ever appropriated them. As a result, insofar as Milton is a conventional pastoral poet (or, in the case of *Paradise Lost*, a conventional theological epic poet) his poetic/Biblical images come to him largely as given elements. And, he passes them on, frequently, in the same way he received them. As such, these images are less and less indicative of his own psychological history or makeup. They have little, if anything at all, to do with his sexual desires, conscious or otherwise.

Despite its tendency to universalize the iconic significance of images in dreams and in literary texts, Freudian interpretation fails to realize the culturally relative nature of its iconology. That kings and queens represent one's parents is a hypothesis likely to arise only in times and places near to kings and queens. It may even be true that royalty dreams themselves will arise only in such conditions. If my memory serves (and Freudians, who think they know my mind better than I do, say it does not), I have *never* dreamed of or written about kings and queens, or even about the President and his wife, for that matter. Their presence and/or absence in my dreams and poetry is of no psychological or sexual significance whatsoever and has no bearing at all upon my relationship to my mother or father. The only small animal I remember dreaming about at the moment is my dog, Zeke. His appearance in my dreams "means" nothing beyond himself. Zeke is Zeke, not my brother, Chris. In the only poem I ever wrote about Zeke, he is himself, nothing more. I reject as the most blatant form of eisegesis any attempt to construe him otherwise. Apart from Freudianism's bold assertions, where is the proof that kings and queens, roses and violets, or dogs and cats "mean" anything at all, in dreams or in art? Exegesis built upon the hypothesis of unconscious metaphor does not deserve to be called literary criticism. Books that unabashedly advocate it do not deserve to be read.

Modern Freudians are not the first of Milton's readers to invent sexual overtones for Milton's words or to imagine a perverse sexuality behind them. The anonymous author of *A Modest Confutation* (1642) thought he detected such things in Milton's *Animadversions*, where he found mention of "old cloaks, false beards, night-walkers, and salt lotion."[6] From these, the author concluded that Milton "haunts playhouses and bordellos; for if he did not, how could he speak of such gear?"[7] Milton met such scurrilous libels with denial, indignation, and (best of all) refutation. He brought "his inmost thoughts to the front" so that, if his "name and outward demeanor" were not sufficient to defend him in the eyes of the reader, then perhaps "the discovery of [his] inmost thoughts" would be.[8] When Milton himself examined his "inmost thoughts," he found very different things there than do the Freudians. Nourished, as he was, on Dante's praise of Beatrice, on Petrarch's praise of Laura, on Spenser's allegory on "Chastitie," and on the Bible's warnings against licentious thoughts and actions,[9] Milton said that he learned "the love and steadfast observation of that virtue which abhors the society of bordellos."[10] More significantly for our point, Milton also said that from such books he learned the practice of "sublime and pure thoughts, without transgression," mental sublimities which kept him above "low descents of mind."[11] Yet, even after he had carefully laid out his "inmost thoughts" to the reader, and even after he had set forth the details of the growth of his mind for all to see, Milton knew that some people would persist in their perverse and unjustified interpretation of his life and words, people who, like Freudian critics, were "good at dismembring and slitting sentences."[12] He also knew that the scope of invention for anyone who read his works in that fashion was nearly unlimited. "By such handicraft as this," Milton asked, "what might he not traduce?"[13]

Freudianism is a mirage in the sphere of literary criticism because it is a mirage in the sphere of human existence and knowledge. It is like that inspiring, but illusory, optical phenomenon of the desert. It has its own peculiar fascination and allure, but it is devoid of almost all objective reference. Freudianism is a deflection of the light of truth, a deflection that gives rise to images of things that do not exist. Its findings, if such they can be called, are merely chimerical. They have no objective or verifiable basis in reality. They are scientifically suspect. I agree with those who say that, when they are subjected to the close scrutiny of empirical testing, Freud's theories have failed miserably.[14]

Freudianism is but one more modern and perverse academic mysticism. It is one more intellectual deviation by which substantial and objective scholarship is woefully bedeviled. It might be that Freudians see what I cannot. It might also be that they see what is not there. That is because psychoanalysis pretends to psychic awareness. It confidently claims to be able to organize and to interpret the mysterious and the irretrievable.

But I am unconvinced. I deny that ids, egos, and superegos exist, either as discreet entities in themselves or as mechanisms or processes in the mind. Ids, egos, and superegos have no independent existence in the human being under analysis. We seem not to have noticed that Freud invented the id, the ego, and the superego; he did not discover them. These "things" are merely a part of the interpretive grid of the Freudian critic, not a part of the author that critic imagines he understands through the author's text. Nor do these "things" relate to one another in the way Freudians hypothesize. The existence of, and interaction between, ids, egos, and superegos are a psychologist's fiction. It is much the same as the old faculty psychology of the Middle Ages, which posited emotion, intellect, and will as separate faculties within us. The faculty psychologists had fallen into the functional fallacy. They reasoned that because I emote, think, desire, and do, that I *have* an emotion, an intellect, and a will. But I do not possess, as separate entities within me, these three faculties. Nor do they relate to one another in the ways imaged by Thomas Aquinas, John Duns Scotus, or

William of Occam. We know better, now that Locke has undeceived us. But, having escaped that misconception, we have fallen into another: Freud's fabrications concerning our inner composition and function have led us back into the Middle Ages. Sadly, some modern scholars do not know enough to perceive the gaffe. They *welcome* it.

Some Freudians try to explain the admittedly elusive character of these inner phantoms by telling us that "the names, id, ego and superego, actually signify nothing in themselves. They are merely a shorthand way of designating different processes, functions, mechanisms, and dynamisms within the total personality."[15] In addition to sounding like an expedient adopted at the last moment to protect a cherished but endangered theory, this explanation is manifestly absurd. It speaks as if "processes, functions, mechanisms, and dynamisms" were "nothing in themselves." This is mere verbal sleight of hand. Despite this Freudian's convoluted language, a process is a thing. To process is an action. An action is a thing. But, we are told, "processes, functions, mechanisms and dynamisms," when referred to by the words "id," "ego," and "superego," are "nothing in themselves." If the Freudians had said simply that ids, egos, and superegos are nothing, we all could have agreed. But they did not. Freudian criticism is not known for stating the obvious and then stopping.

Put another way, I deny that Freudian criticism is methodologically sound. After all, it is not real authors we are psychoanalyzing but, rather, ancient bits of yellowing paper, or else modern editions of them. When a psychoanalytic critic poses questions to a text, it is not the author who responds. *Comus*, for example, is not written in answer to questions posed to Milton about the Oedipal pressures churning within him. If such questions were posed to Milton, and if he desired to answer them at all, we have no reason to think that he would point to *Comus* in response. In the end, it is *the Freudian critic himself*, not the author under examination, who both poses the question and answers it. And, when he answers it, he answers it in the way a schoolboy invents an off-color joke, by foisting unintentional sexual overtones upon someone else's words. Furthermore, because these sexual overtones cannot be ascribed to the author's conscious intention itself, they are relegated to his *unconscious* mind, as if such things actually existed and were accessible to us through texts, and as if the concept of an unconscious mind was not, in some sense, a contradiction in terms.

I am not saying that a text cannot answer questions toward which it was not specifically addressed. Such answers, when they are to be found, are to be identified or extracted with the greatest possible care, always bearing in mind that, though we might wish it otherwise, many things from the past are not easily retrievable through texts, if at all. In a theological poem like *Paradise Lost*, a poem that is intended to "justify the ways of God to man" (I, 26), the poet's *theology* is both present and largely accessible. His unconscious psychological motivations and his psychic history (especially as interpreted by Freudian critics) are neither. *Paradise Lost*, after all, is not about Milton. Neither does it concern his alleged constituent psychological "functions" — id, ego, and superego. I begin to think that those who find such things in theological poetry have become so skilled at reading between and behind the lines of a text that they have lost the ability to read the lines themselves.

Because of its method, I deny that Freudian criticism is actually criticism. If criticism is, as my dictionary says, "the art of judging or evaluating with knowledge and propriety the beauties and faults of a work of art or literature," then Freudianism, I repeat, is not criticism. Studies that abuse literary texts by making them a means to the solution of other, non-literary, problems are not genuine literary criticism. Their pursuit may, indeed, proceed via literature, but it is not legitimately a literary pursuit. True literary criticism must make literature its focus, not merely the vehicle of the critic's own private agenda or interests.

Some Freudian interpreters try to maintain their claim to legitimacy by insisting that their "discoveries" bear upon our understanding of the text because they bear upon our understanding of the author. They proceed, they say, from text to author to text. Perhaps they do. But I deny that what they find at either end of their return trip is truth. Forays into the extraliterary do not always lead us back into the perimeter. In fact, they often end in foreign ports. Freudian criticism, despite the claims of some of its practitioners, is just such a foray. While a critic needs (and should welcome) all the help he can get from other disciplines, the critic must be sure that what is received actually constitutes hermeneutical assistance and not hindrance. Not every hand is a helping hand.

Perhaps Freudian interpreters do not take sufficient account of the fact that every intellectual discipline is fraught with ambiguity. As a result of this ambiguity, every discipline entails a number of schools of thought and each of those schools of thought, in turn, is colored by various shades of disagreement concerning interpretation and/or implementation. As an interdisciplinary study, Freudian criticism is doubly tenuous. On the one hand, it is racked by tensions and conflicts in psychology in general and in Freudianism in particular.[16] On the other hand, it also is buffeted by the warfare within literary criticism. I, for one, believe that Freudian criticism fails on both sides of its double life. It is bad science and it is bad criticism; bad science because of its natural inability to subject its conclusions to scientific verification (It is, we are told, a "postdictive science," not a "predictive" one.[17]) and bad criticism because it mistakenly thinks that not only is a writer accessible to us in his text, but so also is his *subconscious.*

My belief that Freudian criticism is an interdisciplinary failure should not be taken to mean that I oppose interdisciplinary research in general or "extrinsic" criticism in particular. In fact, I am very much in favor of them. I do not oppose Freudian criticism because it takes things into account other than the text; rather, I oppose Freudian criticism because what it takes into account is Freudianism. External frames of reference are not necessarily faulty; Freudian ones are. Freudian hermeneutics respects no boundaries. It exhibits no caution. It posits forces, factors, and functions in things that may not even be things. As usually practiced, Freudian criticism has usurped the subject matter. In becoming psychographers, Freudian critics often have become less than literary critics. Despite claims to the contrary, Freudian criticism's primary pursuit is not the explication of the text at hand. Its objective is almost always one well beyond the text, even well beyond the author's intention or even his consciousness. Those who write three hundred page monographs on the "psychogenesis of *Paradise Lost*"[18] are doing a great deal that lies beyond the pale of literary criticism. Not surprisingly then, Freudianism's grotesque fabrications do not enhance our understanding of our language's great theological works of verbal art. Freudianism has not succeeded in deepening our understanding and appreciation of *Paradise Lost*, for example, because Freudianism has shown itself incapable of detecting either beauty or sanctity. It detects only the earthquake of sexuality and its aftershocks. Sanctity, despite the title of one Miltonist's book, is not a complex.[19] Nor, despite the same book, are complexes sacred. Put another way, Freudian criticism often misconstrues theological art because it misunderstands the origin or generation of art. Art, to Freudianism, is traced to fantasies: to wish fulfillment and day dreams.[20] Such a causal connection, however, is utterly insupportable and is the merest of conjectures. As George Watson has explained concerning Freudianism's wildly speculative theories of literary causation and generation, Freud

> "compares the human mind, where 'it is the rule rather than the exception for the past to be preserved', to the city of Rome as it might appear if most of its ancient monuments had not vanished, with pagan temples standing among medieval and Renaissance buildings and modern thoroughfares. In history itself, the past may die and leave no trace. But in the individual mind, in the Freudian view, memories are stored and stand ready for use. Looked at from the angle of the literary historian, such a view seems like an ecstasy of Victorian historical enthusiasm. The most biographical critic before Freud — Sainte-Beuve, for instance — would not have ventured so far as to suppose that remote infantile experience, and even prenatal experience, could be formative in what ultimately appears as a work of literature. He would have been content, more modestly, with the outward facts about the schooling, reading, and acquaintanceship of the poet whose portrait he drew. The Freudian critic would intensify these biographical elements to the point of seeing the poem as minute evidence of the past of the poet; not of one past only, or the experience immediately preceding the act of creation, but of a whole succession of states of mind stretching back into childhood and causally interconnected."[21]

Obviously, human beings are interested in, and motivated by, much more than sex. I imagine that a great deal of theological poetry, perhaps nearly all poetry, has a source other than infantile sexuality and its alleged repercussions. Only a schoolboy's fascination with things genital allows us to posit sexual causation for art in such a facile manner. I say, along with C. S. Lewis, that "poetry is not a substitute for sexual satisfaction, nor sexual satisfaction for poetry."[22] I reject as perverse supposition the assertion that the motive for poetic creation lies beneath the consciousness and is linked to internal sexual turmoil, especially for Milton, whose poetic craft is conscious, deliberate, meticulous, precise, decorous, purposeful, and highly intellectual. The unarticulated methodological arrogance of such Freudian suppositions is staggering. Though Milton himself says that his poetry was motivated by a love for God, for country, and for freedom, and that it was intended to promote all three, the Freudian critic, who must imagine himself clearly aware of the many complicated factors within Milton that escaped even Milton's own notice, can see not only what the poet repressed, but why he has done so and what exactly was its artistic and theological residue. The Freudian critic believes he can identify and explain, with precision and confidence, what prompted a certain blind Englishman to write a theological epic poem more than three hundred years ago. Milton's plain affirmations to the contrary notwithstanding, we are told "that the Oedipus complex is the generative center of his character and his art."[23] And, as if that staggering insight were not enough, we are assured that "this could be predicated of *all* authors who are not psychotic."[24] Perhaps I am hopelessly skeptical, but I hesitate to say things about *all* writers of nearly any category, especially something that pertains to their character and their art.

But this is one of those places where Freudian criticism breaks down so noticeably. It allows the Freudian critic to assert what the author denies and to deny what the author affirms. It entitles the critic to operate as if he knows Milton's motives and character better than Milton did. It is arguable, of course, that such a critic does not know Milton at all. The poet himself might prove to be very different from all the Freudian (or non-Freudian) speculations about his long-dead psyche and its hidden "processes, functions, mechanisms, and dynamisms." Unlikely as it is that Milton will return to dispel such myths (or that many Freudian critics would recognize him if he did) the fearless psychoanalyzing of writers who have been in their graves for centuries will continue unrestrained.

Perhaps it is its unrestrained nature that renders so much Freudian interpretation fiction and not fact. In that system of literary analysis, after all, the wall dividing those two realms is virtually nonexistent. Even if ids, egos, and superegos existed, Lewis Carroll's Alice does not possess them. She does not even possess a *she*. She does not exist. That minor consideration, however, has not prevented critics from psychoanalyzing her, or Hamlet, or Captain Ahab. But, though it is frequently attempted, one cannot profitably psychoanalyze the non-existent. That the Electra complex has no real connection to the psychic development of a fictional character like Alice, a character who has no psyche to develop, has not kept Freudian hermeneutics out of Wonderland. Freudian hermeneutics seems to specialize in fictional characters, characters like the Milton that it imagines stands behinds his theological poems, spewing forth a stream of unconsciously sexual and/or pornographic metaphors. Perhaps one of the reasons Freudian criticism proceeds as confidently with fictional characters as it does with historical persons is because Freudian criticism is not rooted in verifiable reality. In its hands, historical persons *are* fictional. After all, we have only the psychoanalytic critic's (not unbiased) word that such a Milton ever existed. Or, to paraphrase I. A. Richards, despite what psychoanalytic critics might assert, the imagined mental processes of a writer are not a very profitable field for investigation because they are too happy a hunting ground for unbridled speculation.[25]

Its nonfactual nature accounts for some of Freudian criticism's apparent profundity, a profundity which arises from its ability to see what is not there. Readers of Freudian criticism, for example, some-times come away from a Freudian work surprised at all *they* missed when they read the *Faerie Queene* or the Pentateuch,[26] especially when compared to all the Freudian critic claims to see. But, *seeing* is the one thing Freudian criticism does not do — unless one classifies exegetical hallucination as vision. Though they tell us that the iconic significance of flowers and puppy dogs is unknown or unrecognized in the writer's own consciousness and that it lies buried deep within the recesses of his psyche, though they tell us the psyche operates by means of the mysterious transference of hidden "psychic energies" (whatever *they* are) between the inscrutable "processes, functions, mechanisms, and dynamisms" we label id, ego, and superego, despite all this shadowy ambiguity — or perhaps because of it — Freudian literary analysis often fails to exercise anything remotely resembling skepticism or modesty concerning its hypotheses. (Evidence for this is the fact that Freudians often label their ideas "conclusions," not "hypotheses.") It apparently matters little that the verification of Freudian theories concerning literary cause and effect, if it exists at all, lies well beyond (or below) what many cautious and reasonable scholars would allow as either relevant or analyzable data. In this light, one may be permitted to speculate that the Freudian critic's own imagination (as it feeds upon a number of perverse schoolboy speculations concerning literary meaning and origin) has been doing duty in place of a close, responsible, treatment of the text itself, as understood against its historical and literary background.

Freudian hermeneutics proceeds by hooking up a sexual and/or pornographic view of psychic reality to a religious text like *Paradise Lost*, a poem that draws upon the long standing conventions of epic genre and upon the content of the Bible and its traditional interpretation. It then tries to interpret that poem in light of the view of psychic history it posits for the author, a history based both upon its hypothetical id, ego, and superego paradigm and upon its assumptions concerning the iconic significance of unconscious metaphor. This imagined psychic history, in turn, is brought back into play not only in conjunction with the poem's unconscious meaning, but also as an explanation for the poem's very existence. In other words, the hypothetical psychic background that Freudians deduce *from the text* is used as a hermeneutical aid *for the text* from which it was derived. It proceeds by transforming its highly suspect hermeneutic for dreams into a hermeneutic for verbal art. This truncated and misshapen method brings us, exegetically, exactly nowhere. Understanding an epic poem from a Freudian slant is not to be identified with understanding an epic poem.

All this is not to say that suffering people have never been aided through psychoanalysis. They certainly have. But their improvement is not justification for Freudianism as an exegetical device. In fact, their improvement is hardly justification for Freudianism as thera-py. These instances of therapeutic success do not offset the instances (and they are legion) where not only no healing occurred, but actual damage was inflicted. Some studies have shown, in fact, that Freudian therapy's healing powers are hardly better than no therapy at all.[27] I would expect as much from any therapy not rooted in reality.

Finally, if I may be permitted to turn the tables for one paragraph and to psychoanalyze the psychoanalysts, I speculate that Freudian criticism is itself a wish fulfillment. Perhaps Freudian critics want to make this fallen world understandable when it often is not. Perhaps they want to make the world simpler by imposing upon it their own narrow system of causes and effects. But they cannot and they have not. And, they don't know they've failed.

That, at any rate, is why I no longer believe I ought to read ev-ery book about John Milton. Some simply do not repay the time and effort required to study them seriously. The time I waste on such books is time I could have invested studying genuinely useful books about Milton, books by Masson, Hanford, French, Kelley, Verity, and Lewalski, to name but a few. In short, I have reconfirmed for myself what Milton had earlier discovered about useless books: "if the com-pendious recital of what [one man misthought] was so tedious and unprofitable, then surely to sit out the whole extent of their tattle in a dozen volumes would be a loss of time irrecoverable."[28]

Should you wonder why I stop here, having merely exposed one method of how *not* to read, but not having explained how reading *should* be done, I reply that I need not bother. Such a demonstration has already been produced — twice.[29]

The justification for that hermeneutic is the subject of the next chapter.

END NOTES

1   Calvin S. Hall, *A Primer of Freudian Psychology* (New York: New American Library: A Mentor Book, 1954, 1979), p. 40.

2   John T. Shawcross, *With Mortal Voice: The Creation of "Paradise Lost"* (Lexington: The University Press of Kentucky, 1982), p. 178 n. 3.

3   Ibid., p. 18.

4 Ibid., p. 20.

5 Ibid., p. 179 n. 9.

6 John Milton, *The Complete Prose Works of John Milton*, 8 vols., Don M. Wolfe, General Editor (New Haven: Yale: 1953-82), 1: 886. The words to which Milton refers come from the preface of *A Modest Confutation*.

7 Ibid., p. 886.

8 Ibid., pp. 888-889.

9 Ibid., pp. 890-892.

10 Ibid., p. 891.

11 Ibid., p. 890.

12 Ibid., p. 894.

13 Ibid.

14 One of the most devastating critiques to date of Freudianism's failures is Hans J. Eysenck, *The Decline and Fall of the Freudian Empire* (Washington: Scott-Townsend Publishers),1985/1990. See also Hans Eysenck and Glenn Wilson, *The Experimental Studies of Freudian Theories* (New York: Barnes & Noble, 1974); Thomas Szasz, *The Myth of Psychotherapy* (New York: Doubleday, 1978); David E. Stannard, *Shrinking History: On Freud & the Failure of Psychohistory* (New York: Oxford University Press, 1980), Andrew Salter, *The Case against Psychoanalysis* (New York: Henry Holt, 1954), and Richard Webster, *Why Freud was Wrong: Sin, Science and Psychoanalysis* (London: Fontana, 1995).

15 Hall, pp. 34, 35.

16 Oddly, some Freudian critics will use the variegated nature of current Freudian studies as a defense against my strictures. In conversations with me, they often say that my negative judgments do not take into account the fact that Freudianism is a spectrum, not a monolithic entity. But that defense will not do. It serves only to underscore my contention that most Freudian conclusions are neither demonstrable nor convincing, even to other Freudians. The anarchy within Freudian studies has been recognized by many scholars. For example, Jacques Barzun, *Clio and the Doctors: Psycho-history, Quanto-history & History* (Chicago: University of Chicago, 1974), p. 71, observes: "The theorists of psycho-history invoke Freud and speak of psychoanalysis or of dynamic psychiatry as if those names covered unified teachings. Yet a slight acquaintance with the literature is enough to show that radical conflicts exist."

17 Hall, p. 53.

18 William Kerrigan, *The Sacred Complex: On the Psychogenesis of "Paradise Lost"* (Cambridge: Harvard, 1983).

19 Ibid. According to Allan Bloom, *The Closing of the American Mind* (New York: Simon and Schuster, 1987), p. 193: "Freud's psychoanalytic theory . . . wants to found itself on biology and at the same time to account for spiritual phenomena," and it does so "to the detriment of both."

20 Sigmund Freud, *Introductory Lectures on Psycho-Analysis*, trans. Joan Riviere (London: Heron Books, n.d.), Lecture 23, p. 306.

21 George Watson, *The Study of Literature* (London: Allen Lane, 1969), pp. 157-158. Elsewhere (p. 18) in the same text, Watson makes another pertinent observation concerning the modern criticism of *Paradise Lost*: ". . . Milton, if he could know that interest in his epics is no longer primarily theological, would be contemptuous in the last degree."

22 C. S. Lewis, *Selected Literary Essays*, ed. Walter Hooper (Cambridge at the University Press, 1969), p. 295. As T. S. Eliot taught us, "nothing in this world or the next is a substitute for anything else; and if you find you must do without something, such as religious faith or philosophic belief, then you must do without it," quoted in F. W. Bateson, *Essays in Critical Dissent* (London: Longman Group Ltd., 1972), p. 194.

23 Kerrigan, p. 6.

24 Ibid., emphasis added.

25 I. A. Richards, *Principles of Literary Criticism* (San Diego: Harcourt, Brace, Jovanovich, 1925), p. 29.

26 For an example of a psychoanalytic interpretation of the Pentateuch, see Sigmund Freud, *Moses and Monotheism* (New York: Random House, 1939).

27 From among the many scholars and studies that support this conclusion, see, for example, the two articles by Thomas Oden: "A Populist's View of Psychotherapeutic Deprofessionalization," *Journal of Humanistic Psychology* 14 (1974): 3-18; and "Consumer Interests in Therapeutic Outcome Studies: A Reply to Herron," *Journal of Humanistic Psychology* 15 (1975): 74-84.

28 Milton, p. 944.

29 I believe one does best by combining the insights of C. S. Lewis, *An Experiment in Criticism* (Cambridge: Cambridge University Press, 1961); and E. D. Hirsch, Jr., *Validity in Interpretation* (New Haven: Yale University Press, 1967).

"I should be glad if I sent my reader away with a new sense of responsibility to the language."
C. S. LEWIS
Studies in Words

The Ethics of Meaning: The Case for a Conservative Hermeneutic

If you are a student, please read carefully. I will explain how you can prevent any teacher who believes that a text means what the reader says it means rather than what the author says it means from marking any of your work wrong ever again, regardless of whether your work is in the form of short answers, essays, or research papers.

The payment I seek for doing so is not primarily financial. Rather than money, my reward is to stifle those literary critics and those literary theories that undermine Western tradition, at least those parts of Western tradition preserved for us in language and in texts. In other words, the wealth I seek is not monetary. I want to preserve the wisdom, the truth, and the freedom that our forefathers bequeathed to us in our culture's foundational documents.

Put differently, I want to hear the voices of the founding fathers in the Declaration of Independence and in the Constitution, not the voices of activist liberal judges who think that heeding the intentions of the framers is simply to fall slave to the dead hand of the past. I also want to hear the voices of the poets and the sages, who speak to us across the centuries in the greatest works of verbal art ever produced, not the deconstructive ramblings of the self-appointed destroyers of language and literature who seem to occupy so many seats of power and influence in the humanities departments on so many college campuses. Finally, and most importantly, I want to hear the voice of God and the voices of his apostles and prophets in the Bible, not the voices of modernist exegetes who think that the Bible's meaning has nothing to do with the intention of either the God who inspired it or the people who wrote it.

I want to do so, on the one hand, because I value the theological, political, and cultural legacy left me by those men and women who made the civilized world what it is. I am firmly persuaded that the best of the past deserves — indeed requires — our protection, especially now, when the mindless mantra chanted on so many American campuses seems to be "Hey-Hey, Ho-Ho, Western Civ. has got to go!" I do so because I value the patrimony of freedom, of truth, and of salvation left for us in the texts that make both civilization and hope possible. I do so because I agree with Confucius that when words lose their meaning, people lose their freedom.

I want to do so, on the other hand, because I value the teaching profession, which, without a suitable hermeneutic, becomes impossible, as the following considerations make evident.

I. THE HERMENEUTICS OF PEDAGOGY

Before I keep the promise I made at the outset of this essay and explain how to insulate yourself from all your professor's criticisms, and before I tell you how to preserve the meaning of the most important and enduring texts in the world, I want to tell you a story[1].

Some years ago, a good friend of mine was caught in a London downpour. Fighting his way slowly, but resolutely, along some unfamiliar English side street, and bitterly longing for the umbrella he somehow had misplaced, my friend turned a fog-shrouded corner and on an overhead shop sign spied the words "umbrellas recovered." "Ah," my friend thought to himself, "perhaps this man can help me recover mine!"

A moment's reflection, however, revealed the folly. No matter how intensely my friend wished otherwise, "recovered" meant "repaired" or "refurbished," not "retrieved." The meaning of that word was the one intended for it by the shopkeeper who made the sign, not the meaning imagined or desired by the drenched pedestrian who was reading it. That is how shop signs, telephone books, love letters, travel brochures, and — Dare we say it? — even novels and epic poems are written and should be read. A text means what its author intends it to mean, not what a reader wants it to mean. In Alexander Pope's words, one ought "to read every work of wit in the same spirit as its author writ." That is the meaning of meaning. If something on an umbrella shop sign is unclear, perhaps a quick perusal of the information displayed on the shop window will help, or else a glance inside. That is the beauty and function of context.

I stand over against those literary critics, activist judges, and modernist biblical exegetes who mistakenly insist that a text, whether poetry or prose, has a life of its own, or that what a text means is what it means to the reader and not what its author intended it to mean. That is, I deny the hermeneutical assumption that a text can be rightly understood apart from solid grammatical/historical exegesis. I do so because, methodologically, any interpreter who maintains otherwise must necessarily compromise himself every time he turns away from the text at hand and opens a dictionary in order to trace down a term with which he is unfamiliar. And who among us has not done so? My desire, of course, is not to steer readers away from the *Oxford English Dictionary*; it is to steer them away from the unfortunate hermeneutical inconsistency that has racked modern literary criticism — the sort of criticism that tells us a great deal more about the presuppositions and world view of the reader than it does about the great works of writers like Dante, Erasmus, or Milton.

As a student and devotee of literature myself, I want to know more about great authors and great books, not about the predilections and prejudices of people who read them many centuries after the fact. The interpreter's work is to point out and to elucidate the literature at hand, not to foist upon it the interpreter's own peculiar world view or that of the one small segment of contemporary society that interpreter represents.

In short, I oppose non-intentionalist and non-historical exegesis.

Who cannot see the hermeneutical fortress that non-intentionalist and non-historical readers try to build for themselves? By positing, on the one hand, an autonomously existing text, subject neither to time nor place, and by positing, on the other hand, a subjective meaning for that text, a meaning unrestrained by either authorial intention or historical milieu, critics who deny authorial intention insist, in effect, that any text's meaning reduces to whatever *they* say, though, what they say seldom, if ever, accords with what other readers of the same school say. By adopting this autonomous, indeed libertine, hermeneutical subjectivity, modern critics assert both that the text itself is independent (nothing controls *it*) and that so are they (nothing controls *them*). They no longer need hearken, they think, to Spenser when they read *The Faerie Queene*, to Shakespeare when they read *Romeo and Juliet*, to James Madison when they read the Constitution, or even to the apostle Paul himself when they read the epistle to the Romans. The meaning of all texts, new or old, great or small, sacred or secular, is now to be concocted free hand, by anyone so inclined.

But I, for one, ardently oppose this arrogant intrusion into the texts of others. I oppose the shameless hijacking of someone else's words for our own self-seeking ends. The time has come to put both the text and the modern interpreter back under authority. I believe it is of more than etymological significance that the word "authority" derives from "author." In short, I am saying that to call authorial intention a fallacy is itself a fallacy.

Yet, nearly all the literary critics with whom I have ever spoken say precisely that: authorial intention is a fallacy.

But, if authorial intention is a fallacy, if meaning is the reader's prerogative, then graded instruction of any kind is an injustice because it credits the student with the instructor's insight, on the one hand, and it holds the student responsible for the instructor's mistaken meanings, on the other. If authorial intention is not the measure of meaning, then teachers can no longer count students wrong when *the teachers themselves* are responsible for what the student's test answers or research papers actually mean. After all, no student ought to get a lower grade simply because the instructor gave that student's answer or essay an incorrect or inappropriate meaning. One could quite as easily give the student's writing the correct meaning so that the student in question, indeed all students, might make the dean's list every semester.

If the professor gives the student's words what the professor deems an incorrect meaning, then the error ought to be charged to the *professor*, not the student. In that case, teachers who give their students F's are failing their own courses. Under such a method of interpretation, the incorrect meaning of all mistaken answers on all tests is the responsibility of the grader.

Furthermore, because in this system of interpretation meaning is the prerogative of the reader and not the author, no professor can properly prevent any student from giving the professor's course syllabus, the professor's lectures, the professor's assignments, or the professor's test questions whatever meanings the *student* sees fit. On the basis of the professor's own hermeneutical principles, no objection could be effectively raised against such a student practice. Nor could any teacher ever again chide any student for failing to follow instructions, because the teacher's instructions mean not what the teacher intended them to mean but what the student determined they ought to mean.

The professor cannot escape this difficulty by saying that authorial intention applies to syllabi but not to epic poems or to elegies because syllabi are prose and epics and elegies are not. Both this dichotomous view and the double hermeneutic to which it gives rise assume that words mean not only a *different thing* in a prose passage than in a poetic one, but that words mean in a *different way* in a prose passage than in a poetic one, neither of which is demonstrable. Such professors argue as if subordinate clauses and indirect objects somehow functioned differently in a line from Keats than they do in a line from Faulkner, which is nonsense.

Put differently, if my professor told me I could be graded down on a test or a paper and that mistaken answers could be attributed to me rather than to him because my answers were in prose, I would simply write all my answers in iambic pentameter (or, more troublesome for the instructor, in free verse) — then, on the instructor's own basis, all errors revert to the instructor because the instructor's own theory of interpretation states that in poetry meaning is the prerogative of the reader.

And if a professor who holds that prose meaning differs from poetic meaning were unable to say definitively and precisely what exactly poetry is, and if that professor could not objectively or conclusively distinguish what was truly poetry from what was merely poetic — that is, if that professor affirmed that whether or not a text was poetry was a matter of private judgment and not a matter of absolute fact — then that professor still could not extricate himself from his pedagogical dilemma because identifying a student's answer as prose and not as poetry would be a subjective literary judgment on the part of the professor and would reflect more on that professor than on the student. In such a case, the professor would be able to count the student's answer wrong only because that professor had subjectively categorized that student's answer as prose. If the student insists that his answer is poetry, the professor's attribution of error to the student remains self-condemning.

Thus, if you are a student, pay close attention to what I am about to say. It will ensure that you never again miss another question on any test or receive a poor grade on any essay or any paper from any teacher who denies authorial intention or who says that poetry means subjectively but that prose does not.

According to your professor's own rules of interpretation, when you are assigned to write an answer or a paper about a poem, that poem means what *you* say it means, not what anyone else says it means — not even the poet or your professor. By the professor's own rules, meaning is your prerogative. The text means what you say it means.

If your professor says that prose texts mean objectively and that poetic texts do not, then write all your answers in poetic form. In that way, all wrong answers are the result of your professor's interpretation, not your intended meaning. If your professor wants to continue to mark himself or herself wrong, that is up to your professor. But your professor cannot continue to mark *you* down because of your professor's own mistaken meanings. If your professor wants to grade you, he must deny his own interpretive method and he must relinquish his hegemony over the meaning of your texts and begin to read everything in a new way.

In short, if authorial intention is wrong, then you are not; only your professor is. If authorial intention is not wrong, then all those who have opposed it up until now are wrong, which includes most modern professors of literature.

Some professors try to extricate themselves from this hermeneutical and pedagogical mare's nest by insisting that the meaning of a text lies neither with the author nor with the reader, but with the text itself. But this unabashed textual positivism will not do. It conveniently overlooks the obvious fact that a text has a meaning (indeed a text has existence) only because an author put it there. A text does not somehow create its own meaning. Nor does a text create itself; an author has a meaning and creates a text in order to preserve that meaning and to communicate it. Neither texts nor meanings are autonomous. To think otherwise is to apply to textual meaning Satan's error in *Paradise Lost*, which is to ascribe to something not God that it is "self-begot, self-raised/By [its] own quick'ning power" (*Paradise Lost* V, 860-1).

Put differently, to assert that a text is autonomous is bad theology because a text is the product of a writer. Because that writer is necessarily subject to the limitations of time, space and causation, one simply cannot ascribe to any creation of a creature (i.e., one cannot ascribe to the text) the self-sufficiency and independence that reality and theology deny to the creature himself (i.e., the author).

II. THE HERMENEUTICS OF CONSERVATISM

You see, (to move from theology to economics) Adam Smith was right.

Prosperity follows in the wake of the division of labor. As long as every worker is constrained to satisfy all his needs and desires for himself, his lot in life will be significantly poorer. He cannot raise his own sheep and cotton in order to provide all his own clothes. He cannot extract his own iron ore from the earth and then smelt it and shape it in a steel mill of his own construction and operation in order to make his own automobiles and passenger trains. He cannot grow his own bananas and coconuts so that he will have tasty little morsels to sprinkle on his cereal or his ice cream. He cannot produce, direct, and act in his own television programs and movies, or build and operate his own television sets and movie theaters in order to keep himself entertained. He cannot design, develop, test, and deploy his own system of nuclear weapons in order to protect himself from foreign aggression. In order to have a more pleasant, more prosperous, and more secure existence, he needs the things that others can provide for him better than he can provide them for himself. Because the division of labor affords a degree of specialization, expertise, and efficiency not available in alternate economic systems, some people are able to do for others what others are not able to do for themselves nearly so well, if at all. As a result, those who engage in the division of labor are far better off than those who do not.

By the same token, I propose that we all are better off, not only pedagogically but *in virtually every way*, if we employ a division of labor with regard to our fundamental texts, whether literary, political, or sacred. If each one of us had to write our own *Paradise Lost*, our own *Canterbury Tales*, our own *Divine Comedy*, our own *Reflections on the Revolution in France*, or our own Psalms, rather than permitting Milton, Chaucer, Dante, Burke and David to do so for us, we would each be immeasurably impoverished. We could never do for ourselves what that collection of great minds and valiant spirits has done for us in their world-shaping texts. As it is in economics, so it is in hermeneutics — prosperity follows close upon the division of labor.

In hermeneutics, the division of labor runs like this: The author has in mind something he thinks is true or beneficial and which he desires to communicate. He selects language and a genre that he deems appropriate for his message, which he then writes down. A reader, interested in what he imagines this text will say, picks it up and begins to read. If the author has formed his mental concepts clearly and cohesively; if he has selected his terms and his genre with careful precision; and if the reader has expended the effort needed to understand the text from the author's point of view (that is, if the reader has properly discerned the author's intended meaning); genuine communication occurs. In such a case, the notions received by the reader from the text will closely approximate the intentions built into it by the writer.

But if the author's ideas were not clearly defined in his own mind; or if the author has chosen terms and a genre ill-suited to his purpose; or if the reader has been careless in his work as an interpreter; or if he feels it his prerogative to ignore the intentions of the writer altogether; a failure of communication predictably results. In such cases, what the reader claims to get from the text is not gotten from the text at all. It is simply manufactured *ad hoc* in the reader's own mind. That failure to communicate results from a breakdown in the division of labor within the literary enterprise. It results, on the one hand, from writers not taking seriously their proper task of clear conception and precise articulation. It results, on the other hand, from readers abandoning their proper task of consuming meaning in favor of usurping a role not truly their own — that of producing meaning. That wrongheaded method of procedure does not work well in the marketplace, where buyers and sellers freely exchange goods and services; it does not work well in the classroom, where students study Wordsworth and Shakespeare; it does not work well in the judge's chambers, where judges interpret the Constitution and its attendant amendments; and it does not work well in the pulpit, where preachers interpret and expound the word of God.

As long as we require the reader to do the job of the writer, and as long as we continue to confuse the role of the interpreter with that of the author, we will remain culturally, politically, and spiritually poorer because this backwards-working hermeneutic lays upon every one of us the tremendous burden of reinventing our entire cultural heritage anew. It lays upon us the necessity of reinventing the meaning not only of our foundational texts, but of all texts whatsoever, because (according to this theory of reading) no text has a meaning until the reader gives it one. The Bible means nothing; the Constitution means nothing; *Hamlet* means nothing; traffic signs mean nothing; marriage vows mean nothing; even the perverse scrawls on rest room walls mean nothing until the reader gives them a meaning — a meaning quite cut off from, perhaps even antithetical to, the author's intention.

To consign the manufacture of meaning to the reader requires the reader to create the meaning of all texts *de novo*, to reinvent the literary wheel, the legal wheel, and the theological wheel each time the reader picks up a text. To insist that texts mean what their readers say they mean and not what their authors intended them to mean effectively strips the reader of his entire cultural patrimony by forcing him to create for himself what the apostles, the prophets, the sages, and the framers have made for him already but (according to this view) foolishly preserved for him in the form of a text, not realizing that simply by preserving it for him in verbal form they have actually sequestered that patrimony from him forever and sentenced him to remake the great works of the Western world all over again, freehand.

If this hermeneutic is correct, no messages are possible. No sentence you ever heard, no statement you ever read, had any meaning until you gave it one. Though perhaps you thought otherwise, if this method of interpretation is correct, Plato has never spoken to you in the *Republic*, nor Thomas in the *Summa*, nor God in Christ. Your wife, your husband, your Lord, have never really whispered "I love you." It was only your own voice all along. You simply did not recognize it. You have never really talked to anyone; you talked only to yourself using someone else's words. If this hermeneutic is correct, all conversations, despite their appearance, are monologues.

If this hermeneutic is correct, you are surrounded by a world of empty texts, waiting for you not simply to discover their meaning, but to invent it.

If this hermeneutic is correct, no text has been, or ever could be, misconstrued. If this hermeneutic is correct, no author and no speaker can raise any complaint about being misunderstood or misrepresented. The meaning of their words, according to this theory, is simply not their prerogative. Over the meaning of their own words, they exercise no claim.

According to this theory of interpretation, the position I advocate in these pages — the idea that authorial intention, not the reader's interpretation, is the true measure of meaning — is fundamentally and expansively wrong.

According to this misguided theory of interpretation, you can tell me, now that I am finished with this essay, just what I meant by it, but did not realize or intend. I invite you to do so.

Tell me what this essay really means.

Then I'll tell you what your interpretation really means — and it will surprise you.

I guarantee it.

I know you won't mind.

END NOTES

1   This story appears in slightly modified form in Michael Bauman, *Milton's Arianism* (Frankfurt: Verlag Peter Lang, 1987), 341.

POLITICAL THEOLOGY

" . . . the mysterious dynamic of history resides in man's choice of gods.
In the service of his god — or gods (they may be legion) — a man expends
his energies, commits his sacrifices, devotes his life. And history is made.
Understand Communism, then, as a religion; or miss
the secret of its power!"

LESTER DEKOSTER
Communism and Christian Faith

" . . . look what the grounds and causes of a single happiness to one man,
the same you shall find them to [be for] a whole state."

JOHN MILTON
Of Reformation

"A noble nature desires to be instructed, and will not endure to be coerced.
Merely to use coercion is for tyrants; merely to suffer it, for donkeys."

ERASMUS
epistle 1153

Reality, Religion, and the Marxist Retreat

Reality is resilient. Ignore it, reshape it, mistreat it as we may, it bounces back. After many decades of abuse at the hands of its socialist reformers, the world of hard economic fact and of unchanging human nature has again raised its head to assert that true wealth resides not in measurable, divisible, allegedly manageable lumps of dead matter, and not in the state-controlled means of production, but in the creativity and genius of the human mind freely doing what it was designed to do: "replenish the earth and subdue it" (Gen. 1: 28).

We humans have tackled the task of replenishing and subduing the earth in many ways, very few of which have met with success. Each of us enters the world with little else than a fallen nature, and most of us exit this life in virtually the same condition. Poverty, ignorance, and bondage are not the exception in human history, they are the norm. Only rarely and with great difficulty have we ever extricated ourselves from their vice-like grip. When we do escape, it behooves us to ponder carefully how that escape was orchestrated, and how it might be reproduced for the sake of our fellows. By means of such careful reflection, we discover that the secret to sustained economic prosperity is nothing else but what Michael Novak labelled "democratic capitalism," that happy combination of self-government under law coupled with an extensively unencumbered marketplace.

No other political and economic system has been able to deliver political freedom and economic prosperity in anything like the lavish way democratic capitalism has produced them.

The proof is not hard to find. One need only look as far back as World War II to discern that the free market greatly outperforms the command economy in any and all of its partial or plenary manifestations. Japan, for example, was on the losing side the war effort and suffered nuclear destruction — twice. Its land area and population are both comparatively small. Its natural resources are significantly limited. Nevertheless, Japan's economy and its standard of living far outstrip those of the Soviet Union, which, like Japan, suffered extensive damage during the war, but which, unlike Japan, did not rise from the ashes like a phoenix, despite the fact that it was on the winning side of the conflict, despite the fact that it was given all of Eastern Europe as a gift (a gift which its primitive economic system could neither sustain nor retain), and despite the fact that it has more people, more land and more natural resources than Japan.

A similar comparison could be made between North and South Korea, mainland China and either Hong Kong or Taiwan, East and West Germany (while they were divided), and India and South Africa (the largest and second largest examples of apartheid in the world). Both the production performance and the standard of living of First World free market economies consistently dwarf those of Second World socialist systems.

Even if one were to focus only on countries of the Third World, where the problem of poverty is most acute, the evidence is unambiguous: those nations that place greater reliance on the market process, such as Malaysia, Hong Kong, and South Korea, embarrass those nations that rely on state-directed production and consumption, such as India, Tanzania, and Mozambique.

One cannot attribute the unmatched Third World prosperity of free market nations to the foreign aid they have allegedly received from the West. Nor can one blame the backwardness of those nations that do not flourish on the lingering effects of colonialism. Some of the most well developed nations of the Third World are former colonies, like Singapore, Hong Kong, and Malaysia, while some of the very poorest nations of the Third World, like Ethiopia, Nepal, Tibet, and Afghanistan, were never Western colonies at all. In fact, some of the wealthiest nations in the world, the United States, Canada, and Australia among them, are themselves former colonies. Furthermore, massive amounts of Western aid have been poured into countries that remain resolutely poor, like Kampuchea, Uganda, Pakistan, and Nigeria. They remain poor because most of the reasons for national poverty are domestic and systemic. Until the underdeveloped nations unleash the productive forces of the marketplace, they and the millions of poor whose wretched lot it is to live within their borders will continue in unrelenting want.

But market economies are not so. As Brian Griffiths observes,

> It so happens that as a matter of history it was the market economy which brought about the transformation of the Western world from widespread poverty to the level of prosperity which it now enjoys. In the mid-eighteenth century, life in England was comparable to that in many Third World countries today: low real income, little education, poor housing, widespread disease and short life expectancy. By the end of the nineteenth century, the situation had changed dramatically. Real incomes had quadrupled, education was widespread, the housing stock had grown dramatically and life expectancy had increased. In no small measure this was due to the ability of the market economy to harness the inventiveness and entrepreneurial resources of ordinary people ... [M]arket economies create wealth more efficiently than either state-owned or state-planned economies. It is true in developed countries; it is also true in developing countries.[1]

In other words, if as a Christian one is intent upon easing the conditions of the poor and pushing back the boundaries of poverty and destitution, then democratic capitalism has far more to recommend it than any other system of political economy ever devised. Under no other system have the poor been raised as far so quickly, and in such great numbers. Marxism, by contrast, is the cause of sustained poverty, not its solution. In short, to condemn democratic capitalism, one must first misrepresent its history.

But though democratic capitalism flourishes, the human past in general has by no means been a story of unrelenting prosperity and freedom; it is a litany of tyranny, famines, illiteracy, plagues, war, oppression, infant death, and mere subsistence. For most of the people who ever lived, life is exactly what Thomas Hobbes said it was — nasty, brutish, and short. The life we enjoy in the modern Western world is a rare commodity in human history. It is a blessing of immense magnitude, seldom given, and never so lavishly as now.

But, like most of the blessings we enjoy, freedom and prosperity do not come to us fully formed, directly from the hand of God. God is a sharing God; He rarely does anything on His own the doing of which He can share with His creatures. Freedom and prosperity are no exception. They are mediated blessings, mediated by the development of human insight, effort, and sacrifice, which alone can produce the life we enjoy. Thus, as a Christian theologian, I acknowledge both the divine source of our blessedness and the human means whereby it was actualized. I thank God; and I recognize that liberty under law and a marketplace controlled by little else than the morally enlightened preferences of its freely engaged participants constitute the *sine qua non* of political freedom and economic prosperity.

Democratic capitalism succeeds where other systems fail because it is more firmly rooted in the inescapable facts of economic scarcity, of incomplete knowledge, and of human imperfectability. That is, among the various competing systems of governance and production, democratic capitalism takes the fullest account of reality. It understands that human desires normally tend to outstrip the supply of goods and services available to satisfy those desires. It understands that none of us knows all we need to know in order to make the very best use of the means and the goods available to us (much less to make the wisest possible economic decisions for countless thousands, perhaps millions, of people with whom we are utterly unfamiliar, as must be the case in any system of central planning). It understands that we humans are an incorrigibly selfish lot. Democratic capitalism has learned to take these factors into account by devising a system of exchange that harnesses human self-interest in the service of others and in the satisfaction of their desire and needs. More than two hundred years ago, Adam Smith captured this fact so memorably:

> As every individual, therefore, endeavors as much as he can
> both to employ his capital in the support of domestic indus-

try, and so to direct that industry that its produce may be
of the greatest value; every individual necessarily labors to
render the annual revenue of the society as great as he can.
He generally, indeed, neither intends to promote the public
interest, nor knows how much he is promoting it. By prefer-
ring the support of domestic to that of foreign industry, he
intends only his own security; and by directing that industry in such a manner as its produce may be of the greatest
value, he intends only his own gain, and he is in this, as in
many other cases, led by an invisible hand to promote an end
which was no part of his intention. Nor is it always the worse
for the society that it was no part of it. By pursuing his own
interest he frequently promotes that of the society more ef-
fectually than when he really intends to promote it. I have
never known much good done by those who affected to trade
for the public good.[2]

But the Marxists have not learned that important economic lesson, nor any number of a vast array of lessons that they could have and
should have learned from the world around them and from Marxism's
own dismal record in that world. No religion, no political system, and
no means of production can prosper if it is not firmly rooted in things
as they are rather than things as we would like them to be. Precisely
here Marxism fails. Rather than beginning with the hard facts of reality, and rather than constructing a theory of governance and production that takes those facts into account by conforming their thoughts
to extra-mental reality, the Marxists foolishly believe that political
and economic institutions can be molded at will to conform to the
political vision in their heads. It cannot. Of Marxism's numerous cognitive failures, I mention but five.

I. MARXISM ENTAILS A FAULTY VIEW OF HUMAN NATURE
Marxists do not seem to realize that human institutions arise from
human action; that human action arises from human nature; and that
human nature is notoriously intractable. The problem of the human
heart is at the heart of the human problem. The human heart, the Bible
says, is desperately wicked (Jeremiah 17:9). But this the Marxists do
not comprehend. They seem not to know what Alexander Hamilton

knew: the science of public policy is the knowledge of human nature. Try as they may, the Marxists cannot succeed so long as human nature remains what it is: marginally (sometimes extensively) unloving, ungiving, and untamed. Marxism cannot succeed because it has no way to harness human depravity for the service of others. Instead, it depends upon altruism where little or none exists, and it supplies no incentive for that altruism to be cultivated.

But democratic capitalism is not so. Unlike Marxism, democratic capitalism enjoys unprecedented success because it takes into account the undeniable fact of human nature. People, being what they are, respond to incentives. Democratic capitalism succeeds where other systems fail or flounder because within it the interests of the individual coincide with, and serve, the interests of others, by means of incentives. In democratic capitalism, one does not normally succeed without first serving the needs and interests of others in a way that others find acceptable and at a price those others deem fair.

Within Marxism, however, the needs and desires of the private individual are cut loose from those of society at large. In Marxism, the individual's incentives toward productivity and creativity are vitiated, if not eradicated, because no matter how hard he works he will not get further ahead, and no matter how poorly he works, he will not lose. As Ludwig von Mises made clear,

> In the socialist system, in which all the fruits of the various individuals' labor are appropriated by the supreme office of production management and then redistributed among the comrades without any regard for the worth of their individual contribution, there is no inducement for an individual to exert his strength . . . The superiority of the capitalistic system of production is due to the fact that it remunerates everybody according to his contribution to the satisfaction of his fellow men. It thus stimulates everybody, within the system of the division of labor, to exert himself to the utmost. The better a man serves others, the better for him. In the capitalistic market economy the consumers are supreme. In his capacity as a producer of commodities and services everybody is forced to serve the consumers.[3]

Because it ignores human nature, socialist production falls off; needs are not met; people are not satisfied; poverty is not reduced. If understanding the nature and limitations of human beings is the beginning of political wisdom, then the Marxists have yet to begin.

II. MARXISM ENTAILS A FAULTY VIEW OF CAUSE AND EFFECT

The Marxists do more than ignore that which cannot be ignored, they also confuse cause and effect by believing the fallacy that economic conditions and the social and political circumstances that attach to them serve to shape everything and everyone. They have never stopped to ask themselves what (or who) changes economic conditions, and why.

Public policy and political theory are enacted only by real and identifiable human beings, not by any alleged impersonal forces of change set loose in the world at large. Individual human beings are the true movers and shakers in political affairs, not "the spirit of the age," not the "the winds of freedom and equality," not "historically determined class struggle," not even "ideas whose time has come." *People* are responsible for hatching failed economic policies, for inciting Marxist revolutions, and for inter-racial oppression, on the one hand, as well as for the acquisition and maintenance of political freedom and material prosperity, on the other. Until the Marxists recognize from whence arise both human failures and human successes, they will continue to generate ill-conceived policies. It can be no other way. No answers are possible until the Marxists discover who is answerable; and until they discover who is answerable, they chase illusory excuses and imaginary scapegoats. Human actors excepted, nearly everything is a mirage in the events of the political arena and of the marketplace. Behind nearly every political and economic result, both good and bad, lies a human cause.

But Marxist taxonomy and the worldview it embodies permit no such conclusion. Marxist nomenclature ignores the obvious fact that only individuals exist. Rather than beginning with the irreducible fact of the fallen human individual, rather than building its theory on the basis of individual dignity, worth, autonomy, and sinfulness, Marxism sees only classes, aggregates, and masses, never realizing that such things are merely their own interpretations of reality, and not reality itself. As Marc Bloch observed in a different context, a nomenclature that is thrust upon the external world rather than derived from it will always end by distorting the world because it raises its own failed interpretive categories to the level of the true and the eternal.

Classes, as such, do not exist. Only fallen individual human beings exist. Classes are a sociologist's fiction, a shorthand method of identifying and interpreting the great many billions of individuals who now live or who have lived upon this planet. In that way, Marxist theory is the political and sociological equivalent of philosophical realism and, as a result, has most of philosophical realism's attendant strengths and weaknesses, reification among them. I cannot explain it any more plainly than has Rose Wilder Lane:

> In the human world there is no entity but the individual person . . . So far as Society has any existence, it exists when boy meets girl, when Mrs. Jones telephones Mrs. Smith, when Robinson buys a cigar, when the motorist stops for gasoline . . . when the postman delivers the mail and the labor bosses discuss a strike . . . and the dentist says 'Wider, please.' Human relationships are so infinitely numerous and varying every moment, that no human mind can begin to grasp them. To call these relationships Society, and then discuss the welfare or progress of Society, as if it existed as a bee swarm does, is simply to escape from reality to fairyland.[4]

Such ideas are not new. Centuries ago Aristotle understood that those with money and those without were likely to be mentally and socially crippled by the distorted way they viewed each other as only either rich or poor, rather than as individual human beings. Modern Marxists are subject to the same ancient interpretive delusion to which Aristotle alluded. Marxist taxonomy binds Marxists — and those over whom they rule — in the chains of error. The Marxists not only see aggregates where only individuals exist, they also see only imperialists, revolutionaries, the bourgeoisie, and the proletariat. That is, the Marxists not only fall afoul of the fallacy of aggregation, they apply laudatory or pejorative labels to the aggregates they have created, and thereby applaud or condemn millions of individuals for no other reason than that those individuals happen to fall into one or the other artificial category. For such "offenses" millions of people, quite literally, have died.

But, though people rule the world, and not impersonal forces or faceless masses, one must not conclude that therefore ideas are either unimportant or inconsequential. As Richard Weaver properly observed, ideas have consequences. But ideas do not have consequences apart from the people who conceive them, refine them, and apply them. Thus, on their own, ideas do not lead us places; we take them somewhere. Only to the extent that people act upon their beliefs do ideas have consequences. People do not always do so; but when they do, *they themselves* are the active agents in history, not their mental conceptions.

III. MARXISM ENTAILS A FAULTY VIEW OF JUSTICE

The Marxists mistakenly believe that justice is synonymous with equality. It is not. Justice is not having the same as your neighbor, regardless of differences in skill, investment, effort, ownership, worth, and chance. Nor is justice the same as confiscating the personal property of some in order to give it to those who have no moral or legal claim upon it. Justice is not synonymous with either equality or coercive redistribution. Justice is having what is yours by inheritance, by hard work, by legal purchase, and by good fortune, provided such possessions have come to you apart from coercion and deceit. Justice is the same as equality only for those people and in those circumstances that are truly equal. Such people and such circumstances, however, are exceedingly rare. We human beings, and the varying circumstances in which we find ourselves, are not equal. Whatever else they may be, things that are all the same are not human. Things that are not truly the same are not equal. To misunderstand this fact is to misunderstand justice. To misunderstand justice is to set a course for political and economic failure. As Brian Griffiths explains,

> To aim for after-tax equality of income as a major objective of economic policy has three basic difficulties associated with it. By blunting the incentives of economic life to start with, it would discourage enterprise and reduce the real income of the society as a whole. Next, it would seem to many unfair not to allow differentials in wages based on such things as training costs, risk, mobility, hard work, and innovation. Finally, the kind of society which typically decides to abolish

161

inequality of income and wealth ends up creating inequality based on political power because of the discretion it invests in government.[5]

But the Bible makes no such error. Rather than denouncing economic differences, the Bible presupposes them, as Christ's parable of the talents (Matthew 25: 14-30) demonstrates. In it, Christ indicates that God's just judgment of human beings is based upon their wise stewardship of the varied gifts (financial and otherwise) that He has entrusted to them, not upon either the allegedly egalitarian initial allocation of those gifts or upon their egalitarian final disbursement. Shrewd investment, not redistribution, calls forth the divine encomium "Well done, thou good and faithful servant" (vv. 21, 23).

The specific political economy a Christian finally endorses cannot be pulled from a hat. Rather, one's political view is chosen by careful reflection upon Christianity's fundamental truths and upon the relationship of those fundamental truths to the presuppositions of the political or economic theory under consideration, as well as upon that theory's historical record. But of those varied historical and philosophical considerations, the ethical must predominate. Mere productivity and efficiency are not enough. Christians can properly endorse only those policies that are just both in their ends and in their means. Thus, while assisting the poor is an admirable and biblical endeavor, coercion and theft are not. The biblical means of alleviating another's distress is not coercive redistribution by the state, it is that act of selfless charity practiced by the good Samaritan: personal involvement and compassionate private largesse (Luke 10: 30-37). The good Samaritan himself came to the aid of his suffering brother. He did not lobby Congress to fund another massive, ineffective and wasteful giveaway, made possible only by a large-scale, coercive confiscation of private property. Those who depend upon the state to be an effective means of philanthropy must first ignore the fact that the modern state is not normally an agency of Christian love. Quite the contrary; the modern state has been the cause of more deaths (approximately 100 million) in this century than in all other centuries combined. Nor do the socialist redistributers of other people's property seem to realize that despite his good intentions, Robin Hood was a thief.

IV. MARXISM ENTAILS A FAULTY VIEW OF PRIVATE PROPERTY

By abolishing private property rights, Marxism has cut economic rewards loose from risk taking, from effort, and from saving. Human beings simply cannot be relied upon to make the careful and painstaking evaluations necessary to assess the real possibilities for success or failure before taking entrepreneurial risks when neither the profits gained from such risks nor the losses incurred from such risks are theirs. Nor can investment capital be accumulated except from the profits of prior endeavors, the use of which has been sacrificed for the present in order to make possible (but not certain) greater prosperity in the future. In a low-efficiency system like Marxism, where profits already tend to be very small, workers will be unwilling to work harder to raise a company's profit margin or to endure intensified deprivation for the purpose of funding future endeavors that are not likely to be successful, or, if they are successful, will not yield profits to them but to the state. A socialist economy does not permit people to reap for themselves the rewards of their hard work, shrewdness, and abstinence. For that reason, if for no other, socialism will never be as successful as democratic capitalism. When private property rights disappear, so does the entrepreneurial spirit. Incentive is tied inextricably to ownership.

The Marxist denial of private property rights is not only inefficient, it is unbiblical and contradicts the clear teaching of both testaments. In the Hebrew scriptures, for example, the Decalogue forbids both theft and the evil desires that frequently give rise to theft by declaring "Thou shalt not steal" and "Thou shalt not covet" (Exodus 20: 15, 17). As John Chamberlain correctly explains,

> "Thou shalt not steal" means that the Bible countenances private property — for if a thing is not owned in the first place it can scarcely be stolen. "Thou shalt not covet" means that it is sinful even to contemplate the seizure of another man's goods — which is something which socialists, whether Christian or other, have never managed to explain away. Furthermore, the prohibitions against false witness and adultery mean that contracts should be honored and double-dealing eschewed. As for the commandment to "honor thy father and thy mother that thy days may be long," this implies that the family, not

the state, is the basic continuing unit and constitutive element of society.[6]

The New Testament is no different. In his parables on the talents (mentioned above), on the unjust steward (Luke 16: 1-13), and on the pounds (Luke 19: 11-27), Christ was concerned to underscore the virtue of properly managing and utilizing one's resources in the best interest both of oneself and the Kingdom of God. From these and other passages, it is clear that Jesus does not condemn private property, work, business, investment, saving, or wealth. He does, however, condemn covetousness, greed, and neglecting both the needs of others and those of one's own soul. Christ is well aware of the spiritual hazards of wealth, and He warns us against them. But that does not mean that money is evil or that possessing it is wicked. The *love of money*, not money itself, is the root of all evil (1 Timothy 6: 10). By the same token, spiritual hazards also attach to poverty, such as crime, envy, and bitterness. After all, it is not the poor, but the poor in spirit — that is, the repentant — who inherit the Kingdom of Heaven (Matthew 5: 3). Jesus condemns not wealth, but avarice. In the former instance, you have money; in the latter instance, it has you.

In short, the New Testament does not view private property as a problem in itself. Rather, it endorses it. In the one instance where the New Testament-era Christians practiced community of goods (Acts 2: 44), the experiment seems to have proved a failure, for shortly afterward we discover that bureaucratic miscarriage in the redistribution of goods as well as increasing poverty in the ranks (conditions not at all unrelated or atypical of socialist systems on any scale) led to complaints and to divisions among believers (Acts 6: 1). In other words, socialism is a system that not even the apostles themselves could make work.

But here I must digress for one paragraph. Like the Marxists, the secular libertarians make a fundamental error with regard to private property. They do so by believing that their bodies and their lives are in fact their own, and that, because they are their own, they can do with them as they please. But the secular libertarians are wrong. Neither the bodies we inhabit nor we ourselves belong to us. These things are doubly, even trebly, God's. That is, what a man makes belongs to a man. He owns the fruit of his labor. What a man purchases is his. He owns what he buys. By the same token, we ourselves are God's. He both created us and purchased us from sin at the cost of his own Son. In Paul's words, "You are not your own; you were bought with a price" (1 Corinthians 6: 19, 20). Furthermore, we know we must not despoil a man of his home. Our bodies, so to speak, are the home of God. As Paul asks in the same passage, "Do you not know that your body is a temple of the Holy Spirit within you, which you have from God?" (1 Corinthians 6: 19). We also know that ownership entails the privilege of both use and disposal. Because it does, and because we are God's, the secular libertarian cannot do with (or to) himself anything he sees fit and then try justify his actions on the grounds that they injure no one else and are therefore morally acceptable. They are not. Secular libertarians expropriate from God what is rightfully his — the very action those same libertarians properly condemn when done to them by the state. Nor can a feminist any longer claim that the fetus growing within her is her own body and that she may do with her body whatever she pleases. Abortion, in other words, not only despoils the rights of the one growing within her, it is a trespass against the property rights of God. So also is suicide.

Marxists make egregious errors regarding the expropriation of private property, but that failing is not exclusively Marxist.

V. MARXISM ENTAILS A FAULTY VIEW OF THE NATURE OF WEALTH

The Marxists have believed for too long that the inevitable scarcity of economic goods, on the one hand, and the equally inescapable condition of human depravity and the ignorance, poverty, and misery to which it gives rise, on the other hand, were somehow susceptible to solution by the state-sponsored machinations of an oppressive interventionist government and the command economy it always produces.

Marxists seem to focus more on the egalitarian redistribution of wealth than on the most effective means of producing that wealth. They seem not to understand that one cannot redistribute what has not been produced. If one's system of production does not create the goods, then no matter how one slices the pie, the economic status of the nation will not be raised. Nor do the Marxists seem to understand that some of the most fertile repositories of wealth are not susceptible to reallocation and redistribution, such as inventiveness and know-how. A great deal of Western wealth (especially the means to future Western wealth) resides not in material things but in the technological brilliance and innovativeness embodied in so many of its best and most valuable workers. That brilliance and innovativeness cannot be appropriated by the state and reassigned and redistributed at will.

With such Marxist errors Christianity cannot and does not agree. Because Christianity and the world of hard extra-mental fact both have their origin in God, Christianity and reality sing the same song, as it were. Because they do, Christianity is not conformable to the incomplete list of Marxist delusions noted above. But because both Christianity and democratic capitalism are rooted in the way things really are, they are compatible with one another. After all, if one were to tune all the pianos in a piano warehouse to the same piano, all the pianos in the warehouse would be in tune with one another.

Put succinctly, capitalist values closely approximate Christian values, as George Gilder has so ably demonstrated in his excellent *Wealth and Poverty*. First, Gilder argues, capitalism is based upon giving. Successful capitalistic enterprise consists of providing wisely conceived, conveniently distributed, readily available, agreeably priced goods and services that others could not have provided so well or so cheaply for themselves. That means that capitalism does not reward selfishness. Instead, it forces upon the selfish a necessity to seek and to serve the interests of others, to offer to them a product or a service they desire at a price they think is fair. If a capitalist fails to take into account the needs of others and the prices they are willing to pay to meet those needs, that capitalist goes out of business. *Capitalists work for the consumer, not for themselves.* They give the consumer what the consumer wants, not what they themselves want. As Thomas Taylor correctly observed, "virtually every person in a modern economy devotes his skills and energies to a highly specialized activity that provides a product or service to be used by someone else."[7] As a result, capitalists stay in business only as long as the consumer permits them to do so. The marketplace is not the arena for unbridled selfishness; it is the stage upon which we learn to consider others and their needs. The market rewards those who serve and those who give, not those who do not. Capitalist prosperity hinges not upon our selfishness, but upon our successfully focusing upon, analyzing, and satisfying someone else's needs. We succeed in the marketplace only insofar as we advance the cause of our fellows and invest our resources and our efforts in that advance. If you neglect your neighbor's needs; if you refuse to put your time, talent, and treasure to work providing for his convenience; your enterprise comes to nothing. If you carefully consider and then appropriately satisfy your neighbor's needs you will enjoy the fruit of your labors. Whatever else we may call this attention to meeting the needs of others, it is not selfishness. The marketplace is a school for virtue, not a subsidy for vice.

The critics of capitalism do not understand this because they do not understand either the market-wide beneficial effects of economic competition or the inescapably civilizing effects of the marketplace. Nor do they understand that after a freely entered market exchange *both* parties are better off, otherwise no exchange would have taken place. Competition is a struggle for excellence that results in better products at lower and lower prices to the consumer. The marketplace tames those who compete there by requiring them to be courteous to customers; to accommodate other people's needs and desires before their own; and to deal fairly and honestly with all the people with whom they trade; or else to fail.

Second, Gilder argues, faith is a capitalist virtue. In the marketplace one finds no guarantees. Investments sometimes fail. Try as you may, the entrepreneurial gifts which you offer your neighbor might be rejected. As Gilder explains,

> . . . there is no demand for new and unknown goods, no demand for the unforeseeable fruits of innovation and genius . . . If a product is new, it may create demand, perhaps over time. But the demand does not already exist, except in the mind [and hopes] of the entrepreneur.[8]

Entrepreneurs, in other words, walk by faith, not by sight. They learn to believe in things not seen.

But this chapter is not the place to rehearse at length the case that Gilder himself has made so convincingly and in greater detail elsewhere. Suffice it here to say that Gilder has demonstrated that, like Christianity, democratic capitalism places a premium not only upon such things as faith and giving, but also upon hard work, strong traditional family ties and roles, creativity, and experience. Marxism does not. Its refusal to do so raises the most fundamental question of all: Can you ignore the moral laws of God or (what is the same) the laws of nature and still prosper? The answer to that fundamental question, as the dismal history of Marxism indicates, is no. Given the hard facts of nature and the immutable God by whom that nature was established, one could easily believe that the political and economic meltdown now underway in Marxist nations around the world was inevitable. It ultimately can be no other way. As Dorothy L. Sayers correctly observed, "There is only one real law — the law of the universe; it may be fulfilled by way of judgment or by the way of grace, but it must be fulfilled one way or the other."[9]

From every indication now available to me, Karl Marx was wrong. The future does not belong to the proletariat. It belongs to the free. Marxism is in retreat worldwide because it ignores reality and because the reality it ignores is resilient and will have its way.

But because human beings tend to be relentlessly obtuse, error is resilient too. We human beings hold to our errors sometimes with prodigious tenacity and often with a ferocity to match. In the words of Malcolm Muggeridge,

> [Some] minds are prepared to believe anything, however preposterous, to overlook anything, however villainous, to approve anything, however obscurantist and brutally authoritarian, in order to be able to preserve intact the confident expectation that one of the most thoroughgoing, ruthless and bloody tyrannies ever to exist on earth can be relied on to champion human freedom.[10]

Because error is resilient, the free nations of the West must be circumspect and deliberate in their continued self-defense. Christians must not be derelict in their duty to preserve the manifold blessings of liberty and prosperity because it remains to be seen whether or not a new strain of Marxist virus will breed in the presently rotting corpse of Soviet tyranny. That new strain, if it arises, will be more virulent and robust than any we have yet known. We must not let that genie out of the bottle.

END NOTES

1 Brian Griffiths, *The Creation of Wealth: A Christian's Case for Capitalism* (Downers Grove: IVP, 1984), pp. 11, 13.

2 Adam Smith, *An Inquiry into the Nature and Causes of the Wealth of Nations* (Indianapolis: Liberty Press, 1976/1981), p. 452.

3 Ludwig von Mises, *Money, Method, and the Market Process*, edited by Richard M. Ebeling (Norwell: Kluwer Academic Publishers, 1990), pp. 223, 221-222.

4 Rose Wilder Lane, *The Discovery of Freedom* (New York: The John Day Company, 1943), pp. 5, 6.

5 Griffiths, ibid., p. 78.

6 John Chamberlain, *The Roots of Capitalism* (Indianapolis: Liberty Press, 1959/1976), pp. 70, 71.

7 Thomas C. Taylor, *An Introduction to Austrian Economics* (Auburn: The Ludwig von Mises Institute, 1980), p. 18.

8 George Gilder, *Wealth and Poverty* (New York: Bantam, 1981), pp. 45,49.

9 Dorothy L. Sayers, *Creed or Chaos? and other Essays in Popular Theology* (London: Methuen & Co. Ltd., 1947), p. 52.

10 Malcolm Muggeridge, *Confessions of a Twentieth-Century Pilgrim* (San Francisco: Harper & Row, 1988), p. 87.

"Where there is no law, there is no freedom."
JOHN LOCKE

"Rabbi Hananiah, prefect of the priests, says: Do thou pray for the welfare of the empire, because were it not for the fear that it inspires, every man would eat his neighbor alive."
THE MISHNAH

"It is simply true that he who pauses to choose the right word will find out what he means to mean, and he who can't will make it clear to his reader that he is ignorant and thoughtless."
RICHARD MITCHELL
The Gift of Fire

"Why, then, do men cease to be Communists? One answer is: Very few do."
WHITTAKER CHAMBERS
Witness

Christianity and Leftist Radical Chic: Critiquing Evangelicalism's Attraction to Ellul and Anarchy

Theologians quickly discover that death and taxes do not exhaust the list of life's inevitabilities. Not only do we die and pay; we think[1] — however well or however poorly. Because such considerations are foundational and pervasive, among the things we cannot avoid thinking about are our relationship to the transcendent, if any, and our relationship to our neighbor, whether near or far away. That is, human nature and human relationships being what they now are, human existence is inescapably theological and political. Thus, the question is never whether or not we will have a theology or a political ideology, but whether or not the theology and the political ideology we have are any good.

Ellulism — the theology and politics of Jacques Ellul — I am convinced, is seriously defective. It is, nevertheless, widely held and respected among evangelicals. The burden of this essay, therefore, is to bring its flaws to view and thereby to explain why I believe about it as I do. My agenda will be threefold: first, to expose its exegetical shortcomings; second, to reveal its political and philosophical inadequacies; and third, to trace its ideological roots back to their source.

I. BIBLICAL ANARCHISM?

According to Ellul, the gospel should not be tied to any prevalent political or economic ideology. To do so, he says, is to degenerate Christianity, which "was originally an anti-ideology."[2] To do so also entails a dangerous conformity to the world, which Ellul sees as a transgression against our freedom in Christ.[3] But, Christianity is not the politically or economically ideology-free (or even ideology-neutral) religion Ellul describes. It most assuredly does have political and economic proclivities, or tendencies, of a definite sort, though they are not the sort Ellul identifies or prefers. To them I will return later. Furthermore, Ellul, as a Christian anarchist, does not escape committing the "error" (his word) of fusing Christianity to a political ideology, a practice about which he has warned others. He himself has fused the radical politics of the anarchist left with a skewed vision of Christianity and of Scripture.

Ellul is convinced that both testaments inculcate anarchism. This he repeatedly declares in the process of "reconciling anarchism and Christianity." "I do not intend," he writes, "to abandon the biblical message in the slightest, since it seems to me . . . that biblical thought leads straight to anarchism — anarchism is the only 'anti-political political position' in harmony with Christian thought."[4] "Both the Old and New Testaments," he contends, "take exception to *all* political power."[5] "The biblical view," Ellul writes, "is not just apolitical but antipolitical. . . it refuses to confer any value on political power. . . it regards political power as idolatrous, inevitably entailing idolatry. Christianity offers no justification for political power."[6] "We must uphold the sure and certain fact," Ellul asserts, "that the Bible brings us a message that is against power, against the state, and against politics."[7] By so arguing, however, Ellul has improperly recast the Bible into a left-wing manifesto. This transformation he tries to support with what, to me at least, seem grotesque exegetical contortions that deface the biblical teaching on government.

A. Old Testament

According to Ellul, the Old Testament "*always* challenges political power in itself where the 'nations' are concerned . . . The government of a foreign people never appears in the Old Testament as legitimate or satisfactory."[8] But, as is almost embarrassingly obvious, the Old Testament never impugns "political power in itself" among Gentile nations; rather, it excoriates the abuses those powers sometimes perpetrate. Nor, contrary to Ellul, does the Old Testament challenge the political legitimacy of all foreign regimes, regardless of whether or not the reigning polities were monarchical, oligarchical, or even (as was the case in some portions of ancient Greece) ostensibly democratic. It does not challenge Gentile regimes based upon whether or not those regimes were legitimated, or whether or not they ruled by the free consent of the governed, which, along with hereditary rule (and apart from any direct command of God), seem to me to be the only bases upon which genuine political legitimacy could ever be established. In the Old Testament, the question of Gentile political legitimacy is not in view, much less is it *always* decided in the negative, as Ellul insists. Furthermore, the application of the very concept of political legitimacy to Old Testament times and conditions is itself a largely anachronistic application.

Ellul's own anarchist assertions, he believes, are taught not only in the Old Testament in its entirety, but also in 1 Samuel 8, which he identifies as "the main text" on the issue of political power, a chapter he contends "boils down to three objections" to government, one of which he claims is that "political power is *always* dictatorial, excessive, and unjust."[9]

First, Ellul's assertion that 1 Sam 8 is the foundational Hebrew passage on this issue is highly debatable, if not roundly mistaken. One could argue, as Robert Filmer did three hundred years ago in his *Patriarcha*, that Genesis 1 and 2 formed the basis of Old Testament teaching on government and that from those chapters one discerns that the universe itself is both hierarchical and monarchical (not anarchic).[10] What the universe is, written large, as it were, the family is, written small. And government, Filmer argued, ought to take its cue from the family, of which it was intended to be the national manifestation or extension. The family, at least as Filmer understood Genesis, was monarchical in that the authority of the husband (or father) is singular and unrivalled. The king is, and ought to be, Filmer reasoned, the father of his nation and should rule (and be honored) accordingly. The point here is not that Filmer's monarchicalism is correct. (I do not think it is. John Locke disposed of that.) The point is that 1 Samuel 8 is not the unquestionably proper point of departure or locus of debate, as Ellul too easily assumes. Nor is the point insignificant for, as Aristotle taught us long ago, he who wishes to succeed must ask the right preliminary questions. The right question here is where properly to begin.

In that light, both Filmer and Ellul notwithstanding, other theologians argue that the place to begin is in Deuteronomy, and that the Deuteronomic code itself is an extensive and elaborate constitution[11] for ancient political power, dealing as it does with property rights, family relationships, labor, freedom, and crime and punishment. Among the numerous relevant passages to which those theologians point are Deuteronomy 17: 8ff (wherein the Israelites are commanded to obey the judicial decisions rendered by the judges and the Levites, upon pain of death), Deuteronomy 16: 18ff (wherein civil judges are expressly said to be given by God), and Deuteronomy 17: 14ff (which not only permits an Israelite monarchy and gives rules for its conduct, but actually indicates that God himself will select the king). Thus, it is not true, as Ellul alleges, that before the incidents in 1 Samuel 8 "the people of Israel have been without political organization,"[12] or that human government and political power are *always* evil and *always* opposed by God. Instead, the case was simply that Israel, at that time, did not have a human monarch at its head. Prior to 1 Samuel 8, Israel was a theocratic monarchy, not an instance of pre-Christian, divinely ordained anarchism. This point is underscored by practices in the age of judges that followed the second giving of the law, an age in which the theocratic monarchy was still (in theory, at least) in full force, but in which major portions of political power had been delegated by God himself to human beings and widely dispersed among them. To the advocates of this view, the books of Deuteronomy and Judges are pivotal, not 1 Samuel 8.[13]

One could also equally well argue that Genesis 9, wherein capital punishment is prescribed and delegated to humans to enact at their discretion, is the God-ordained origin (and endorsement) of even the most extreme political power — that of the power of life and death over one's fellows. Perhaps all Christian theorizing ought to begin there, beneath God's ancient imprimatur.

Still other exegetes argue that by employing the suzerainty covenant ritual practiced by other nations while himself dealing with the chosen nation of Israel, God was indirectly (though not inadvertently or indiscriminately) endorsing human government and that such passages are crucial, not incidental, to our understanding of the Old Testament's teaching on political power. Nor have I made mention of such diverse Old Testament texts as Exodus 18: 13ff (in which civil judges are appointed to administer God's statutes); Exodus 21: 23ff, (the famous *lex talionis* passage requiring human intervention for the proper administration of justice), or 2 Chronicles 19: 5ff (which indicates, among other things, that judges rule not for man but for God himself).

In short, that 1 Samuel 8 is the pivotal Old Testament text is not at all clear. While theologians commonly find starting points other than 1 Samuel 8, and while those starting points (and the conclusions to which they lead) differ, anarchism is rarely named among them, as Ellul argues it ought to be.

Yet, even if one were to begin with 1 Samuel 8, one could not conclude, as does Ellul, that it endorses anarchism or that it teaches that "political power is always dictatorial, excessive, and unjust." The passage in question deals with Israel's decision to have a human king once Samuel is gone. Their desire for a human king is spiritually wicked, not because political power is always and everywhere inescapably evil, or because monarchy is inherently vile, but because the Israelites already have God as their king. It simply and plainly is untrue that in 1 Samuel 8 "monarchical organization is formally condemned" or that this chapter condemns it "with ad hoc arguments that are always valid."[14] This chapter makes *no statement whatever* about the allegedly universal perversity or dictatorial propensities of political power, in general, or of monarchies, in particular. Ellul's anarchism cannot be found anywhere in this text. By contending otherwise, Ellul is failing in precisely the same way about which he himself warned others: "Anytime we read the Bible to find arguments or justifications, we wallow in Christian ideology."[15]

Ellul's anarchism runs counter not only to the Old Testament, but also to the Jewish tradition and liturgy to which it gives rise. Jewish believers, for example, consider it their sacred duty to pray for the welfare of the civil government and of the society of the land in which they happen to live. This duty has been enjoined upon them by the prophet Jeremiah (29:7) and reinforced by the Mishnah (Avot 3:2:

"pray for the welfare of the government"). The Jewish prayer for the welfare of the ruling powers of state, be they royal, executive, representative, or judicial, is a part of the Sabbath morning service and is recited after the reading of the Torah and before the Law scrolls are returned to the Ark. According to the *Metsudah Siddur*, this prayer traditionally begins: "He Who grants deliverance to kings, and dominion to princes, His kingship is a kingship of all worlds; He Who rescued David, His servant, from the evil sword, Who put a road through the sea, and a path amid the mighty waters; may He bless, preserve, and guard, help, exalt, and make great, and raise high our Sovereign." Clearly, these are not the petitions of anarchism.

B. New Testament

Not surprisingly, Ellul insists that, like the Old, the New Testament also teaches anarchism. For example, the miraculous catching of a fish with a coin in its mouth, a coin sufficient to pay the temple tax for both Jesus and Peter (Matthew 17: 24ff), Ellul describes as an "absurd miracle,"[16] one designed "precisely to show that the obligation to pay the tax is ridiculous." By it, Ellul improperly insists, "Jesus held up power to ridicule."[17] But, Jesus's intention, as He himself clearly indicates, is *not to give offense* (v. 27). Ridicule is perhaps the furthest thing from his mind — though not apparently from Ellul, who goes on to argue that the payment of such taxes is a matter of indifference; we are free to pay or not to pay. "Doctrinally I should not," he writes, "but out of love I will"[18] — as if the demands of Christian belief and of Christian love were somehow different.

Similarly, the standard pro-government views that most theologians take toward Jesus's famous injunction to give to Caesar those things that are Caesar's and to God those things that are God's (Matthew 22:21), Ellul characterizes as "unbelievable conclusions."[19] Jesus's words, according to Ellul, as any "pious Jew of Jesus' time" would surely recognize, mean that, because God is the master of everything, "Caesar is the legitimate master of nothing, except for what he makes himself," and those things, Ellul asserts, "belong to the order of the demonic."[20] But, considering that the question posed in this passage to Jesus by the Jews concerned the right of Caesar to rule the Jewish homeland and not whether or not all government is illegitimate, and considering that the demonic order is nowhere in view, either in this verse or in the entire chapter from which it comes, Ellul's anarchist conclusions are simply gratuitous. Ellul here is arguing as if all political power is and only could be exercised after a Machiavellian model; as if all political measures were Draconian, and as if the only acceptable alternative to Machiavelli and Draco is anarchy — all of which are patently false. Although Jesus's words clearly rule out any facile identification of the divine and the political, they do not rule out the political altogether or relegate it to the realm of the irremediably perverse. They are, quite to the contrary, an explicit sanction of government, though not of all that governments have done. Christ's words clearly indicate the possibility (and implicitly reveal the advisability) of loyalty to both God and government. In no way should this passage be construed as a vilification of all political power for all time and in all circumstances. Such assertions are simply the idiosyncratic contortions of Ellul's bizarre dance upon the text. They are not the carefully ascertained teaching of the text itself; and they are not exegetical scholarship.

When Jesus later declares that his kingdom is not of this world (John 18:36), Ellul again finds what he believes is grist for his anarchist mill. These words, Ellul writes, teach that "apart from the Kingdom of God, any power exercised is evil" and "should be obliterated." With these words, Ellul argues, "Jesus . . . launches a fundamental attack on power."[21] But Jesus, of course, has said or done absolutely nothing (here or elsewhere) so politically doctrinaire or irresponsible as that. In fact, Jesus tells Pilate something quite the opposite: "You would have no power over me," Jesus said, "if it were not given you from above" (John 19: 11). Pilate's power, of course, was political. It was also far reaching, including even the power to judge matters of life and death. We have it on the highest authority, furthermore, that Pilate's power was given to him *by God himself.* In other words, the dominical utterance to which Ellul alludes has nothing at all to do with the establishment or endorsement of universal political anarchy or the iconoclastic overthrow of all political power. Those things can be found nowhere in Scripture, much less here in John's gospel. They are the result only of Ellul's egregious and misshapen interpretation.

Ellul then dismisses out of hand what most exegetes would identify as the *locus classicus* of the New Testament's teaching on government: Paul's word in Romans 13 that we ought to submit ourselves to the governing authorities because, as rulers, they have been established by God himself as a force for good. This passage, says Ellul, is "much too celebrated."[22] He writes:

> "This text, it seems to me, should be reduced to its real meaning: rather than giving us the last word on the matter of political authority, it seeks to apply love in a context where Christians detested the authorities."[23]

In spite of Ellul's imaginative supposition, we have no evidence whatever that either Paul (who was imprisoned repeatedly by the authorities) or the Roman Christians to whom he wrote, ever "detested the authorities." Indeed, some of those to whom Paul addressed his admonition were themselves quite possibly *active agents in the government and part of the ruling authority*, as a number of biblical considerations might lead us to believe. Detesting political authority is a characteristic of Ellulism, not of apostolic Christianity.

In short, the anarchism that Ellul espouses, and with which he labels both Testaments and Christ himself, is not the political ideology of Scripture; it is the yield of Ellul's own anarchic hermeneutic, a hermeneutic that refuses to submit itself to the precise verbal parameters established by the language of any given biblical text. If the Bible entails any sort of political orthodoxy, it is not anarchism.

II. The Philosophical and Practical Implications of Anarchism

Because ideas have consequences, and because bad ideas have bad consequences, an anarchistic reading of Scripture is not without its untoward effects. Relying on exegesis of this sort, for example, enables one unabashedly to insist, as does Ellul, that "the state's prosperity *always* implies the death of innocents," and that "a person can exercise political power only if he worships the power of evil."[24] But, by this logic, voting — the supreme act of power in any democratic republic — would be unspeakably wicked and ought to be resisted by all Christians as a point of true spirituality and moral responsibility.[25] The same would apply (in most free nations) to paying taxes, to military service, to sending letters (and to delivering them), to pledging allegiance, to testifying in court, to serving on a jury, to filing a lawsuit, or even to purchasing and using a library card at a public library, all of which are exercises of, and participation in, political power. Furthermore, simply by saying publicly what he does, Ellul himself "worships the power of evil" because the exercise of free speech and of public discourse are *political acts of power*, as the ancient Greeks well understood and as has been re-emphasized in modern times by Leo Strauss and those who identify with Strauss's school of political theorizing, among others. Furthermore, because publishing, preaching, teaching, and persuading are powerful political actions, because these avenues of expression are open to Ellul primarily because his government (and others) protect his freedom of speech, his academic freedom, and the freedom of the press, and because Ellul continues to practice those liberties and to value them highly, he must not say, as he does say, that "political power never has any value in itself."[26]

But here as elsewhere, Ellul's thought has been misdirected and imprecise. As his exaggerated language frequently indicates, his theological and political beliefs often are inadequately nuanced. For example, Ellul speaks of "the radical incompatibility of the gospel and the state,"[27] which, in light of the fact that he lives in a country that guarantees his right to believe as he chooses, and in light of the fact that so many European countries have Christian churches that spread the gospel at home and abroad — churches that are protected by the state, is a grossly distorted exaggeration. Had he mentioned only the incompatibility of the gospel and *some* states, his remark would have been more credible. As it is, however, one has a good deal of difficulty working up any confidence in Ellul's theological and political judgments because of their habitually exaggerated verbal configuration.

But faulty exegesis, internal inconsistency, and imprecise language are only part of the problem of Ellul's anarchism; it is also eminently unrealistic. That is, rather than arising form an observation of what human existence is really like and deducing, as Thomas Hobbes did in the seventeenth-century, that life in a fallen world is typically nasty, brutish, and short; and rather than tying his political theorizings to that fundamental diagnostic fact, Ellul seeks to foist onto an already ruptured world the ineffective anarchic vision concocted in his own head, unchecked as it is by human reality or the biblical text. In other words, because it is not subject to the dictates of any external restraint, Ellul's political theory, in effect, is *epistemologically* anarchistic.

Put differently, Ellul has succumbed to what Jeane J. Kirkpatrick, former U.S. ambassador to the United Nations, has characterized as the unfortunate disjunction between political ideas and human experience. When such disjunctions develop, she says, irresponsible political and economic theories proliferate. These theories, which she labels "the rationalist perversion," "tend . . . to be abstract and unembarrassed by the need for empirical indicators of their major assumptions." "Rationalist theories," she observes, "are speculative rather than empirical and historical; rationalist reforms seek to conform human behavior to oversimplified, unrealistic models."[28] Rationalist theoreticians ignore the fact that human institutions arise out of human behavior and that human behavior is notoriously intractable. This same ideological unperturbedness precisely describes Ellul, who is undaunted by the acknowledged unlikelihood, perhaps impossibility, of his anarchistic political vision:

> "We must not become discouraged, [he writes,] if our anarchist declaration fails to lead to an anarchist society, or if it does not overthrow society, destroying its whole framework . . . In spite of everything, in spite of this human reality, we want to destroy power. *This is the Christian hope in politics.*"[29]

All this flies in the face of historic Christian wisdom, both ancient and modern, and it ignores the fact that Christianity is, as it were, a reality game. The Bible deals with real people in a realistic fashion. It stares directly upon human nature and does not blink. Jesus, as C. S. Lewis rightly perceived, was a thorough-going realist, though He is seldom given credit for being so. Augustine, while he understood perhaps better than anyone that the City of Man could never become the City of God, never slid from anti-utopianism into anarchism.[30] Thomas Aquinas, far from being an anarchist, was an ardent proponent of the *respublica hominum sub Deo.* He believed that the proper purpose of human law was to propose and to uphold the ideal of good conduct and to help habituate men toward its performance. But by doing so, however, Thomas Aquinas was not therefore an idolator of the state, contrary to Ellul's scathing verdict on those who hold such a view. Thomas knew that "no matter what high ideals, how fine the structures and laws, how good and beneficent the ruler, the political community is no substitute for . . . religion" and that "politics is not a way of salvation." He also knew that "for the Christian, politics is neither all-important nor unimportant." In short, Aquinas understood what Ellul does not: the Christian "cannot let politics fall to the perverters by default."[31] Even Dante, perpetually abused as he was by government, argued to subject the world to one state;[32] Ellul (by contrast) unrealistically argues to eliminate political power altogether. Calvin, too, understood the realism and practical wisdom of a God who works *in our world on our behalf*, and therefore he set about actively trying to bring the revealed will of God to bear upon the political and social concerns of Geneva.[33]

Ellul's is just the sort of impracticable and unbiblical political philosophy that Karl Rahner criticized for mortgaging the present for the sake of a generation of people who were never born and who never will be.[34] As the old maxim indicates, politics is the art of the possible. It is not an impractical affair disconnected from human reality. Christian political theory, to paraphrase Algernon Sidney, does not seek for that which is perfect, because it knows that such a thing is not to be found among men. Rather, it seeks that form of government that is attended with the fewest and most pardonable shortcomings, and it knows that anarchism is not that form which it seeks. Christian political theory deals with possibilities, not with unreachable goals or with speculations about the politics of the eschaton, at least as we imperfectly anticipate them.

Furthermore, simply because human government is imperfectible, Christian political theorists and politicians do not relegate politics and the state to the secularists and to the secular, as does Ellul, who writes that we do not "have to work out a Christian doctrine of the form of government or the economy," and that "another way that is closed [to Christians] is that of wanting to christianize society or the state. The state is not meant to be Christian. It is meant to be secular."[35] To Ellul, participation in politics and in the structures of "the powers that be" form no necessary part of Christian life and faith. "In fact," writes Ellul, "no directly biblical or theological argument seems to support participation."[36]

The proliferation of views like Ellul's has had a disastrous effect. Partly because Christianity is made to seem not only unpolitical but anti-political, most universities feel free to construct an entire curriculum in political theory that operates as if Christianity were either nonexistent or else an accumulation of merely irrelevant data that can be safely ignored. Theology seems to them to have no bearing upon the integrity or content of the discipline of political science. Yet, Ellul appears not to understand that, because they are the chief mechanisms of providing and preserving liberty, peace, and prosperity, the state and political power cannot be considered a matter of indifference by responsible Christians, or as something from which Christians can detach themselves with moral impunity, as if such institutions and concerns were theologically neutral or somehow fell outside the scope of necessary Christian action and reflection.[37] Ellul does not understand that, while the political considerations surrounding life, liberty, and property (to invoke the Lockean triad) are not of ultimate or transcendent importance, they have a genuine significance that cannot be downplayed or made to appear as falling somehow beyond the purview of Christian revelation and theology. That such considerations are not ultimate concerns should lead us to advocate a limited state, not no state whatever. Ellul has not come to grips with the fact that not one shred of evidence exists that demonstrates that the anarchist principles he advocates would make the world more free, more prosperous, or more secure. To procure these desirable political and economic conditions requires "the active presence and participation of the Christian in the affairs of state and society,"[38] not the radical secularization of all political endeavors. Secularization is the enemy of modern Christianity, not its political ally.

As John Stuart Mill once chided Jeremy Bentham, the cardinal error in most misguided political theories is the belief that politics can be reduced to a few simple, overarching formulas, a reduction that leads to an inflexible (and often universal) misapplication of half-true truisms, much to the distress and disadvantage of those upon whom they are imposed. Ellul's anarchism is just such a simplistic theory. What he does not seem to understand about his call to abolish all power is the self-stultifying fact that *the abolition of power can be accomplished, imposed, and maintained only by means of power*, for, Montesquieu observed more than 200 years ago, it takes a power to check a power. Freedom never was, is not now, nor ever shall be (so far as we have evidence to tell) possible without political power.

Freedom and political power are not antithetical realities in a fallen world. Ellul seems not to recognize that there can be no freedom without justice and that in a fallen world there can be no justice without power. He seems not to understand that while freedom is, in most cases, a desirable political condition, anarchism is simply freedom gone to seed. It is freedom improperly extended beyond the boundaries of political wisdom and foresight, the two indispensable characteristics of any good political theory. There is no freedom without order, and there is no order without law and law enforcement. As Goethe has observed, only law can give us freedom. Freedom without law endures as long as a lamb among hungry wolves. Therefore, because order is a political requirement of the first rank, if anything in politics is demonic, it is not Caesar or money (as Ellul says); it is that spirit that cannot bear authority and seeks to destroy it utterly.

Because moral order in society is predicated upon virtue and not merely upon freedom, the absence of virtue is far more troubling to a Christian political theorist than is the presence of power. For the sake of virtue alone, therefore, one must resist the drive to abolish all power. The variously coercive powers of family, of church, of state, and of school are not inimical to virtue; rather, they help secure it and make it possible. The eradication of all power results not in virtue, order, or prosperity, but in chaos. Unencumbered freedom (even freedom hiding behind the adjective "Christian") is not the political panacea or objective toward which we ought to be ineluctably moving. Instead, we should desire to do what must be done and what can be done, both of which require power. Political freedom, while itself highly desirable, is largely neutral with regard to the advancement of moral virtues and can be detrimental to them. The abolition of political and economic power is not the inescapable precondition of virtue, either that of the powerful or that of the powerless. In fact, the withering of established political and economic institutions has often been the precondition of history's most heinous misdeeds, as it was during the French Revolution. In light of such considerations, therefore, Christians need to realize that the alternative to totalitarianism and to statism is not simply anarchism. As the framers of the American Constitution understood, our guiding principle ought to be a rule of law, not of men; and our political objective ought to be a limited government, not no government at all. By radicalizing politics the way it does — that is, by advocating anarchism in the face of the fact that human beings are inescapably political and societal *by nature*[39] — Ellulism goes Niebuhr one better: It posits not simply a Christ against culture, but a Christ against creation.

Destruction of the state is the opiate of anarchists. It has no part in the Christian agenda. It cannot produce a better world; it can only destroy the one that is. That is why Ellul's anarchistic vision is unfit for human habitation. It relentlessly confuses the force of law with the law of force.

But if, as I have argued, Ellul's political ideology does not derive from Scripture, from whence does it arise? And if it does not resemble the teaching of the Bible or of historic Christianity, to what does it bear the greatest affinity? The answer to both questions is the same — Marxism. Ellulism has Marxist roots and Marxist branches. That is, Ellulism shares with Marxism a plethora of presuppositions, methods, and conclusions. Because it has been done so well and so often,[40] to refute each of Ellul's capitulations to Marxism would both fall outside the scope of this essay and be a useless redundancy. I simply say here that both Ellulism and Marxism are characterized by an ideological correspondence that includes (but is by no means limited to) agreement in the following concepts, procedures, and goals, the delineation of which will be the focus of the final portion of this essay.

III. Marxist Roots and Branches

Historians of Christian thought have repeatedly noticed the difference between the theology and piety of Martin Luther and those of Ulrich Zwingli, the two greatest of the first generation of Protestant reformers. Luther's theological distance from Rome, while considerable, is markedly less than Zwingli's. This difference scholars often account for by noting that, prior to his conversion to Protestantism, Zwingli was never the intensely ardent Roman Catholic that Luther once was. Thus, while Luther brought with him into Protestantism all of his Catholicism that the Bible did not expressly prohibit, Zwingli brought of his only what the Bible expressly commanded. To the Zwinglians, Luther's break with Rome was imperfect and incomplete because he continued to tolerate what, to the Zwinglians, was too much Roman residue.

This inability or unwillingness to make a sufficient break with one's own past is not an isolated phenomenon. For example, scholars also have noticed the Manichean inclinations of the mature Augustine and the lingering Rosicrucianism in Charles Williams's Christian novels. Jacques Ellul, too, it seems to me, has made an imperfect and insufficient break from his own Marxist past and from the ideology that necessarily attaches to it, as the following observations will indicate:

A. Human Alienation
Rather than endorsing the version of alienation expressed by such Christian thinkers as Luther, Schleiermacher, or Kierkegaard (not to mention St. Paul), Ellul opts for the version articulated by Marx, a version that is not only Ellul's "starting point" on the subject, but a version he characterizes as "perspicacious and even prophetic." "I firmly believe," writes Ellul, "that it is in terms of the tradition that goes back to Marx that we must consider man's present condition."[41]

B. Anti-capitalism
Like Marx, Ellul views free-market capitalism as a radically flawed, even internally contradictory economic system. To them, it is riddled with exploitive malfunctions so great that they cannot be considered mere imperfections in an otherwise harmonious and productive system. Also like Marx, Ellul believes that capitalism has produced a class of workers who, because they live by wages, are related to their employers by a cash-nexus, which reduces their capacity to work to the subhuman level of a mere commodity,[42] something Marx characterized as wage slavery. Ellul rarely rises above the standard Marxist caricatures of capitalism. For example, he absurdly states that "massacres" are "required to maintain capitalism;" that "workers" are "starved by the capitalist system;" and that for the Christian "allegiance to capitalism is virtually impossible."[43] Capitalism's alleged failures aside, both Marx and Ellul have been forced to acknowledge its unparalleled powers of production.

C. Determinism

In some cases, Ellul not only agrees with Marx, he surpasses him, as he does on the question of human freedom. According to Marx, "It is not the consciousness of men that determines their existence, but, on the contrary, their social existence determines their consciousness."[44] But Ellul believes that "in this regard we need to probe much deeper than Marx did in his criticism of formal democracy . . . For our choice is never free. We are conditioned by a number of factors that cause us to elect this or that representative, to sign this or that manifesto, to buy this or that newspaper. The man who chooses is always alienated man, man subject to many necessities. Hence his choice is not an exercise of freedom. For it is not he who chooses. The choice is made by his cultural setting, his upbringing, his environment, and the various psychological manipulations to which he is subject."[45] One wonders, is Ellul himself somehow exempt from this allegedly pervasive mind control, or is he affirming that his own ideas are merely the mindless dictates imposed upon him by his environment?

D. Money

Like Marx before him, Ellul believes that money is an inescapably and universally alienating power, one that estranges both those who have it and those who do not. Concerning the role and function of money in society, Ellul believes that "the analysis of Marx is perfectly correct."[46]

E. Dialectical Methodology

Like Marx, Ellul believes that only the dialectical method is able to deal successfully with the continuously changing data with which reality presents us. To both Marx and Ellul, dialectical analysis is indispensable. "I am a dialectician above all," Ellul declares, "I believe nothing can be understood without dialectical analysis."[47] In order to rescue the biblical writers (who, at least on a consensus view, lived prior to the era of dialectics and apart from its influences) from the wholesale dismissal that his radical view entails, Ellul quite remarkably claims that the dialectical method can be traced back to its beginnings *with the Hebrew prophets* in the eighth century BC. Ellul, in effect, even goes so far as to jettison, in principle, almost the entire tradition of biblical exegesis: "only dialectical thinking can give a proper account of scriptural revelation, such revelation itself being fundamentally and intrinsically dialectical."[48]

F. Revolution and Liberation

At times Ellul sacrifices Marx's opinions for Lenin's, as he does when he compares Leninism's view of revolution and liberation to his own view of the work of Christ:

> "It seems to me that the familiar analysis of Marx, according to which a revolution consonant with the meaning of history brings liberation to the alienated, offers points of similarity but cannot be used because it insists on self-liberation. Lenin's doctrine is better in this regard, since it gives the party a mediatorial role on behalf of the proletariat. The work of the party with reference to the alienation of the proletariat corresponds figuratively to that of Jesus Christ with regard to the alienation of man. Since the proletariat cannot liberate itself with its feelings of revolt and spontaneous reactions, the work must be done from above. The proletariat comes into the act when it recognizes the reality and is thus in effect de-alienated already. Along these lines the work of Jesus Christ is a revolutionary action in the sense that it is a revolt against alienating forces."[49]

Time and space would fail were I to identify the full range of Ellul's Marxisms, including as it does Marxist assumptions on such things as the nature of religion, sociological nomenclature (and the Marxist taxonomy of class structure and class struggle, as well as the Marxist class analysis that attaches to it), egalitarianism, socialism, the nature of merchandise, and socio-political revolution, among many others. One does not wonder, therefore, that Ellul pronounces Fernando Belo's leftist revolutionism a political choice "which we do not question," or that Ellul believes that Belo's view of the "radical opposition between God and Money, God and the State" and "God and Caesar," is not only true, but "truly evangelical."[50] Nor is it at all surprising that in Ellul's *The Ethics of Freedom*, Karl Marx is the most often quoted author, even though this is a text on Christian ethics and even though Marx is not a Christian.[51] One can tax Ellul with the same charge he himself levels at Belo: he "appears not to suspect

[that] Marx's thought is a whole — a precise, integrated unit, based on a thorough method. Once one has adopted it, one cannot mix it with other methods and concepts." Nevertheless, Ellul himself adopts Marxist "methods and concepts" and believes that Belo's choice to be a Communist "clearly merits our respect."[52]

It does not.

Not all, perhaps not even most, of the choices humans make are respectable or are worthy of a Christian's considered approval. Some choices are ignorant and inadequately informed; some are counterproductive; some are wicked. Belo's attachment to Marxist principles is all these things. It is no more admirable than the choice to become a slave trader, which I consider to be very much the same thing. Marxism has been the ideological justification for the imprisonment, enslavement, destitution, and murder of countless millions of human beings. It has spawned the most atrocious crimes of history, and its marriage to colossal evil seems both indissolvable and inevitable. Marxism's historic evil towers over all others. Since World war II, more human beings have been murdered under Marxism between the western borders of what once was East Germany and the eastern shores of China than in the entirety of the rest of recorded history, stretching back as it does more than four millennia. When compared to Stalin's penchant for mass extermination, even Hitler seems an amateur.

But, am I inventing a Marxist Ellul? Not at all. As Ellul himself confesses, he was converted to Marx after reading *Das Kapital* in his teens. Reading Marx "answered almost all the questions I had been asking myself," he writes. "It seemed to me that the method of Karl Marx . . . was superior to all that I had encountered elsewhere."[53] Nor has Ellul's attachment to Marxism proven merely the skewed judgment or passing infatuation of an uninformed youth. Ellul has "remained unable to eliminate Marx."[54] "I totally agree," writes Ellul, "with a Marxism that offers a method of interpretation — one of the best interpretations, in fact, I believe the best — of the world of the nineteenth and twentieth centuries."[55] Ellul himself boasts that large and significant portions of his own work and the methodology by which he produced it is consciously patterned after that of Marx: "I was certain, absolutely certain, that if Marx were alive in 1940 he would no longer study economics or the capitalist structures, he would study Technique. So I began to study Technique, using a method as similar as possible to the one Marx used a century earlier to study capitalism."[56] Ellul identifies Karl Marx and Karl Barth as the twin fountains of his own twofold intellectual origin.[57]

In short, a man who does not reject socialism,[58] egalitarianism, or the dissolution of the state, but who does reject the teachings of the historic Christian church and the legitimacy of *every* government, past or present, regardless of its form, its history, or its ideals, has not *really* rejected Marxist ideology — despite his claims to the contrary. Simply by distancing himself from other Marxists, Ellul has not thereby distanced himself from Marxist ideology. He has merely subjected it to a marginal reconstruction, as if Marxist methods of analysis could be separated from their philosophical presuppositions and their ideological underpinnings and implications, and as if Marxist methods came from nothing and could lead nowhere. When Ellul opposes the Marxists, it is still an intra-camp affair. When he attacks Communist ideologues, he puts his own work under siege. He is not sufficiently alarmed by the pervasive Marxist ideology of his own position.[59]

The crisis in Ellul's thought is that there is no crisis in Ellul's thought, much less a proper resolution.

END NOTES

1 That, for some, thinking is inescapable has been memorably depicted in Ayn Rand's "The Simplest Thing in the World," in Ayn Rand, *The Romantic Manifesto,* (New York: New American Library, 1971) pp. 173-185.

2 Jacques Ellul, *Jesus and Marx: From Gospel to Ideology*, (Grand Rapids: Wm. B. Eerdmans, 1988) p. 2. Ellul's view of the allegedly anti-ideological character of Christianity is so extreme that he argues that "God's biblical revelation" is "the destruction of all religions [and] beliefs" (Ibid.). That Christianity itself is, on any common sense view, a religion and entails beliefs seems not to matter.

3 Ibid., pp. 3, 4.

4 Ibid., p. 157. Note that Ellul's anarchism moves beyond politics without partisanship to politics without politics. Ellul seems undisturbed by the stunning verbal antinomy here employed, or by the impossibility of an anti-political *political* philosophy, something no more possible or reasonable than

an anti-mathematical mathematics. See also Jacques Ellul, *Anarchy and Christianity*, (Grand Rapids: Wm. B. Eerdmans, 1991) p. 4, where he affirms that anarchism "seems to be the position which in this area is closest to biblical thinking" and ibid,. p. 45.

5 Ellul, *Jesus and Marx*, p. 171 (italics added to emphasize Ellul's characteristic practice of overstatement).

6 Jacques Ellul, *The Subversion of Christianity*, (Grand Rapids: Wm. B. Eerdmans, 1986) pp. 113, 114.

7 Ibid., p. 121. "I believe that the biblical teaching is clear," he adds, "it always contests political power," Ibid., p. 116.

8 Ellul, *Jesus and Marx*, p. 163 (italics his). Ellul here stands over against the Jewish rabbis, both ancient and medieval, one of whom, Menahem ben Solomon Ha-Meiri (1246-1306), comments concerning the epigraph that heads this essay: "Rabbi Hananiah emphasizes that we must pray [on behalf of the government]; and this is intended not merely in behalf of a Jewish government, but *in behalf of Gentile ones too.*", Judah Goldin (ed.), *The Living Talmud* (New York: New American Library, 1957) p. 120 (emphasis added).

9 Ellul, *Jesus and Marx*, 165 (italics added).

10 Robert Filmer, *Patriarcha; or The Natural Power of Kings*, in John Locke, *Two Treatises of Government* (edited by Thomas I. Cook, New York: Hafner, 1947) pp. 249-308.

11 See J. H. Hertz (ed.), *The Pentateuch and Haftorahs* (London: Soncino, 1973) 2. 823.

12 Ellul, *Jesus and Marx*, p. 165. My argument here, of course, in one way, depends upon the traditional dating of the Pentateuch. In another way, however, it does not, for we are dealing here with the identification of primary passages, or passages of prime importance, not simply with chronological priority.

13 According to Ellul, the rule of the judges was "apolitical" and "nonstatist," *The Subversion of Christianity*, p. 114.

14 Ibid. Ellul's characterization of other portions of the Old Testament are no less unreliable. For example, he believes that the prophets "offer no political opinion" and "never engage in politics at all," Jacques Ellul, *The Ethics of Freedom*, (Grand Rapids: Wm. B. Eerdmans, 1976) p. 373.

15 Ellul, *Jesus and Marx*, p. 3.

16 Ellul, *The Subversion of Christianity*, p. 114. Elsewhere Ellul describes this miracle as "somewhat magical and absurd," *The Ethics of Freedom*, p. 372. See

also *Anarchy and Christianity*, pp. 63ff.

17 Ellul, *Jesus and Marx*, p. 167.

18 Ellul, *The Ethics of Freedom*, p. 372.

19 Ellul, *Jesus and Marx*, p. 167.

20 Ibid., p. 168. According to Ellul, *Anarchy and Christianity*, (p. 58) not only is politics demonic, it is absolutely devilish. He insists that "all that has to do with politics and political authority belongs to the devil . . . Those who hold political power receive it from him and depend upon him." This view leads Ellul into a grotesque interpretation of Christ's assertion to Pilate that Pilate's political power comes to him "from above" (John 19:11). "Jesus is telling Pilate," Ellul writes, "that his power is from the spirit of evil" (ibid., p. 69). See also Ellul, *The Subversion of Christianity*, p. 114.

Further, that Caesar (or any government) is not the creator of money, as Ellul seems to think (*Jesus and Marx*, p. 167ff), is something economists have known for over two hundred years, since the work of Adam Smith and Adam Ferguson, who argued that money antedates government and that it arises from human action, not human design. Government eventually recognizes the prevailing medium of human exchange (often rare metals, because they are durable, dividable, and conveniently carried) and then adapts itself and its political mechanisms to it. But government, Caesar included, does not create money. To think otherwise is to confuse legal tender with money, a common mistake. Government cannot even dictate the use of money, as the U. S. government discovered at great cost when the American public generally declined to use the newly minted Susan B. Anthony one-dollar coin. See, for example, Adam Smith, *An Inquiry into the Nature and Causes of the Wealth of Nations* (Indianapolis: Liberty Classics, 1981) Bk.1, ch. 4.

21 Ellul, *Jesus and Marx*, p. 168.

22 Ellul, *The Subversion of Christianity*, p. 113.

23 Ellul, *Jesus and Marx*, p. 170. Ellul also fails to deal adequately with New Testament texts like I Corinthians 6:1,2; Colossians 1:15,16; Titus 3:1; and 1 Peter 2:13-17, passages he often declines even to mention. He also neglects to mention that the New Testament teaches that just as God gave Jesus to Israel, *so also did He give Israel both judges and kings, such as Saul and David* (Acts 13:20ff).

24 Ellul, *Jesus and Marx*, pp. 172, 168. See also *Anarchy and Christianity*, p. 46, where, with predictable exaggeration, he insists that today we are "confronted with the crushing of individuals by the state under every regime," and

ibid., p.61,62, where he affirms that there "can be no political power without tyranny" and that "there can be no such thing as good political power."

25 Ellul himself questions the biblical propriety of voting: "But where do we find the epistles recommending voting at elections . . .?", Ellul, *The Ethics of Freedom*, 372. See also ibid., p. 374 and Ellul, *Anarchy and Christianity*, p. 14: "Should anarchists vote? . . . For my part, I think not. To vote is to take part in the organization of the false democracy that has been set up forcefully by the middle class. No matter whether one votes for the left or the right, the situation is the same." He continues (p. 15): "Conscientious objection is objection not merely to military service *but to all the demands and obligations imposed by our society*: to taxes, to vaccination, to compulsory schooling, etc." (emphasis added). He believes as he does about military service because he mistakenly thinks that there is no "difference between private crime and war" (ibid., p. 39), as if the entire just war tradition in Christian thought could be dismissed with a wave of the hand as a tragically misguided ruse to justify international thuggery.

26 Ellul, *Jesus and Marx*, p. 166.

27 Ibid., p. 171.

28 Jeane J. Kirkpatrick, *Dictatorships and Double Standards: Rationalism & Reason in Politics*, (New York: Simon and Schuster, 1982) pp. 10, 11.

29 Ellul, *Jesus and Marx*, pp. 174, 175 (italics his). Ellul has apparently not noticed that the startling juxtaposition of the words "anarchist society" seems to constitute an oxymoron. That his anarchist vision is impossible and impractical, and that he holds it nevertheless, Ellul readily admits in *Anarchy and Christianity*, (p. 19): "The true anarchist thinks that an anarchist society — with no state, no organization, no hierarchy, and no authorities — is possible, livable, and practicable. But I do not. In other words, I believe that the anarchist fight, the struggle for an anarchist society, is essential, but I also think that the realizing of such a society is impossible."

30 For an introduction to Augustine's political views, see Herbert A. Deane, *The Political and Social Ideas of St. Augustine* (New York: Columbia University Press, 1963) and R. A. Markus, *Saeculum: History and Society in the Theology of St. Augustine* (Cambridge: Cambridge University Press, 1970). Unlike Ellul, "Augustine envisioned the total Christian society, with believers having essentially captured all nominally secular institutions, including government." See Doug Bandow, *Beyond Good Intentions: A Biblical View of Politics*, (Westchester: Crossway, 1988) p. 125. Ellul regards the views of Augustine

and those thinkers whom I name subsequently as grossly mistaken. In *Anarchy and Christianity*, (p. 7) Ellul insists that "We have to eliminate two thousand years of accumulated Christian errors, or mistaken traditions."

31 Clifford Kossel, S. J., "Some Limits of Politics, " in George W. Carey and James V. Schall, S. J., editors, *Essays on Christianity and Political Philosophy*, (Lanham, MD: University Press of America, 1984) pp. 35, 38, 39. For an introduction to Thomas Aquinas's political views, see F. Aveling, "St. Thomas Aquinas and the Papal Monarchy," in F. J. C. Hearnshaw, editor, *The Social and Political Ideas of Some Great Mediaeval Thinkers*, (New York: Barnes & Noble, 1923/1967) pp. 85-106; Ernest L. Fortin, "St. Thomas Aquinas," in Leo Strauss and Joseph Cropsey, editors, *History of Political Philosophy*, (Chicago: The University of Chicago Press, 1963/1981) pp. 223-250; and George H. Sabine, *A History of Political Theory*, (New York: Henry Holt, 1937) pp. 247-257.

32 For an introduction to Dante's political views, see Etienne Gilson, *Dante and Philosophy*, (New York: Harper Torchbooks, 1963) pp. 162-224; Thomas G. Bergin, *Dante*, (New York: Orion, 1965) pp.177-194; James Burnham, *The Machiavellians*, (New York: John Day, 1943) pp. 1-26; and Dante's own *On World Government* (Indianapolis: Bobbs-Merrill, 1949/1957).

33 For an introduction to Calvin's political views and to those of Calvinism in general, see W. Fred Graham, *The Constructive Revolutionary: John Calvin & His Socio-Economic Impact* (Atlanta: John Knox, 1971); William C. Innes, *Social Concern in Calvin's Geneva* (Allison Park, PA: Pickwick, 1983); Harro Höpfl, *The Christian Polity of John Calvin* (Cambridge: Cambridge University Press, 1982); E. William Monter, *Calvin's Geneva* (New York: John Wiley & Sons, 1967); and George L. Hunt, editor, *Calvinism and the Political Order* (Philadelphia: Westminster, 1965).

34 Ellul is well aware that he stands over against mainstream Christian wisdom on this issue, which he calls "the Constantinian heresy" of aligning the affairs of the church with those of the state. He contends, with typical overstatement and imprecision, that "Christianity's historical sin has been to recognize the state. This sin continues, no matter what form the state takes, no matter who holds power," *Jesus and Marx*, p. 172.

35 Ellul, *The Ethics of Freedom*, p. 375. Elsewhere Ellul writes that "it is idealistic and fanciful to think that Christianity can permeate or modify the structures of society," Jacques Ellul, *What I Believe*, (Grand Rapids: Wm. B. Eerdmans, 1989) p. 43.

36 Ellul, *The Ethics of Freedom*, p. 374. Ellul sometimes writes as if he thinks

Christians can properly participate in the political, but not in politics. The difference is merely semantic. It simply substitutes an adjective for a noun.

37 Surely Adam Smith is correct when he says, "The administration of the great system of the universe [and] the care and happiness of all rational and sensible beings is the business of God, and not of man. To man is allotted a much humbler department, but one much more suitable to the weakness of his powers, and to the narrowness of his comprehension — the care of his own happiness, of that of his family, his friends, his country," John Haggerty, editor, *The Wisdom of Adam Smith*, (Indianapolis: Liberty, 1976) p. 38. For the care and nurture of such things, Ellul's anarchist principles are clearly insufficient.

38 Thomas Molnar, "The Medieval Beginnings of Political Secularization," in Carey and Schall, *Essays on Christianity and Political Philosophy*, p. 53.

39 Ellul denies that human beings are either political or social creatures by nature: "I believe that for millennia people lived as though grafted upon the natural environment, and that at that time they were not social animals," Ellul, *What I Believe*, p. 101. For an assertion that political institutions and relationships also are unnatural see his discussion on the following page. For an interesting alternative to Ellul's idiosyncratic views concerning the social nature of man, see Eberhard Jüngel, *Theological Essays*, (Edinburgh: T & T Clark, 1989) pp. 139ff.

40 The literature on the inadequacies of socialism, in general, and of Marxism, in particular, on the one hand, and of the comparative superiority of capitalism, on the other, is enormous. See David Conway, *A Farewell to Marx* (New York: Penguin, 1987); Friedrich A. Hayek, *The Road to Serfdom* (Chicago: The University of Chicago Press, 1944); [Even though Hayek has been honored as the Nobel laureate in economics, Ellul insists that the fundamental premise of this book is one that "no one accepts," Jacques Ellul, *The Technological Society* (New York: Vintage, 1964) 178.] Friedrich A. Hayek, *The Constitution of Liberty* (Chicago: The University of Chicago Press, 1960); Ludwig von Mises, *Socialism* (Indianapolis: Liberty Classics); Eugen von Böhm-Bawerk, *The Exploitation Theory of Socialism-Communism*,(South Holland, IL: Libertarian, 1975); Eugen von Böhm-Bawerk, "Unresolved Contradiction in the Marxian Economic System," in Eugen von Böhm-Bawerk, *Shorter Classics of Böhm-Bawerk*, (South Holland, IL: Libertarian, 1962) pp. 200-302; H. W. B. Joseph, *The Labor Theory of Value in Karl Marx* (London: Oxford University Press, 1923); Milton Friedman, *Capitalism and Freedom* (Chicago: The University

of Chicago Press, 1962); Tibor R. Machan, *Marxism: A Bourgeois Critique* (Bradford, England: MCB University Press, 1988); Thomas Sowell, *Marxism: Philosophy and Economics* (New York: William Morrow, Inc., 1985); and Frederic Bastiat, *Selected Texts on Political Economy* (Irvington-on-Hudson, NY: The Foundation for Economic Education, Inc., 1964). That capitalist values and presuppositions are Christian or else are compatible with Christian belief and practice, see George Gilder, *Wealth & Poverty* (New York: Bantam, 1981); Franky Schaeffer, editor, *Is Capitalism Christian?* (Westchester, IL: Crossway, 1985); Ronald H. Nash, *Poverty and Wealth: The Christian Debate Over Capitalism* (Westchester, IL: Crossway, 1986); and Michael Novak, *The Spirit of Democratic Capitalism* (New York: Simon and Schuster, 1982). For an account of Marx's own personal failings, see Paul Johnson, *Intellectuals* (New York: Harper & Row, 1988) pp. 52-81.

41 Ellul, *The Ethics of Freedom*, pp. 24, 26, 27. Later in the same text (p. 48) he writes that "one of the merits of Marx is to have brought to light the universal character of alienation."

42 See Ellul, *The Ethics of Freedom*, pp. 500ff. Capitalism's power to produce goods and services and its ability to raise the standard of living of those that live under it Ellul judges as detrimental or evil. See Ellul, *What I Believe*, pp. 61ff. Elsewhere Ellul states, "Capitalism is a historical fact that is obsolete. It may well last another century, but it has no more historical importance." See Jacques Ellul, *In Season, Out of Season: An Introduction to the Thought of Jacques Ellul* (San Francisco:Harper & Row, 1982) p. 176. In a similar vein, Ellul writes, "Capitalism, in spite of all its power, will be crushed by . . . automatism." See Ellul, *The Technological Society*, p. 82. Ellul's understanding of capitalism is abysmally distorted.

43 Jacques Ellul, *Money and Power*, (Downers Grove: InterVarsity, 1984) pp. 14, 16, 20.

44 Quoted in Sabine, *A History of Political Thought*, p. 695.

45 Ellul, *The Ethics of Freedom*, p. 113.

46 Ibid., p. 38. See also p. 154 and Ellul, *Money and Power*, p. 20. Furthermore, as K. L. Billingsley pungently comments, "Unlike Christian writers such as Jacques Ellul and Tony Campolo, I don't believe that money is evil in itself. (Strange that, believing this, these people don't give their books or videos away free of charge.)" See K. L. Billingsley, *The Seductive Image: A Christian Critique of the World of Film*, (Westchester: Crossway, 1989) p. 77. The same criticism of Ellul has been made at greater length and with more force in

Nash, *Poverty and Wealth* pp. 157-163.

47 Quoted in Daniel B. Clendenin, *Theological Method in Jacques Ellul* (Lanham, MD: The University Press of America) p. 24.

48 Jacques Ellul, "Epilogue: On Dialectic," in Clifford G. Christians and Jay M. VanHook, editors, *Jacques Ellul: Interpretive Essays*, (Urbana: University of Illinois Press, 1981) p. 297. The same essay appears in slightly modified form in Ellul, *What I Believe*, pp. 29-46. In it (p. 29) he writes that "dialectic is so much a part of my way of thinking and being that [when I talk about it] I am talking about myself and my studies rather than about an academic mode of exposition or a philosophy." See p. 35 for his assertion concerning ancient Hebrew dialectics. According to Ellul, both "Christianity and biblical thought are dialectical." See Ellul, *In Season, Out of Season*, p. 202. As David W. Gill comments, "Ellul's thought . . . is thus very *dialectical*." See Ellul, *Money and Power*, p. 8.

49 Ellul, *The Ethics of Freedom*, p. 68.

50 Ellul, *Jesus and Marx*, pp. 86, 89.

51 If Ellul's index is to be trusted, Marx is cited 44 times (p. 513), or nearly as many times as Matthew, Mark, Luke, and John (and therefore Jesus) combined.

52 Ellul, *Jesus and Marx*, pp. 94, 86.

53 Jacques Ellul, "From Jacques Ellul," in James Holloway, ed., *Introducing Jacques Ellul*, (Grand Rapids: Wm. B. Eerdmans, 1970) p. 5. As Ellul himself recounts the event elsewhere, "I borrowed *Das Kapital* from the library and started reading it, you can easily see that the effect this reading had on me was not purely due to chance. I was eighteen years old. I discovered a global interpretation of the world, the explanation for this drama of misery and decadence that we had experienced. The excellence of Marx's thinking, in the domain of economic theory, convinced me." See Ellul, *In Season, Out of Season*, p. 11.

54 Ibid., p. 16.

55 Ibid., p. 60.

56 Ibid., p. 176.

57 See Ellul, *What I Believe*, p. 30 and Ellul, "Epilogue: On Dialectic," p. 292.

58 As he writes (ibid., p. 8), "I like the Socialists, . . . and I could wish that they would bring about a true Socialist revolution, as I have often said." In *Anarchy and Christianity*, p. 3, Ellul insists that he regards "anarchism as the fullest and most serious form of socialism."

59 My recitation of Ellul's Marxisms in this essay is far from complete. One could also add, as Ellul himself does, that both his reluctance to offer political solutions for current problems and his dramatic style of political exposition consciously follow the example set by Marx. See Ellul, *In Season, Out of Season*, pp. 196, 223. Among his numerous other Marxisms, Ellul also identifies "Marx's analysis of democracy, which I hold to be true." See Ellul, *The Technological Society*, p. 403. All this notwithstanding, pro-Ellul evangelicals continue to resist any linkage of Ellulism with its pervasively Marxist roots.

"People are prone to look for something new, and all too often the new lacks the profound, substantial meaning enshrined in traditional forms."
WOLFHART PANNENBERG

"So long as we speak in language based on erroneous theory, we generate and perpetuate error."
F. A. HAYEK

". . . we think in the interplay of information and the assimilation of what we have grasped through language. In this respect, language makes it possible to think."
EBERHARD JÜNGEL

"Although it is not routinely understood in this way, thought is talk. . . When the power of saying is small, the power of thinking is small. . . If our words are few, we can say little. And if our words are mostly the words of communication, those words that name publicly visible things and events, then we can make sayings that are mostly ways of pointing to something. We have not the words to make sayings about our sayings."
RICHARD MITCHELL

"Why shouldn't we quarrel about a word? What is the good of words if they aren't important enough to quarrel over? Why do we choose one word more than another if there isn't any difference between them?"
G. K. CHESTERTON

Verbal Plunder: Combating the Feminist Encroachment on the Language of Theology and Ethics

I don't like being ripped off. The more valuable something is to me, the more I hate to lose it. As a historian of theology and as a literary critic, I value words and their meaning and I value tradition. I won't give them up without a fight. If someone wants to steal something from me and I can stop them, I will. This essay is my way of saying that I've had enough, and I'm not going to take it anymore.

Not long ago, a small and vocal band of feminist thugs tried to pull off one of the greatest acts of verbal plunder in the history of the Western world. By means of a linguistic subterfuge that prohibited any term that happened to strike them as sexist, they tried to abscond not only with 1/3 of all our generic personal and possessive pronouns (No more "he" and "his," for example.), they also tried to swipe any and every descriptive term beginning with the letters m-a-n. And, because crime breeds crime, they fell quickly from larceny into slander by identifying as sexual bigots and chauvinists anyone, past or present, who failed to pay homage to their idiosyncratic rules of usage. As much as I hate to endorse anything to do with Freudianism, it seems to me that some feminists suffer from acute pronoun envy.

But I will not be bullied out of my words or my heritage by the verbal, philosophical, or cultural heresies of those who are dedicated to undermining the great tradition that brought us the good, the true, and the beautiful, on the one hand, or redemption and hope, on the other. I know what that mob of word pirates is up to, and I want to tell them to keep their hands off my legacy and to stop spreading lies about my friends. Anyone who thinks that Jesus, Dante, Petrarch, Michelangelo, or Milton were sexist pigs simply because they did not speak, write, or paint according to the aberrant rules propounded in the latest feminist manifesto had better think again. Some people not only have no respect for their own language and tradition, they have none for anyone else's. They smear those who, in ages past, "spake full well in language quaint and olden," people whose verbal art and commitment to truth I am unwilling to abandon, condemn, or reshape in some generic mold of feminist design. I do not trust the minds and methods of feminist teachers who, by means of their anachronistic slurs, bear false witness against the past and its towering figures. Nor do I want them teaching my children. I will not entrust my descendants to those who abuse my ancestors. Wisdom, beauty, and truth are hard won things, the gaining of which took generations. To overthrow them or to undervalue them simply because those who discovered them do not worship at the altar of one's own linguistic special interest group is both insupportably arrogant and reckless.

More than 1500 years ago, in his monumental *City of God*, St. Augustine understood the principles by which modern propagandists operate: if you want to undercut an opponent's argument, simply compromise his language. This is done best by stealing your opponent's words and making them your own. When you do so, your opponent is forced either to stop and explain what he means every time he uses the words you co-opted, or else to find a whole new set of unfamiliar terms with which to advance his case. Either option is doomed to failure. Neither audience attention span nor media sound bites are sufficiently long to accommodate his necessarily lengthy and labyrinthine efforts at re-educating the populace to his newly acquired taxonomy. By stealing his language, you have stolen the verbal flags and banners around which he can rally people to his cause. Without those flags and banners he is speechless. By pilfering his verbal arsenal, you have left him without weapons and without defense.

That is precisely what the feminist word thieves are trying to do. They have taken traditionally generic terms of representation like "he," "his," and "mankind" and *redefined* them so that they can be understood *only* as sexist or gender specific. In much the same way that weasels suck the contents out of eggs, the feminists suck out all the content of words. Then they go the weasels one better. Rather than leaving the empty shell of a word behind them after they have emptied it of its previous meaning, they proceed to refill that mangled word with *a definition of their own choosing*. For example, according to one prominent feminist handbook, the "only acceptable nonsexist usage" of the word "man" is in reference to an adult male. But that is a feminist weasel word, one from which the feminists have sucked out its prior meaning and replaced it with one of their own. According to my *Webster's Dictionary*, the word "man" is not a male word. In fact, the concept of maleness does not enter until the third definition. Contrary to the self-serving assertions of the feminist verbal revolutionaries, traditional usage is not ideologically patriarchal in either definition or usage. For my money, Noah Webster is a far better guide to language than Gloria Steinem, Betty Freidan, or Starhawk. My point (if it is not obvious) is this: rather than having a command of language, the feminists want to command language.

Read my lips: I'm not buying it.

I will defy all those who insist on taking the language and the literature of Western tradition to the verbal veterinarian in order to have them neutered. Not all changes are progress, and neutered language is one of those changes that is not. Neutered language is no improvement. It is not more accurate, more picturesque, more powerful, or more communicative. Neutered language is not preferable. None of us is better off because standard word usage has been castrated.

Feminists insist on rejecting traditional verbal usage because they think it is exclusivistic and that it leaves out half of humanity — namely women. Their response to this imaginary impropriety is to represent the human race in neutered language — which merely succeeds in eliminating *all* of us, because human beings are not androgynous, and they are not neuter.

If you look carefully, you will discover that much feminist language is not inclusive. You also will notice that a great deal of feminist language (and the ideology that accompanies it) is not neutral; it is overt feminist sexism. I don't know about you, but I've had enough of books like *Jesus as Mother*. If any change is needed now, it is to have feminist language and literature spayed. I intend to be a recruiter for, and a front-line warrior in, the resistance movement determined to stave off the feminist encroachment upon legitimate verbal conventions, and I intend to be an environmental activist in the fight against semantic pollution. I will stridently oppose all those whose verbal fetish is exposing the supposed genitals of standard English. I, for one, will not be party to the humorless, even unhuman, triumph of feminist androgyny, and I will not sanction the willful blindness of those who insist upon seeing only the imaginary sameness of all things, because things that are all the same, whatever else they might be, are not human beings.

Have the feminist word bandits never learned that grammatical gender is not the same as sex? One does not make a sex statement when one calls the race "man" any more than when one calls a ship or a nation or liberty "she." Genitalia are not in question. Sex and grammatical gender must not be equated. If you insist on equating them when the author you read or the speaker you hear has not, you will misread or mishear. In that sense, some feminists can misunderstand in seven languages. Their verbal fetishes make it inevitable. In their monomaniacal quest to expose the verbal genitals of every great writer, they miss the beauty and truth and power of the world's finest works of verbal art and, in the process, make themselves beggars and complainers at the great feast of language and literature. Their ill-conceived sexist jingoism does little else than make them whistlers, hecklers, and foot stompers in the rhapsody of words played out for us by the finest verbal performers of all time. I, for one, am scandalized by their audacious efforts to teach the old Muses new tricks and by the manner in which they pretend to stand in ideological and artistic judgment over them. Great words and great works judge us, not vice versa.

As a grammatical category, the concept of gender first reached maturity in ancient Greece, where it seems not to have developed as a reference to sex, but rather as a classification of kind. Must I remind feminists that while there are only two sexes, Greek has three genders (a distinction of which the Greeks were well aware and heartily endorsed)?

Furthermore, the same non-sexual character of grammatical gender is repeated in modern language. In German, for example, the word for "girl" is grammatically neuter while the word for "turnip" is feminine. This does not mean that the Germans confuse their women with their vegetables. Such ideas are laughable to us because when feminist propaganda is not blaring in our ears we easily understand that grammatical gender is a semantic classification and that a semantic classification is not the same as biological sex. You must not impose a sexual orientation upon words where one does not exist.

If the words "man" and "mankind" were really male words, then it should be the men, not the women, who ought to be offended by the use of allegedly male terms to refer to the race indiscriminately because by employing a masculine word for a generic meaning our culture would be demonstrating that it thinks nothing at all of defacing or erasing maleness. If generic words really were male words, then masculinity is being defaced everyday by everybody — and no one seems to object, least of all the feminists.

The feminist word fetish sometimes reaches ridiculous extremes, as even the feminists themselves have had occasion to acknowledge. *The Nonsexist Wordfinder* actually feels compelled to stop and remind its feminist readers that the words "*amen*," "*boy*cott," "*Man*hattan," and "*men*opause" are not sexist words! I never thought they were; but apparently enough feminists did so to require such a warning.

The feminist verbal agenda is the academic equivalent of an urban renewal project: it is intended to clean things up and to modernize them, but all it does is to serve as the seedbed for future blight. The feminist wrecking crews long ago began to demolish the venerable landmarks of language, literature, and theology. They intend to replace the Victorian richness and character of our language's architecture with the androgynous homogeneity and boredom of the cinder block, steel, and glass ugliness of endless rows of antiseptic, off-white, cloned cubicles of androgynous language. They want to replace the hallowed halls of ivy with the long, gray, dimly-lit corridors of an ill-conceived, allegedly gender-neutral taxonomy. These inhospitable corridors they will pervasively and perpetually serenade with a politicized, propagandized, amorphous Muzak that permits you to hear all the notes, but never the music. The feminists intend to level the great books, the great authors, and standard English just as thoroughly as the Allies did Dresden. The great tragedy is that the feminists have met with so much success and with so little resistance, especially in political affairs and in the affairs of academia.

We are the victims of a feminist "Newspeak" that is designed not to portray or to depict reality more accurately, more graphically, or more comprehensively, but simply to meet the ideological needs of feminism and to further its own radicalized political agenda. The unabashed purpose of feminist Newspeak is, to paraphrase George Orwell, not merely to denigrate standard English, but to make the worldview of standard English impossible and, literally, unthinkable. This is done partly by means of new words, but primarily by means of junking the old words, or by stripping them of their old meanings. Feminist Newspeak is designed, to paraphrase Orwell again, to *diminish* the range of human thought and to make it impossible to formulate in one's mind what feminists misrepresent as the moral heresies and injustices of Western tradition.

You see, because thoughts and words are so intimately interconnected, when someone steals some of your words, they also steal some of your ability to formulate, or to conceive, certain thoughts. The fewer the number of words from which you have left to choose, the fewer the number of thoughts it is possible for you to think and to express coherently or compellingly. In the aftermath of the feminist plunder of the English language, anti-feminist arguments and reasons become impossible because the words and thoughts necessary to conceive and to sustain those arguments have all been stolen. Language control is thought control. The feminist Newspeakers are trying to induce a culture-wide case of selective amnesia; they want you to forget major portions of the accumulated wisdom of many centuries of Western tradition and of the language in which it was conceived and preserved so that you will more willingly drink deep from the boiling cauldrons of cultural and theological heresy, and of feminist social revolution.

Make no mistake about it, the feminist word warriors are thought police. They will confiscate your words — and your thoughts — and they will deface those words and thoughts they leave behind. Feminist Newspeak is not merely a form of ideological censorship, it is verbal plunder and mental vandalism.

That is my first point — the feminist word warriors have damaged English language and literature. My second point is that they have done the same thing to theology and to ethics.

They've even kidnapped God Himself and had Him neutered. The Father, Son, and Holy Ghost have been exchanged for God, Jesus, and the Spirit, as if the Son were not God, as if the revelation in Scripture could be altered at will, and as if heresy were a trifle. They had better re-read St. John and the creeds of Nicea and Chalcedon. When Christ taught his disciples to pray using the words "Our Father who art in Heaven" (Matthew 6:9), He was not being an unreconstructed chauvinist simply because He wisely refrained from employing the neutered language of the *New Lectionary*. My point here is not merely that Jesus spoke of God as Father, but that He apparently never spoke of Him as anything else — and that matters.

Jesus did not merely continue the patriarchal theology of the Old Testament, He widely and deeply intensified it. In the whole of the Hebrew Scriptures, God is almost never actually addressed as "Father." He is described as " Father" only occasionally. But Jesus himself alone calls God "Father" more than 160 times, and except for the cry of dereliction on the cross, which is a quotation from the Old Testament, Jesus never calls Him anything else. The feminists, in other words, are fighting with Christ, and they must be made to realize this. We not only have Christ's explicit instruction to call God "Father," we have His constant example. I remind you that no one knows the Father except the Son and those to whom the Son reveals Him, and the Son has revealed Him to us as Father. If you reject that revelation, then, in some profound fashion, you can not know God. If you reject that revelation, the God you know is somehow other than, and different from, the heavenly Father of Jesus. As Adolf Harnack observed, Jesus did not make God our Father, He showed us that God is Father.

Put differently, in their mad efforts to rid orthodox Trinitarianism of what they mistakenly identify as sexism, feminist theologians have junked the Father, Son, and Holy Spirit and replaced them with the Creator, the Redeemer, and the Sustainer. That is, they have replaced divine ontology with function, which is a heresy. After all, it is not only the Father who creates; it is not only the Son who redeems; and it is not only the Spirit who sustains. Each of the three divine Persons is intimately involved in each of the three functions arbitrarily singled out here by the feminists as the means of distinguishing and identifying the Persons of the Godhead. This feminist subterfuge is no more helpful than distinguishing the right fielder, the left fielder, and the center fielder as the one who runs, the one who throws, and the one who catches, respectively. All outfielders do all things. To jettison the the three Persons of the Trinity in favor of three arbitrarily selected functions of the Trinity is simply to fall into a new variation of the old Sabellian heresy of modalism, which denied that God is authoritatively revealed to us as three Persons, but which affirmed instead that God merely fulfills three functions and plays three roles. It seems to me that to be baptized into the name of the Creator, the Redeemer, and the Sustainer is to be baptized into another religion, and not into Biblical or historical Christianity.

But the feminists are not only Sabellians, they are Marcionites. That is, like Marcion, they too have utterly rejected the authoritative witness of the Hebrew Scriptures. Like Marcion, the feminists denigrate Yahweh and they despise the picture He gave of Himself to pious ancient Jews in the Old Testament. Furthermore, they despise the picture those pious ancient Jews have left of God for us. The feminists accuse the ancient Jews of doing, indeed severely criticize them for doing, precisely what they themselves unashamedly do: remake God in their own image. The feminists reject the God of the Jews because they think He is merely the culture-bound product of a political and sexist agenda. I reject the God of the feminists for precisely the same reason.

Winston Churchill is reported to have said that whatever name the Iranians choose to call their country, in English it ought to remain "Persia." Likewise, whatever tortured pronouns the feminists invent to refer to God, the good theologian will continue to call Him "He."

Feminist theology, I am convinced, is a flight from Biblical reality. God has made us male and female, not androgynous. God has made the male of the species not better, but head. God has revealed Himself to us as He. When God became incarnated, He became a man, that is, a male. That Man is the source and model of the Christian priesthood. The sexuality of Christ is neither accidental nor incidental. It is the result of divine choice. If you don't like it, argue with God.

In his excellent *The Closing of the American Mind*, Allan Bloom pointed out that Western scholars properly criticize the loss of academic integrity among their Soviet counterparts, who seem to revise their textbooks every time a new regime comes to power. Whenever the academy capitulates to the whims of government or of modern culture, Bloom says, it is the death of learning. Because theological feminism has merely baptized the gender fixation and egalitarian political agenda of the feminist left, theological feminism is the death of genuinely Biblical learning. Even though it sometimes means not to be, feminist revisionism is anti-Scripture. Too many feminist theologians believe that when the Church listens to the Bible the Church becomes deformed, not reformed. They are wrong. The feminist theologians have yet to learn that it is far better to listen to the Heilege Geist than to the Zeitgeist, that is, to the Holy Spirit of God than to the spirit of the age.

But it is not revelation that the feminist theologians crave; it is relevance. They have not understood that all that is revelation is inescapably relevant, but that being relevant is no guarantee of being revelation. The feminist theologians have never learned that to go with the spirit of the age is to go where all ages go and have gone: out of vogue and into a well deserved obscurity in the irretrievable past. They have never learned that to go with the God of revelation is to go where God Himself goes; and God Himself is never out of date. As Vance Havner once said, God is the Eternal Contemporary. Whenever our tomorrows arrive, we will always discover that God Himself has been there before us.

Theological feminism is simply an accommodation to the spirit of the age, not to the core, not to the kernel, of revelation. It finds its authority in something called "feminist experience," and not in Scripture.

The feminists' linguistic lobby, however, has exercised some discretion. Although they have stormed the Bastille of language and literature, and although they have laid siege to the Gates of Heaven and kidnapped its Chief Occupant, they have not yet had the nerve to bombard the walls of Hell in order to claim *its* king as their own. It's funny how calling the Devil "he" doesn't bother the feminists. It doesn't strike them as chauvinistic or sexually bigoted to personify evil in precisely the same language they elsewhere label sexist when used to personify goodness. Nor do they complain on behalf of all little boys everywhere about how psychologically devastating it must be for males to think of evil itself as one of their own kind. Apparently, pronouns are sexist only if they can be construed as anti-feminist.

But make no mistake about it, the feminist encroachment on the language of religion and morality is no mere tempest in an academic teacup. It is far more than the harmless verbal jousting between grammarians and theologians, on the one side, and women's libbers, on the other. It is — and I do mean this literally — a matter of life and death.

That is because language is a deadly weapon.

In the hands of a skilled wordsmith, language can sensitize peoples' consciences to injustice and motivate them to heroic virtue and reform. In the hands of a propagandist, however, it can be the verbal camouflage that hides some wildly horrific crime behind apparent respectability. When the Nazis, for example, resorted to genocidal barbarism in their quest for a "purer" race and nation, they called on their word warriors to help them cloak their wickedness in the language of decency in order to make the unspeakable speakable. Dachau and Buchenwald were painted with the brush of inoffensive clinical jargon. "We have merely implemented," the Nazis said, "the final solution."

Their word ploy was largely and tragically effective. Rather than stating the facts plainly and thereby forcing the German people to face the unimaginable horror around them and to risk life and family to eradicate it, the Nazi's verbal subterfuge provided a respectable wall of words behind which to hide their grotesque villainy. Who, after all, can be opposed to a "purer" nation or to a "solution"?

I can.

Whereas great evils are often disguised by clinical language, accurate words call the ghosts out of the closet. That is why we must learn to call things by their real names. That is why we must beware of every feminist euphemism.

But, even now, decades after Hitler, we fail to speak plainly. We have succumbed to the feminist word ploy, and as a result, *millions of people are dead.*

We let the feminist word warriors hide the fetal holocaust that surrounds us every day just as effectively as the Nazis hid their extermination of the Jews. And they do it the same way. They do not permit themselves to utter the "M" word, even though they commit the "M" act. That is, they do not murder unborn children, they "abort fetuses." That terminology, they wrongly believe, helps to remove their heinous deeds from the realm of the morally reprehensible. It allows them to view themselves and their neighbors with more self-respect and ethical complacency. "After all," they say to themselves, "what nice young woman would ever pay her doctor a handsome sum to murder her unborn baby. That is unthinkable. We merely abort our fetuses because we are unmarried and do not want to sentence our unfortunate and inconvenient offspring to a life of poverty."

Never mind that such a woman is an adultress. Never mind that she sentenced her child to the garbage can. Described in her less graphic and less accurate language, to murder her child seems not only not evil, it seems downright virtuous. As someone else has said, if you brush away the sentimental slush of a thousand sob-sisters, the cold fact remains that this woman wants to kill the child now living within her.

Beware of every feminist euphemism.

Some of the more squeamish among the feminists are unable even to say the "A" word. Though by aborting fetuses rather than murdering babies the feminist's linguistic sleight of hand has hidden the real nature (murder) of their action and the real identity (baby) of their victim, some women require a still heavier dose of verbal opium. For them the feminist word warriors have had to make the accursed deed even more palatable by making it even more impersonal. They have convinced such people that they are merely "terminating a pregnancy," a phrase which eliminates overt reference to any living thing. Unlike fetuses and children, which are undeniably alive, and unlike abortion and murder, which seem to imply nasty things like blood and death, simply to "terminate a pregnancy" sounds as innocuous as ending a radio transmission or pulling into the station after a pleasant railroad journey.

If "terminating pregnancies" is still too shocking a verbal description because the word "pregnant" tends to evoke unfortunate images of happy women large with child, feminist ideologues hide the crime behind an even more impersonal wall of words. They can say that murdering unborn children is nothing more than the voluntary extraction of the "product of conception." If *that* does not work, then they simply talk the way nearly all abortion clinics actually do talk: They resort to an acrostic and say that they are merely " removing the P.O.C." What could be more innocent?

Nearly everything.

Beware of every feminist euphemism.

Pleasant words can be a fraud. A sterile idiom can be a defense mechanism behind which we conceal the grossest reality. But, defense mechanisms do not change that reality. They merely disguise it. The evil facts themselves remain the same. Never forget that the disease you hide you cannot heal. For jargon wizards like the feminists, therefore, and for all who have been morally subverted by the feminist's verbal deception, there remains no therapy. Rather than facing the facts and identifying this slaughter for what it is; rather than calling an unconditional halt to the war they wage on the unborn; rather than confessing their guilt and casting themselves on the immense mercy of God; the feminist ideologues have persuaded millions of women to mask their shame behind a veil of words and to sell their souls to the verbal charlatans and quacks who tell them what they want to hear, not what they need to hear. They hide the crime with a lie.

Because words are inescapably connected to ideas, the feminist abuse of language has given rise to a feminist abuse of moral reason, as well. Let me illustrate.

My mother once asked me to clean up the back room in our basement. Not knowing the magnitude of the task she had set before me, I consented. When I finally got myself downstairs, I opened the wooden door to the back room, flipped on the light, and saw an unimaginable mess of almost legendary proportion: paper, beetles, dirt, bowling pins, cardboard boxes, toys, broken tools, rags, and sawdust. I did what any "rational" 15 year old would do.

I shut off the light and closed the door.

I'm not the only one who ever did that.

Most of us, I dare say, respond to the sometimes ugly face of reality the same way, though after years of practice we have learned to do so with a good deal more dexterity and finesse, so that our indulgent and immoral evasions seem less obvious and less culpable. Sometimes we try to rationalize our indolence and our guilt by telling ourselves (apparently) rational lies. That is, rather than looking at the shocking facts and not wincing; rather than seeing those ugly and disturbing facts for what they are, we rationalize. Though this ploy seems to assuage our consciences momentarily, it does not help. In fact, it does great harm, especially the way the feminist defenders of infanticide employ it.

Feminists not only hide the hideous face of abortion behind a verbal veil of inoffensive language and pretty words, they rationalize their wickedness. They have as many excuses for this barbaric atrocity as they have linguistic feignings to hide it. For example, one often hears the Right-to-Deathers say horrendous things like "Surely we may terminate a pregnancy caused by rape or by incest, may we not?"

No, we may not.

A child does not lose its right to life simply because its father or its mother was a sexual criminal or a deviate. Of course, rape and incest are vicious crimes. Those who perpetrate them must be strictly and decisively punished. Nevertheless, a civilized nation does not permit the victim of a crime to pass a death sentence on the criminal's offspring. *To empower the victim of a sex offense to kill the offender's child is an even more deplorable act than the rape that conceived it.* The child conceived by rape or incest is a victim, too. In America, we do not execute victims.

The Right-to-Deathers think that my argument here is insensitive to the plight of the rape victim and that I would sing another tune were I myself the victim of such a crime. They are wrong.

Because ours is a government of laws and not of men, we must not consign justice or morality to the pain-beguiled desires of victims. They, of all people, might be the least able to render a just verdict or to identify the path of highest virtue. I am convinced that the more monstrously one is mistreated, the more likely it is that revenge and personal expedience will look to that person like goodness. While rape victims most certainly know best the horror and indignity of the crime in question, being its victims does not confer upon them either ethical or jurisprudential expertise. Nor does it enable them to balance the scales of justice or to satisfy the demands of the moral imperative with care, knowledge, finesse, or precision. If one was an uninformed or inept ethicist or penologist before the crime, as most of us undoubtedly are, being a victim does not alter that fact at all. Justice is traditionally portrayed as blind, not because she was victimized and had her eyes criminally removed, but because she is impartial. Rape victims, like all other crime victims, rarely can be trusted to be sufficiently impartial or dependably ethical, especially seeing that they so often decide that the best alternative open to them is to kill the criminal's child. Suffering an evil at the hands of another does not excuse you from the responsibility to acquire knowledge and skill before rendering judgements. Victimization never has any power, on its own, to restore you. It is no substitute for courage, competence, or virtue.

"But does a woman not have the right to her own body?" the Right-to-Deathers ask.

Of course she does. But that is not at issue here. It is not *her* body, after all, that is being murdered; it is someone else's. Like hers, the body being murdered is not canine, not feline, not equine, and not bovine. Like hers, it is human. Like hers, it has a unique combination of twenty-three sets of paired chromosomes. (If, indeed, the body in question were truly hers, its genetic code would be the same as that of her body. It is not. It never is.) Like hers, the body being killed is the human product of human conception. It is not something she may do with as she pleases. Morality dictates that we do not kill human bodies — including our own — for personal convenience. As John Locke taught us, one of the most fundamental rights of all is the right to one's own property; and among the most sacred portions of our property is our own body. To it we have an *almost* exclusive right of function and disposal, a right that no one else can usurp, not even our mothers.

"But don't you believe in abortion rights?" the feminist Right-to-Deathers ask me. "Yes," I reply, "I do believe in abortion rights. I believe *it is the right of every human being not to be murdered by abortion.*"

John Donne was correct — because no man is an island, each man's death diminishes me. That means, among other things, that you cannot diminish the liberty or dignity of one without endangering or diminishing the liberty and dignity of us all. Abortionists, therefore, attack more than the unborn. Abortionists, and the feminist word warriors who defend, them must be resisted. Much depends upon their defeat. The life you save may be your child's. The freedom and dignity you save may be your own. As Confucius observed long ago and far away, when words lose their meaning, people lose their liberty.

To remain free, we must beware of every feminist euphemism and we must unmask every feminist rationalization built upon an abuse of language.

The feminists want to dress themselves up with the lexicon of respectability, but it just won't do. The denigration of Western tradition, the ideological mutilation of standard English, the slaughter of millions of unborn and still defenseless human beings, and the neutering of God Himself are *not* respectable. Those things are supremely wicked and they must be stopped. Feminist Newspeak is simply the diabolical dictionary of the anti-God, anti-tradition, anti-human, feminist left.

Again, I know what they're up to, and I won't have it. Theft and murder are despicable. To throw words away or to mangle them unnaturally and grotesquely so that you can do the same to inconvenient human beings is a monstrous wickedness. Even if I have to stand guard alone, the feminist culture felons are in for a fight.

So go ahead, murderers, word thieves, and slanderers, make my day.

ETHICS

"... *still obscurely fighting the lost fight of virtue, still clinging,*
in the brothel or on the scaffold, to some rag of honor, the poor jewel
of their souls!"
ROBERT LOUIS STEVENSON

"*I dislike the frequent use of the word* virtue, *instead of*
righteousness . . . *it sounds too much like pagan philosophy.*"
SAMUEL TAYLOR COLERIDGE

No God, No Good

At a conference concerning the teaching of moral values in the public schools, a justifiably well-known philosopher from an eastern university asserted that the moral virtues were (1) those values without which we humans do not flourish because they are rooted in human nature, and (2) those values that enjoy a consensus that spans culture, country, and century, something like the Tao described at the end of C. S. Lewis's *The Abolition of Man*. That moral values described or derived in either of these two ways are not really *moral* values, much less moral absolutes, is the burden of this brief chapter.

First, values determined either by human flourishing or by human nature are not truly right or wrong, not properly moral absolutes; they are pragmatism or utilitarianism masquerading as good and coöpting the language of virtue and "oughtness," to which they have no philosophical or theological claim.

As the following analysis will demonstrate, one must not contend that human nature and human flourishing yield moral absolutes, properly so-called, because such a theory fails to account for (1) the origin of human nature, (2) changes in human nature, and (3) the selection of "flourishing" as a category of moral discernment. I shall leave aside the vexed philosophical question of whether or not human nature itself actually exists as an entity in its own right, or if it is merely a philosopher's fiction without any extra-mental reality. I simply note in passing that the theory of morality here under review assumes an answer to this question that, if mistaken, devastates the theory by erasing its metaphysical basis.

(1) If human nature arose as the chance result of a mindless evolutionary process, a process behind which exists no divine mind and no divine plan, then moral absolutes disappear. That is, if human nature is the result of evolutionary accident, and if right and wrong arise solely from human nature, then right and wrong are accidents, not moral absolutes. Biological chance cannot serve as the philosophically proper foundation of right and wrong; it is their undoing. If human nature and human mind are the unintentional outcome of the chance collocation of atoms and of the random meanderings of natural selection (in other words, if the human mind is a mere epiphenomenon contorting and disporting itself for a short while upon the face of physical matter), then we have no convincing reason to trust them as indicators of moral goodness; nor have we any real or enduring right and wrong.

(2) Had the evolutionary process been different, or had the primordial soup been mixed from a different recipe, so to speak, or stirred at a different temperature, human nature might have been radically altered, along with the allegedly moral values this theory insists arise from it. Evolution might well have yielded a quite different array of species than it has, and humans (if they existed at all) might not be the most intelligent species and they might flourish in ways radically different from those that now obtain. That is, one can easily imagine a set of markedly different biological conditions, a set of conditions which demonstrated the physiological supremacy of a non-human species, one that flourished after the fashion of a cockroach. Cockroach-style flourishing would then become the measure of virtue, and not that means of flourishing that we humans sometimes now employ. I take this to mean that the moral absolutes yielded by this system of thought are neither truly moral nor truly absolute. They are simply that set of actions which we perceive to tend most effectively toward the pleasure and prosperity of our own species, which is, to put it bluntly, simply species bigotry parading as morality.

If something noticeably different from us, but something sufficiently close we could still call it human, evolved, then likely a noticeably different set of human actions would yield human flourishing. That altered means of flourishing would then become the definition of right and wrong. But precisely why the actions that conduce to the flourishing of the most intelligent and biologically innovative survivors of natural selection, whatever those survivors happened to be like, should be called morally virtuous is not clear and has not been (indeed, I would say cannot be) established. In other words, what has here been described is not true virtue. It is an intellectual misfire based on the philosophically injudicious assumption that somehow biological might makes right, or that merely by succeeding biologically a species gets to use itself as the measure of good and evil. This is not a system of moral absolutes; it is a system of biological relativism.

That those actions which conduce to the flourishing of the most intelligent and innovative survivors of natural selection (that is, those beings who have managed best to survive the ebb and flow of such things as mutation, catastrophe, retrogression, and adaptation) should be called *moral* merely confuses with right and wrong those actions which seem to some members of a species to permit that species to flourish *at one particular point in its evolution*. Conceivably that species was sufficiently different in its earlier stages of development, and will be sufficiently different in its later stages of development, that those means by which it now flourishes might be radically different both from what they once were and might eventually become. If so, what are now called right and wrong are not moral absolutes, but simply that set of actions perceived as most efficient at the moment. What set of actions will be so perceived in the distant future is still an open question, a question that might receive a starkly different answer then than either it now does or previously did, but which this system must nevertheless consider morally correct and universally binding. In short, to our previous charges of species bigotry and biological relativism we now must add time relativism and moral contradiction — but not moral absolutes.

Put differently, not only does the doctrine of evolution entail the notion that the human species and human nature are essentially mutable, but this allegedly natural mutability is amplified by the very startling, and very real, prospect of the species itself orchestrating and accelerating its own evolution and alteration by means of its scientific experimentation and acumen. Like our alleged natural mutability, this self-conducted mutability is the death knell of any and all moral absolutes supposedly rooted in human nature. When we do acquire the power to modify the nature of the race — and some speculate that our ability to do so is soon to be gotten — will what we produce still be truly and fully human? Will right and wrong then be rooted in human nature as it was or in human nature as it is in whatever it is we shall have made of it? Assuming that the alteration in human nature is accomplished only one person at a time rather than in the entire race all at once, and assuming therefore that *two* sorts of persons with a defendable claim to human nature exist simultaneously, which version of human nature supersedes the other and is to be considered the fountain from which all right and wrong arise? Will those who possess the other human nature be subject to a system of right and wrong that arises from a nature not entirely their own? What if our experiments do not always succeed? That is, what if the treatment does not always "take;" what if it yields occasionally idiosyncratic results that produce far more than merely two varieties of human nature? Which variety takes precedent? Shall we fall into the logical contradiction of having a number of competing sets of moral absolutes, each with different content? Though the answer to such puzzling questions might be difficult to identify, and though the answers to such questions might raise insurmountable difficulties for those who advocate this inadequate system of moral absolutes, the answers given to those questions make no difference at all to our purpose because any answer given them exposes the foundation of this ethical system as shifting sand, not moral bedrock.

Furthermore, if humans did not exist at all (and under the direction of a mindless evolutionary process they easily might not), and if right and wrong arise from human nature, then right and wrong would not exist (regardless of whether we considered right and wrong as either moral absolutes or as the biological relativism that emerges from biological success). In other words, because this theory of ethics ties morality to human nature, the fate of human nature is the fate of morality. That fate, if the second law of thermodynamics is correct, is oblivion. The material world is winding down to something like an amorphous, motionless mass of dead matter at a low temperature, incapable of sustaining life. Along with the demise of the physical universe go this ethical system's alleged moral absolutes, the true name of which we now see is "nihilism." In this system, morality, like everything else, comes precisely to nothing. When human beings cease to exist sometime in the future, as any world view that leaves out God must assert, right and wrong cease to exist at that same moment. In short, what was intended by this philosopher to be the foundation of ethics is really its death warrant.

(3) Why flourishing (and not something else) should be the measure of virtue, cannot be proven. To select flourishing as the measure of moral discernment, or to define flourishing as one thing and not another, is merely to elevate both one's own personal preference for flourishing and one's own definition of flourishing (whatever it happened to be) to the level of an absolute, which they neither are nor ever could be. One might just as easily have selected, as did the Marquis de Sade, private pleasure at the expense of another's pain as the measure of appropriate conduct. One might even prefer death to life, as do virtually all suicides. That happiness or prosperity, and not death, is the proper content of flourishing cannot be established from a merely evolutionary basis, except that one simply assert a preference (pragmatic or otherwise) for the one and not the other. Again, whatever else such private preferences might be, they are not moral absolutes.

Finally, as much as I value the work of C. S. Lewis, in general, and his *The Abolition of Man*, in particular, I would be misusing his book were I to argue from it that, because there appears to be substantial agreement among the peoples of the world about the rules of right and wrong, therefore these rules of right and wrong are moral absolutes. Consensus, regardless of how extensive or how enduring, is no sure measure of morality. All too often the majority has consented, either explicitly or implicitly, to colossal evil. Morality is not determined by nose count. "Majority" is no synonym for "morality."

As Archibald Alexander somewhere observed, virtue is not known by reason alone, but by revelation and by Providence. Sir Philip Sidney's way of saying it was to insist that the only impregnable citadel for virtue was religion. Both were precisely correct.

In a word, if there is no God, there is no good.

HISTORY

"*It is not the remembered but the forgotten past which enslaves us.*"
C. S. LEWIS

"*. . . Christianity is based in a totally unique way on a historical event and a historical figure, the interpretation of which is therefore the central function of the Christian tradition.*"
WOLFHART PANNENBERG

"*We study history in order to intervene in the course of history, and it is our right and duty we do this . . . We must do the right thing in the present, and that is to anticipate the future and be prepared for it in a circumspect manner.*"
ADOLF VON HARNACK

"*I am man; nothing historical do I regard as alien to me.*"
ADOLF VON HARNACK

Justifying History

I have heard it said that the trouble with the younger generation is that it has not read the minutes of the last meeting. As a college history professor, I can attest to the fundamental truth of this observation. When I ask my students to justify this disabling neglect, however, or to explain to me why they have not acquired a mastery of, or even a taste for, history, I am frequently answered with another question: "Why *should* we?" I answer them this way.

First, we study history because, as Carl Becker noted, one of our highest duties is not to be duped. Among other things, the history of mankind is a narrative of frauds and deceits. A detailed knowledge of the past often carries with it, therefore, an acquaintance with the ways of evil, and this acquaintance, in turn, engenders for us a protection. Knowing what we know from history, we need not fall prey to the same old ploys our fathers did. Providence, in other words, has vouchsafed to us a treasure trove of wisdom, gleaned from thousands of years of experience and thoughtful reflection. We are the privileged heirs of a tradition of insight formed in the crucible of our collective past. This tradition is our hedge against transitory circumstances, imperfect knowledge, and narrow perspective. Or, to put it the other way around, "deficiency in historical perspective leads to the ruinous blunders of ideologues." [1] To study history is to gain personal access to that invaluable legacy. Historical study properly pursued has the beneficial effect of granting a person the experience and wisdom of age without its accompanying infirmities or inconveniences. In that sense, historical study can serve as an indispensable aid both in living well and in living freely. History can be both a protection and a liberation.

Second, the study of history enables us to make informed predictions about the likely outcome of various possible courses of action. By noting the differing approaches to past problems in situations that closely parallel our own, and by assessing the results of each, we can predict, within limits, the likely consequences of any particular approach to current difficulties. I say "within limits" because I bear in mind Wordsworth's observation that "we see but darkly, even when we look behind us."[2] Therefore, while historical study, of its own, can never be an infallible guide for tomorrow and does not enable us to prophesy concerning the future, it can enable us to make knowledgeable and mature short-term predictions. More than two hundred years ago, in his address to the Virginia Convention, Patrick Henry made this same point: "I know of no way to judge the future," he said, "but by the past." Or, as the White Queen explained to Alice: "It's a poor sort of memory that only works backwards." In that light, then, history serves to equip us to deal intelligently and vigorously with the future.

Third, not only do we study the past in order to see something of the future, we study the past in order to understand the present. That is, we study the past because someone ought to be interested in (and committed to) finding out the truth about things. Because ideological truth, if it is truth, is not new, and because error is usually old and unoriginal, a thoughtful mastery of the debates of the past serves as a foundation for untangling and resolving contemporary quarrels. Most current philosophical and theological disagreements stem from presuppositions that reach far back into the history of ideas. In that light, Albert Einstein once said that he had only one original idea in his entire life. If true, the implications of that statement are profound. Regardless of how modern we think our problems are, and regardless of how novel we believe our stance toward them might be, the odds are that these arguments, or ones very much like them, have all been argued before, and in much the same way. A great deal of effort has already been expended in solving such problems, and a significant amount of valuable insight has already been expressed on "modern" issues. The ideological expertise of some of the finest minds of the past has been brought to bear on either the very problems that plague us today or on their near relatives. Thus, by schematizing the old debates we not only clarify the current ones, we also enjoy the inestimable privilege of encountering the formative thinkers who shaped the Western World. Of this tremendous deposit of wisdom the Pilgrim Theologian must make the fullest possible use. To do so is not only advisable, it is an inestimable privilege.

Finally, if for no other reason, we study history because it has entertainment value. Unlike some other academic pursuits, history has its own peculiar fascination. People everywhere seem to be buying it, reading it, writing it, and enjoying it. History affords both the excitement of discovery and the satisfaction of acquired mastery. Because of its character as a narrative social science, history can combine in an interesting fashion both the scientist's precision and the storyteller's art. The result of such a union frequently is captivating. Only the incorrigibly obtuse can fail to delight in Huizinga's graphic delineation of the harvest of medieval culture, or in Boswell's Johnson and Bainton's Luther. An almost unavoidable sense of reverence and respect attaches to fondling carefully a delicate four-hundred-year-old book, or to walking where one's grandfather and great-grandfather (or even their ancestors) walked and talked, lived and died. The sensitive mind is profoundly moved when it comes face to face with its own roots. The discovery of one's own spiritual heritage or intellectual pedigree is of supreme importance in helping to develop and to define one's identity. This link to the past, which history supplies, allows us also to move back across time and to traverse vast distances in order to experience, however momentarily, something of life in an ancient and otherwise irretrievable world. History is the closest thing to transcendence that most of us will ever enjoy.

But in this fascination and escape lies one of history's dangers. We are not called to live in the past, romantic though it might seem to us. Nor are we granted leave to sit idly by, wistfully longing for some previous age, allegedly golden. Whenever we do so, we have turned from history to nostalgia — and nostalgia is a failure of nerve. By it we flinch from a daunting present and shrink from an imposing future. Unless our study of history and the wisdom and entertainment it affords can be used to help us deal intelligently and vigorously with our present world, our study has degenerated from an academic discipline to mere sentimentality. Of that there is already enough.

These, then, are the reasons I tell my students we ought to study history. I also tell them that there is one thing better to do with history than to study it, and that is to make it. But precisely here, in making history, or even in changing it, we Christians have proven so ineffective. Others, the Marxists for example, have been able to exert a significant impact upon recent decades even though they promote a bankrupt ideology. We, who have been entrusted with the truth of the eternal gospel of God, and who have been empowered by him, have not. The reason is not far to find. As Lester De Koster explains, "[T]he significant, fateful distinction Marx drew between those who study history only to *understand* it, and those who understand it in order to *change* it, is an essentially Christian distinction, drawn long before Marx's time. Understanding as an *end in itself* . . . is an idolatry . . . If Marxists change history more . . . than do the children of those who once "turned the world upside down," it is because Christians have idolatrously *subordinated* changing history to understanding it, while the Marxists have it the other way around." [3]

That's it — beaten at our own game, injured with our own sword.

The Pilgrim Theologian must know more than history, but not less.

END NOTES

1 Russell Kirk, *The Conservative Constitution* (Washington:Regnery Gateway, 1990), p. 31.

2 William Wordsworth, *The Prelude*, III, pp. 482-483.

3 Lester De Koster, *Communism and Christian Faith* (Grand Rapids: Wm. B. Eerdmans Pub. Co., 1956), pp. 1, 2.

ESCHATOLOGY

"So will it be with the resurrection of the dead. The body that is sown is perishable, it is raised imperishable; it is sown in dishonor, it is raised in glory; it is sown in weakness, it is raised in power; it is sown a material body, it is raised a spiritual body."

1 Corinthians 15:42-44

". . . what we will be has not yet been made known. But we know that when He appears, we shall be like Him . . . Everyone who has this hope in Him purifies himself."

1 John 3:2-3

"Think of yourself just as a seed patiently wintering in the earth; waiting to come up a flower in the Gardener's good time, up into the real world, the real waking. I suppose that our whole present life, looked back on from there, will seem only a drowsy half-waking. We are here in the land of dreams. But cock-crow is coming. It is nearer now than when I began this letter."

C. S. Lewis

"The sages have a hundred maps to give
    That trace their crawling cosmos like a tree,
They rattle reason out through many a sieve
    That stores the sand and lets the gold go free.
And all these things are less than dust to me
    Because my name is Lazarus and I live."

G. K. Chesterton
"The Convert"

Seed Time and Harvest

Not long after my conversion, I was given, in rapid succession, J. Dwight Pentecost's *Things to Come*, Salem Kirban's *666*, and Hal Lindsey's *Late Great Planet Earth*, which I dutifully read cover-to-cover. Had I not been given C. S. Lewis's *Mere Christianity* earlier, I would have acquired, at the very outset, a radically distorted view of Christian life and thought. Except for one, my well-meaning spiritual mentors served to nourish only my taste for the sensational, not my new hunger for God and godliness. While even now I appreciate their zeal and their good intentions, I realize, in a way I did not (indeed could not) realize then, that their conception of Christian nurture and of eschatology were truncated and stifling. They apparently had never learned, and therefore could not impart to me, that eschatology is no beginner's subject. I know now that it is not. I sympathize, for example, with the Protestant reformers' reluctance to address Biblical texts like John's Apocalypse — a book upon which even Calvin himself refused to write a commentary and which both Luther and Zwingli (and St. Jerome before them) rejected as non-canonical.[1]

Evangelical theologians typically pursue their study of eschatology under one of two controlling images: they see it as analogous either to a railroad timetable or else to nature and to natural processes. While I (and the New Testament) generally prefer the latter, the books

I was given to read focused almost entirely upon the former. Nor is the choice insignificant. Very much depends upon the controlling images we employ. As a timetable devotee I was reading Matthew 24 and Revelation 6 as if they were tomorrow's newspaper headlines and reading the *New York Times* as if it were a biblical commentary by F. F. Bruce or B. F. Westcott.

Only later did I learn the hard and humbling lesson that virtually every generation in Christian history thought of itself as the last, and that in *every instance* they were wrong. How could I escape their fate?

Only later did I discover the changing face of Antichrist and the many different names from history that well-informed theologians had assigned him — Pope Julius, Napoleon, Adolf Hitler, and John Kennedy among them. Either those theologians were flatly mistaken or else the Evil One is very much like George Burns in the movie *Oh God!*: he can do any face, any voice.

Only later did I question (and then disavow) the facile identifications I had made between biblical motifs and texts, on the one hand, and current events, on the other. On what demonstrable basis, after all, did I so blithely assume that the political entity produced by United Nations fiat in the late 1940s was the very same entity as that created by God when He called Abram out of Ur millennia earlier, or that was crushed and dispersed by foreign powers in 70 AD? As Russell Kirk observed in a different context, "The twentieth-century democracy of Israel, with its secular parties and western parliamentary structure, bears no resemblance to the Kingdom or to post-exilic theocracy."[2] Don't get me wrong — I don't oppose the modern state of Israel. It is our best friend in that deeply troubled corner of the world, and we ought to support it vigorously and consistently. But eschatology has nothing to do with it.

I had overlooked the cryptic, almost cynical, nature of the answers given by Jesus to any question posed to Him about the timing of the eschaton. He told his questioners that the end would come when people were engrossed in buying and selling, eating and drinking, marrying and giving in marriage; and his listeners (not to mention some of his modern evangelical readers) seemed to act as if they had actually been told something. He would tell them that the end would come when there were earthquakes, wars, and rumors of wars

— a not too helpful reply given that in the two thousand years since He spoke only forty-four have been free of military combat of some sort, on the one hand, and that during those war-laden years we have witnessed thousands upon thousands of earthquakes. The language of theophany, I was slow to learn, is picturesque, not perspicuous. At other times Jesus became far less oblique: He told his questioners that "the kingdom of God is not coming with things that can be observed" (Luke 17:20). But they seemed not to get his point. At least once, He flatly told his listeners that He simply did not know (Matt. 24:36). Only the Father knows the time, Jesus told them, and concerning it the Father has said precisely nothing.

Timetables, in other words, are out. Global eschatology remains what it always has been, a mystery.

But some things about the eschaton can be known, if we know what to ask and how to ask it. As Aristotle once observed, he who would succeed must ask the right preliminary questions. In eschatology, I am convinced, those questions must be personal, not national and not global.

In short, I have taken a lesson from the emphases of economists like Nobel laureate F. A. Hayek[3] and applied it to the study of eschatology. I have deliberately chosen to focus my attention on the individual rather than on the collective. I have turned from macro-eschatology (God's plan for the nations and the world) to micro-eschatology (God's plan for individual people), not only because it is, in my view, a more profitable study, one more suitable for a theological pilgrimage, but because it is a subject upon which Scripture is more clear and accessible.[4] Young theologians, I am convinced, would be better served if they sought to master the Bible's teachings on personal destiny rather than global destiny. And, with regard to micro-eschatology, nature is a far better model than is a bus schedule.

When Paul, for example, explains the coming resurrection to the Corinthians, he resorts to agricultural imagery, to seeds planted in the ground now and to the coming harvest. What is planted (or buried) a material body is harvested (or resurrected) a spiritual one. Jesus does the same. When He teaches micro-eschatology, He also employs natural, or agricultural, images, such as farmers at work separating sheep from goats and wheat from chaff. Even when He addresses

Himself to macro-eschatology, nature images predominate, as when He introduces lessons drawn from fig trees or from the atmospheric conditions that precede a storm.

In that sense, because nature is a fertile source of images and analogies, it can be a useful means of prophetic pedagogy. It also can help to decipher some of the more puzzling micro-eschatological phenomena in Scripture. One such puzzling detail concerning which nature can be an aid actually occurs at least three times in the New Testament: why Mary could not recognize the resurrected Jesus while standing at His empty tomb; why the disciples, fishing from their boat, could not recognize the resurrected Jesus, beckoning them from the nearby shore; and why the disciples on the road to Emmaus could not recognize the resurrected Jesus, the very man about whom they were speaking and to whom they spoke.

Imagine, if you will, a caterpillar and a butterfly, one crawling, the other perched, upon the same twig. Even had he a mind able to do so, the caterpillar would not recognize in his winged companion the same friend with whom he used to share a tasty leaf. The transformation wrought in the cocoon would have masked his friend's true identity. Nor would the caterpillar recognize in his companion his own destiny, even though it stood before his very eyes in all its Monarch splendor. But something in the way that butterfly moved, or something in the way it nibbled at its food in the bright sunlight would stir the caterpillar deeply, would make his heart burn within him. It would awaken the memory of twigs he'd travelled and leaves he'd tasted in the past, and of those with whom he'd shared summer days. The welcome and revered image of his old friend's homely, wormlike countenance would cross his mind, and for an instant, for one brief but electric moment, charged with expectation and softened by nostalgia, he would catch a glimpse of both past and future, and he would understand.

But moments of such transcending significance and insight are rare. Only the keen-sighted or the visionary among us can see the seed that once was in the rose that now is. In the oak trees towering above them they can see the destiny of humble acorns lying in the dirt. They see in the green stalks of corn that sway in the breezes of a warm August morning, while they stand in an Indiana cornfield that fills their vision on every side all the way to the horizon, the very same kernels they buried in the earth just months before. And if, like the caterpillar, they are blessed with a moment of insight, they will see their own destiny. They will learn what graveyards really are: not long lines of weathered headstones standing as silent testimonials to broken dreams or to separation without remedy, but rows and rows of planted seeds, awaiting the harvest of the last day. They will understand that what is harvested far exceeds that which they laid in the ground. They will see that caterpillar and butterfly, acorn and oak, kernel and stalk, bulb and tulip, and egg and rooster, are merely two stages in the development of the same life. They will see that the transformation wrought in the unseen darkness behind the veil of death is so magnificent that what they themselves will become is hardly recognizable in what they now are.[5]

But they have a clue: they know that they shall be like Christ. And they know that some have actually seen the resurrected Jesus and have left behind an account of that amazing sight. Then, the next time they read the inspired description of the awesome Christ in John's vision, they will understand why even Jesus's best friends did not recognize Him at first. And they will catch a glimpse, at the same time, of their own Monarch destiny.

And what will that world be like?

I don't know. But I imagine it will be as startlingly and breathtakingly different from the one we now enjoy as the one we now enjoy is from the dark wetness of the womb we once inhabited, or as the brilliant blue skies and fresh warm breezes in which the violets now bloom are different from the dirt and darkness of the flower bed from which they arose.

End Notes

1   See W. P. Stephens, *The Theology of Huldrych Zwingli* (Oxford: Oxford University Press, 1986), p. 56.

2   Russell Kirk, *The Roots of American Order* (La Salle, IL: Open Court, 1974), p. 20.

3   For a brief introduction to Hayek's economic principles in this regard, see F. A. Hayek, *The Fatal Conceit: The Errors of Socialism* (Chicago: University of Chicago Press, 1989), pp. 94-105.

4   I am advocating an alteration in emphasis, not a full-scale rejection of one sort of eschatology for another. My intention in doing so is threefold. First, I want the young theologian to gain an appreciation for eschatology as a study of God's faithfulness to His promises, not as a dazzling display of God's skill in prediction. Second, I am concerned to preserve a proper emphasis upon the ethical injunctions that invariably attach to God's promises, a consideration that drives us to contemplate the quality of our own Christianity (and eschatology) in social and spiritual categories, not in the disputed details of prophetic sequence or in the title deeds to Middle Eastern real estate. Not without good cause does the Bible consistently couple eschatology with exhortations to purity. Third, I want to spare the young theologians hours of endless wrangling about the nature of the millennium and the time of the rapture, which, though often enjoyable, are equally as often largely unprofitable. By advocating this alteration in emphasis, however, I am not saying that macro-eschatological concerns and categories are unimportant or that they are unrelated to personal eschatology or spirituality. They most assuredly are not. But macro-eschatology is not a beginner's subject.

5   They also will learn something of what Wordsworth (in "Strange Fits of Passion Have I Known") could have learned on his way to Lucy's cottage but did not learn until much later: just as, in the natural order of things, the rising of the sun implies its setting; just as the bloom of the flower implies its fading; and just as birth implies death; even so does the falling of leaves in autumn imply their reappearance in spring. Death, in that light, implies resurrection.

For similar treatments of this theme, see H. B. Swete, *The Life of the World to Come* (London: S.P.C.K., 1919), ch. 5, especially pp. 112-114; C. S. Lewis, "The Weight of Glory" in *The Weight of Glory and Other Addresses* (New York: Macmillan, 1980); and C. S. Lewis, *Miracles* (New York: Macmillan, 1947/1960), ch. 16, especially p. 163.

"It is absolutely safe to say that, if you meet somebody who claims not to believe in evolution, that person is ignorant, stupid, or insane.

RICHARD DAWKINS, OXFORD ZOOLOGIST
in The Blind Watchmaker

Between Jerusalem and the Laboratory: A Theologian Looks at Science

We live in but one world. Science and theology are united in that they both seek to understand that one world and to explain it. They do so according to their own respective method (or methods) of knowing. In that sense, both science and theology are a hermeneutic, or a way of interpreting, the world around us. Because we have but one world to interpret, and not a scientific universe along side a theological universe, only one full and correct answer exists for any well-formed question relating to it. A well-formed question is one that seeks, and helps to make possible, an answer that is both full (that is, comprehensive) and true (that is, accurate). The answer to a well-conceived question, whatever that answer might be, is correct because it comports fully with reality. Answers that do not comport fully with reality are at least partly inadequate, if not flatly wrong. An ill-formed question is one that makes comprehensive and accurate answers not only more difficult to find than they need to be, but might actually make them impossible, as do modern scientific questions, which seek only the material causes to physical phenomena. But as Aristotle observed long ago, the one who would succeed in any intellectual pursuit must ask the right preliminary questions. Questions arising from metaphysical materialism are "the right preliminary questions" only if matter is all that is, or only if matter is all that matters, two propositions that cannot be demonstrated, indeed that are patently false.

The instances where scientists and theologians agree in their description of that one reality which we all inhabit are many and varied. But they are not my concern. Rather, I intend to focus attention on those places (they too are numerous) where scientists and theologians diverge. I do so in order to offer some guidance on adjudicating between the respective truth claims of science and theology and in order to reduce the scope of their future disagreement, as well as its attendant animosity. In the process, I intend to direct my criticisms primarily toward the scientists rather than the theologians. I do so precisely because I am not a scientist. That is, if scientists are to be undeceived about their own shortcomings or blindspots it probably will be because someone who did not share those blindspots was able to point them out. That is my intention: I want to suggest to the scientists that, at least to some outsiders, they sometimes appear narrowly informed, unteachable, and as dogmatic as any ecclesiastical or political inquisition could ever hope to be. I leave it to others to identify for the theologians just what the theologians cannot see and where they fail. Because I do not wish to hold the reader in suspense, much less to be vague or disingenuous, I tell you now that I think much of the adjustment and retrenchment in the sometimes heated dialogue between scientists and theologians needs to be done by the scientists, and that much of the error and unteachability in this dialogue seems to circle around the laboratory and not the seminary. The burden of this essay, therefore, is to explain why I think as I do. I offer but four observations, observations that are, at the same time, both caveats and pleas.

First, the history of both science and theology as intellectual disciplines tends to make me significantly more skeptical about the allegedly secure answers offered by the scientists than I am about those offered by the theologians. That is, science seems a far more fickle pursuit than theology, especially when viewed over time. While Christian orthodoxy seems to have remained stable over two millennia, and while the constant refinement of Christian tenets in the crucible of hard reality seems not to have required any fundamental reorientation in orthodoxy,[1] the record of science is far different. The constant testing of fundamental scientific beliefs has yielded a long series of significant reorientations, some so far reaching as to topple many, sometimes most, of the supporting pillars of any and every previous (and ardently held) scientific world view. The post-Einsteinian worldview is beginning to succeed the Einsteinian, which succeeded the Newtonian, which succeeded the Copernican, which succeeded the Ptolemaic, which succeeded I know not what. What shall succeed the post-Einsteinian (and what shall succeed *that*) we can only guess. If the history of science is a guide to its future, we can be confident something shall and that, whatever it is, it shall depart quite noticeably from its antecedents both near and far. As Austin Farrer once wryly observed, cosmological theories have a short life nowadays.

But not so the Apostles' Creed, which, though it has grown over time, has never required anything resembling a fundamental overhaul, much less several. Liberal theologians of every age (aided by the not inconsiderable efforts of non-Christian thinkers of all sorts) have tried to argue differently and have tried to put orthodoxy under siege. But their dissenting and often idiosyncratic schools of thought themselves have proved transitory and have passed into deserved obscurity. But not the creed. In other words, theological orthodoxy, unlike its several scientific counterparts, has undergone centuries of analysis and assault and survived largely and widely intact. Christian orthodoxy has successfully sustained meticulous scrutiny by both its friends and its enemies and yet has shown itself, and continues to show itself, sufficient to many of the most brilliant minds in history, even over a period of centuries, a claim no scientific explanation of reality can yet make. The scientists in every age, I imagine, suppose they can escape, indeed suppose they have escaped, the fate of their predecessors. They fancy they shall avoid being greatly transcended, though none has yet managed the trick. The face of scientific orthodoxy seems to have a nose of wax.

The transitoriness of scientific speculation and the uniformity and staying power of theological orthodoxy often get hidden behind both the wide diversity of theological beliefs prevalent at any one moment in time, on the one hand, and the absence of many public indications of division within the scientific community, on the other. Widespread theological disagreement seems obvious to the man on the street, who sees the Presbyterian church, the Baptist church, and the Roman

Catholic church all standing tall and serene on their respective street corners, their spires rising toward the heavens. What the man on the street does not see is the underlying unity of the Presbyterians, the Baptists, and the Catholics (to name but a few). He does not readily recognize their common belief in — and devotion to — the same God, the same Christ, the same creed, the same salvation. Nor does the man on the street see the various schools of thought in science, which normally do not erect edifices of difference on tree-shaded side streets in every city and village in the free world. He does not see hundreds, indeed thousands, of buildings (or television programs, for that matter), dedicated to Newtonian or Ptolemaic theories, standing next to the edifices of post-Einsteinianism. Unlike their ecclesiastical counterparts, those Newtonian and Ptolemaic buildings were rarely ever built, and are not now being built, because the scientific world views they represent have been so fully overthrown that they are consigned almost entirely to the dustbin of history. This is not to say that no valuable or enduring elements from within these systems have survived the collapse of the system from which they emerged; it does mean that those systems have been greatly and widely transcended.

Here is my point: While a cross section of views at any one moment yields more agreement among the scientists of that age than among the theologians, a cross section taken over time yields the opposite result, and that result, I argue, is more significant because it reveals both the fundamental staying power of the theological interpretation of the world and the (to date) transitory nature of scientific speculation. Science does not speak with one voice, especially over time. That fact not withstanding, science still seems to me far less likely to take any cues[2] from theology about in which direction to proceed than theology is to take advice from science, which might help explain the transitoriness of the one and the stability of the other. So also might the fact that, unlike nature, God wills to be understood and actively reveals Himself to us.

We apparently are not near the end of scientific intellection, though we are closer now than when Aristotle or Galileo walked among us. We do not know where the next grand turning in the road of scientific learning will lead us, or when it will come, any more than did Ptolemy, Newton, or Einstein. We ought, as a result, to be far more hesitant than we have been to identify scientific results as final. If you contend that scientists do not treat scientific results as final, I simply point to the theory of evolution, which gets treated almost universally not as theory but as established and unassailable fact requiring, at most, not proof, only further nuance. The epigraph by Richard Dawkins, which heads this essay, is a telling case in point, and can be multiplied *many thousands of times*, both in print and in the classroom. It seems to me, Dawkins' arrogance aside, that we ought to be far more wary of Darwin and his hide-bound modern disciples than we now are, because even though those followers of Darwin now admit that Darwin was not entirely right, they too often refuse to admit that Darwin's religious critics are not entirely wrong. Or, to make the point from a different science, one of the positive effects of quantum theory on the dialogue between theology and science seems to be the increasing awareness we gain from it that virtually no physical or geometrical picture of scientific phenomena is wholly accurate, even though such notions or paradigms were (and still are) widely and enthusiastically set forth, whether as models or as heuristic devices. We need to be more measured in the confidence we place in the scientist and in our estimate of what exactly the scientist has actually accomplished.

Second, because scientists are human beings, and because human beings tend to resist the overthrow of their most cherished beliefs, scientific theories, once accepted, are often exceedingly difficult to supersede. The shameful treatment of Pierre Duhem at the hands of his institutional superiors is a well known case in point. All too often, the new, even when it carries great weight of evidence, gets routinely derided as outlandish. That scientists are intellectually conservative, of course, is good. Their conservatism helps protect them from the multiple embarrassments of intellectual trendiness. But that scientists are unduly entrenched, when they are, is lamentable. That entrenchment reveals that scientists sometimes are, like the rest of us, resolutely unteachable. The Dawkins epigraph above is but one example of the entrenchment, perhaps even intellectual bigotry, about which I speak. Scientists who think in that fashion seem to me to be what one dictionary defined as "proof-proof:" the state of mind of one upon whom contrary evidence and argument have no persuasive effect, regardless of their strength. I am not alone in this observation, of course. Many writers, Kuhn and Laudan among them, have shown how dogmatism — yes, dogmatism — characterizes the periods of what we might call *normal* science. Whether we want to admit it or not, there is a remarkably comprehensive scientific orthodoxy to which scientists must subscribe if they want to get a job, get a promotion, get a research grant, get tenured, or get published. If they resist, they get forgotten.

Given how changeable previous scientific worldviews have been, one wonders how chimerical they would have proven without this dogmatism. I am not here debating the relative merits or weaknesses of dogmatism; I simply say that scientists are by no means free from it and should not be treated as if they were, or permitted to speak and act as if dogmatism were a characteristic only, or even primarily, of theologians.

Third, scientists often fail to admit, sometimes even to recognize, that so many of the issues and findings of science are neither purely scientific nor genuinely empirical. Because all empirical endeavors build upon, and proceed according to, various presuppositions, and because those presuppositions and procedures are inescapably philosophical, no scientist and no scientific procedure is truly philosophy-free. Empiricism and the empiricalist procedures that arise from it are philosophy-laden worldviews and techniques, and not necessarily the best. If ideas have consequences, and if (as some philosophers strongly argue) empiricism and empiricalism are highly suspect, perhaps even greatly flawed, then scientists are likely to be misled if they apply these notions uncritically to their work. To put a point on it, if, as some scientists insist, real science is truly empirical and reduces only to empirical methods and to the conclusions reached by using them, then there is no real science, because the theory-independent observation, analysis, and conclusions needed to establish such empirical premises are simply not possible. Because we are not, none of us, presupposition-free, and because (despite much contrary insistence) scientific theories often deal with the unobserved and the unobservable, the laboratory is no philosophy- or theology-free zone. Scientific methods and conclusions cannot be purely empirical because the unavoidable philosophical and theological underpinnings upon which those scientific methods rely are not the result of those allegedly empirical methods.

Put another way, the claim to objectivity and empiricality falls down on both sides — on the side of the scientist and on the side of science. When eating their curry, many people like to build for it a nest of rice. To employ a more American image, people like to mold a bowl in their mashed potatoes in order to hold their gravy. Science, it seems to me, has its nest, its bowl. Science always has its philosophical and theological underpinnings; physics always has its metaphysics — always.[3] To declare science a philosophy-free zone is to have a philosophy; to declare science a procedurally agnostic or atheistic endeavor is to have a theology; to claim that science ought to be value-free is to make a value statement. The question is never whether or not the scientist in a laboratory has a philosophy, a theology, or an ethic when doing scientific work; the question is whether or not the philosophy, the theology, and the ethic the scientist has are any good and are worth having. This problem they cannot escape.

Even in the pursuit of something as fundamental as self-definition, science alone is utterly insufficient. To the question "What is the proper definition of science?" one can give only a philosophical (and, by extension, theological) answer because the question itself presupposes and requires a vantage point from outside science. Because we cannot tell who are the scientists and who are not until we know what science itself is, one cannot answer this question, as scientists too often do, by resorting to the tautology that science is that which is done by the scientist. The question "What is science?" is a question about science, not a question of science. Scientists want, indeed claim, to be empirical. But please note: "empirical" is a philosophical category. Without the aid of the humanities, science cannot even identify itself, much less justify, or even invent, its procedures.

To make the point in a different direction, science is not theology-free, and that is so precisely because science intentionally operates according to a procedural agnosticism, if not procedural atheism. That is, science operates as if God cannot be known or else as if He were altogether irrelevant, if not entirely absent. By its means and its conclusions, science implicitly, perhaps even explicitly, denies that Christ is Lord of the universe, an inescapably theological denial. What I, as a theologian, want to tell my scientific colleagues is that, as Lord of the universe and all that is within it, Christ is not something *in addition* to science, He is Someone *in relation* to it. To operate as if He were utterly irrelevant to the laboratory is to answer, probably without careful analysis and theological acumen, the question raised long ago in the gospels: "What think ye of Christ?" Because Christ is foundational to the universe, He is foundational to science. As Thomas Torrance once explained to me,

> . . . the countries of the Far East and of the Southern Hemisphere want our science and technology, but they have no doctrine of creation. They do not realize that science and technology rest upon, indeed arise from, Christian foundations. This is true both historically and epistemologically. We must show them that it is the Creator God himself who stands behind everything, and that he provides the rational ground upon which the various sciences rest, as well as the world those sciences unlock and help to tame. Theology and technology come as a pair. We must be quite firm about both this and their function in serving and respecting the integrity of nature.[4]

Like it or not, the systematic and procedural denial, not to say the intended destruction, of metaphysics and of theology, is the death of scientific truth, if for no other reason than that it posits a dual or dichotomized universe, which we noted at the outset was untrue. Answers to questions predicated upon that same bifurcated basis, while they are perhaps true as far as they go, do not go all the way, and are not the whole truth.

Perhaps an illustration will serve. No physicist today can reckon with miracles and interventions from outside the material order, or with interventions that break that order open. No theory they devise, no answer they propose, permits such ideas or recognizes such data, even though such data and ideas might be absolutely and comprehensively true. That analytical inability reveals the limitations, indeed the willful blindness, of modern physics. Modern physics does not reveal the limitations of God and his actions, much less God's non-existence or irrelevance, assumptions implicit in scientific method as now understood and practiced. God, if we need to be reminded, works in perfect freedom, and not according to the Kant-Laplace theory of determinedness, or to any of its current or future descendants.

Let me put it more graphically: any intellectual endeavor in which theology is segregated from the other disciplines and relegated to an intellectual ghetto is an instance of Jim Crow come again to the college campus because it explicitly asserts that the best intellectual paradigm is not well-informed academic integration but some framework of "separate but equal," which, as we learned in the old South, meant separate but unequal, not because of actual inferiority, but because of bigotry. By acting as if God Himself were irrelevant to the universe He has made and to our understanding of it, scientists, in effect, practice "disciplinism," a widespread form of intellectual bigotry whereby the research and discoveries of other scholars are systematically disregarded simply because those scholars are members of another discipline. The Queen of the Sciences has been banished to the back of the bus by her own bigoted descendants. The fool has said in his heart that there is no God, and the scientist permits himself to operate as if the fool were right.

Science is not an autonomous set of empirical disciplines. Nothing about science properly, or actually, prevents philosophical or theological concepts from entering into it. Science, like all intellectual disciplines, ought not to conduct its business in an imaginary, air-tight compartment, isolated from all other strivings of the human mind after knowledge. Because too many scientists have cut themselves off from those other strivings, they condemn themselves to discovering all on their own many things already widely known by others. For example, even though such ideas appeared new and revolutionary to some of the unphilosophical practitioners of science, most of Mach's notions were already standard fare in the writings of a number of earlier philosophers. The high price some scientists pay for their intellectual isolationism and prejudice is that they must repeatedly reinvent the intellectual wheel.

But there's more to theology in science than procedural agnosticism and atheism. Our ape ancestors are treated with immense respect, even toadying homage, as the secular Adam and Eve. No attacks upon their status, much less their existence, are tolerated. Read Dawkins' epigraph again. Not to do obeisance to the fossil remains of ancient animals ranks as scientific sacrilege, as scientific heresy. Religion, albeit pagan, has come to the laboratory, and the allegedly secular scientist has become its new high priest.

Furthermore, many of those very scientists who insist on divorcing religion from science seem sometimes especially eager to use their science as a basis for theological (or at least extra-scientific) pronouncements. The literature of science is replete with anti-theistic language and conclusions: The universe was not designed; the universe has no purpose; human beings result from random and mindless natural processes, or so we are repeatedly told.

Put another way, to the adoration of God and of virtue, some moderns have added the adoration of science (or at least what goes by that name). But you cannot deify the scientific method without at the same time devaluing or debasing both theology (the human understanding and application of revelation) and philosophy (the human understanding and application of reason). Many scientists, therefore, without meaning to do so, undermine our only sources of morality and freedom: God and reason. They do so by believing, writing and teaching that only those things that are testable under controlled laboratory conditions qualify as hard knowledge; all else is merely opinion. But even a moment's reflection reveals that if every question of morality, of politics, of philosophy, and of theology is a matter of mere untestable opinion, they can be settled only by force, not by reason. In that way (and in others) scientists sometime lead us to tyranny. Fascism and pseudo-liberalism are the not-too-distant offspring of modern man's widespread belief that science alone is trustworthy and that whatever lies beyond its pale is little more and little else than irrational prejudice, unsubstantiatable conjecture, and transitory emotion incapable of reasoned support. This vision of life most modern persons learned in the science classroom. Too often scientists teach and write as if the only real options available to us are science or mysticism, empiricism or bias, fact or feeling.

Simply because no test tube yields a "should" or an "ought," "should" and "ought" are not thereby banished or made suspect; science is. Moral questions — questions about right and wrong or good and bad — cannot be answered (or even raised) by the scientific methods now prevalent in either the natural or the social sciences. That does not mean, however, that they cannot be answered, have not been answered, or have no answers. It means only that with regard to the diagnostic and fundamental questions of life, science is impotent, though dangerous. The one who has not learned to ask, much less to answer, the fundamental questions of life, is indeed no man at all, but still a child, still benighted. To answer such questions, even to raise them, science is powerless. Consequently, while technical schools and scientific laboratories are important and laudable things, to advertise them as colleges or universities, or to say that those who have passed through them are truly educated men and women, is a lie.

To put the point differently, God is the Lord of the entire world of knowledge, including science and technology. Science and technology that are atheistic in both conception and conduct, that are consciously cut loose from all formal considerations about God and morality, are not your dream come true; they are your worst nightmare. To utilize science and technology wisely or else to become their victims, that is the choice before us. But the wisdom that saves us from our science and technology is no commodity derived from either of them or from both. To paraphrase something C. S. Lewis said in another context, science ceases to be a demon only when it ceases to be a god. It can never cease until it figures out a way to let God be God, even in the laboratory.

Fourth, we ought to be more skeptical than we are both of scientific taxonomy and of the translation of the world outside our heads into numbers. That is, scientists do not simply deal with the world as they find it, they manipulate that world into words of their own choosing, into categories of their own making, into experiments of their own devising, and into numbers. Forcing a creature into one or more categories based upon our intellectual manipulations and speculations regarding its body pattern and parts, or upon our understanding of its physical makeup and upon our conjectures regarding its biological descent, is at least partly arbitrary, partly subjective. Such categories, though helpful and serviceable, are man-made. They unintentionally, and sometimes unwittingly, collapse the distinction between what we discover and what we invent. While the beings that populate such categories most emphatically do exist, the families, orders, classes and phyla into which we have pigeon-holed them do not. Such pigeon-holings are a taxonomist's useful fiction, but *do not exist outside the taxonomist's mind*. That is, while those taxonomical categories are constructs based upon careful observation, they are constructs nevertheless. Of course, I am not saying anything so silly as that there exist no genuine and recognizable differences between a dog and a man, or that *dog* and *man* are useless fictions devoid of all external reference or reality. But let us not too quickly or uncritically identify *useful* as *true* or as *real*, categories that in many cases and ways are quite different.

Yet, not only are we required to accept the taxonomist's scheme of classification as both real and true, we are required to accept that the occupants of these various man-made categories are linked by a long series of non-living intermediate creatures (also duly classified and arranged), most of whom are not found to exist anywhere in the fossil record, a radically incomplete record we interpret according to the taxonomical grid provided for us. (The circularity of this procedure seems to go unnoticed and unremarked.) Furthermore, we are also required to believe that all the seemingly discontinuous and taxonomically divisible groups now alive are the descendants of a common ancestor, another phantom of which (or of whom) we have no direct evidence. Please note that *ancestor* and *descendant* are part of a taxonomical scheme, and are no less so than is *phantom*, a word from which my scientist readers would naturally recoil. Their own language, the scientists must remember, is the source of great recoil as well. It rarely seems to occur to some scientists that the rapid evolutionary branchings posited in some theories are but a euphemism for mystical scientific leaps, though they are called by other names, such as Stephen Jay Gould's *punctuated equilibrium*. Of such leaps I am more than a little skeptical.

Further, not only is taxonomical classification significantly theory laden, it is context dependent and subtly subjective. That which we classify as the observed in one case fails to be so classified in another, even though the thing itself is the same. That is, what is foreground and what is background vary according to the judgment of the observer, an observer who is never context-free or presuppositionless. Thus, scientists are driven back, whether they acknowledge it or not, upon the problem "What is context and what is content?", the answer to which seems to vary from situation to situation depending upon the experimenter and the experiment, even though the aggregation of things involved might be basically the same. Nor are the experiments themselves pristinely empirical and objective, for experiments are highly stylized sets of phenomena, sets from which as many variables as possible have been artificially eliminated by the will and work of the experimenter, however well or however poorly. Of course, I am not saying that the data yielded by such experimentation are therefore untrue, only that they are not pristine. In other words, some scientists need frequently to be reminded of the significantly non-literal and pragmatic nature of their experiments, of their theories, and of the language in which those experiments and theories are conceived and articulated.

Like taxonomy, quantification might itself be a movement away from the world around us, not into it. The translation of things into numbers is, after all, a translation. Neither the words nor the numbers in scientific theories are complete and exact representations of the constitution and behavior of the universe, much less are they the things themselves which they are intended to describe in words or embody in numbers and formulae. Newton had his numbers; Einstein had his; post-Einsteinians have theirs. Newton's and Einstein's formulae worked (so to speak) and were the basis for considerable correct prediction regarding natural phenomena. Nevertheless, on many important points, Newton and Einstein were also quite wrong, something from which their seemingly correct numbers did not and could not save them. I am not reluctant to think that the same fate awaits many of their scientific descendants.

The classification of physical phenomena as suitable and useable scientific data, the arrangement of that data into groups, the translation of that data into numbers, the manipulation of those numbers via computation, and the transformation of the results of that computation into more data and new conclusions are all guided by philosophical deliberations that are prior to and apart from science's alleged empirical nature and militate against it, all of which ought to cause us to hold science's supposedly assured results with less assurance. Judging from the philosophical and theological naiveté of most of the scientists with whom I have ever spoken, those intellectual deliberations might not have been deliberations at all, but merely the unexamined and unacknowledged a priori assumptions of a mind utterly untrained in a number of difficult but acutely relevant fields throughout the humanities.

The related assertion that science is measurement is, of course, a philosophical assertion, an assertion that is flatly unprovable. Indeed, as even a moment's reflection will demonstrate, because it is not itself measurable, this assertion is unscientific on its own terms. It is, in fact, autophagic — it eats itself up. Nor can we prove this assertion by invoking the principle of prediction and thereby assert that a scientific hypothesis is true if it can be shown accurately and successfully to predict the action of physical phenomena. The principle of prediction, while clearly important and serviceable, is at least as closely related to pragmatism as to truth. That is, to be able to predict more accurately than all other theories means only that one's theory is pragmatically preferable, not that it is necessarily true. We must remember that false, or partly false, theories have demonstrated impressive powers of prediction in the past. The ancient Babylonian astronomers, for example, by no means shabby forecasters, were working from premises and principles quite off the mark. In other words, while prediction seems to be a necessary attribute of a true scientific theory, it must not be considered a sufficient attribute. Prediction is not proof, no matter how impressive it seems. Too many scientists, nevertheless, still think, write, argue, and teach as if accurate prediction demonstrated truth. How many times this has been done, is being done, and shall continue to be done, only God knows. But it seems not at all likely to stop. Or, to make the case in a different direction, if prediction were really the reliable indicator of truth that some think it to be, then physics itself, which has an abysmal record of prediction with regard to some individual entities, would be radically undermined. Furthermore, as clear thinking philosophers and theologians understand, pragmatic preference is an utterly insufficient basis for determining the virtue of an action. If pragmatic preference is an exploded mode of justification in ethics, I am inclined to regard it as such in scientific epistemology. Its epistemological failures are not magically eradicated simply because we now concern ourselves with a laboratory.

Those, at any rate, are my observations and caveats. That is how the laboratory looks from the seminary, or at least to this member of it. Having watched many of them in action, I think the scientists would be better served (and would serve better) if they were more humble and more eclectic in pursuit of their worthy enterprise. I should hope that when they do their work the scientists would listen at least as much to those outside the laboratory as they would like those outside the laboratory to listen to them. This, after all, is the golden rule of scholarship.

Finally, though it is clearly beyond both my intention and my competence to dictate to the scientists exactly how their jobs ought to be conducted and in what specific direction they ought to proceed, let me offer but one outsider's opinion, an opinion motivated by sincere goodwill for my laboratory colleagues. I believe that what we need now is not something akin to an aimless collection of more data, but research (of every sort) directed by principles, illumined by ideas. Those guiding principles and those illuminating ideas must, by their very nature, come to science from outside science, at least until we figure out how science ought to be restructured and redefined in order to avoid its current myopia. Science, to be kept serviceable and humane, must be kept humble and teachable. And it must acknowledge its debts, debts it always has.

To the question "Is science enough?" the answer is emphatically "No."

End Notes

1   Creeds are not imposed by simple ecclesiastical fiat. Instead, like scientific definitions in other branches of knowledge, creeds typically undergo what might roughly be described as a five stage development: observation, reflection, articulation, testing, and confirmation or rejection. In the first stage, Christian thinkers examine carefully the text of Scripture (that is, the content of revelation) and the course of their own and others' experience of living in agreement with Scripture, at least as they understand it. Second, they reflect deeply and carefully upon what they have observed, in order to grasp its true significance. Because they must not be content with an inarticulate devotion, to this perceived significance and to their conclusions concerning it, they naturally try to give thoughtful and precise expression. Their newly formulated ideas are then submitted to testing in the twin crucibles of life and thought to see if those ideas can withstand the rough and tumble of genuine human experience and the rigors of systematic intellectual scrutiny. If they cannot, they are rejected, or else modified and tried again. In this informal but ef-

fective way, the Church has invested decades, even centuries, in capturing in precise creedal form the tremendous truths revealed in the historical events connected with Jesus of Nazareth. Of course, this is not to say that creeds have nothing to do with the pronouncements of bishops and councils; they often do. But creeds typically find their roots elsewhere, in revelation and in the life and thought of the church. This is especially true of the Apostles' Creed, which though at some points is still controverted, has been tested by long experience and careful, repeated reflection upon that experience in the light of Scripture and reason. Furthermore, because the Apostles' Creed has grown out of centuries of biblical exegesis, human experience, and reflection, it continues to be both relevant and reliable. It continues to ring true because, like all good theology, it is deeply rooted in divine revelation, on the one hand, and human reason and reality, on the other.

2   What might be the precise nature and content of such cues I cannot now say. How philosophy and theology ought ideally to be introduced into the sciences is a question the answering of which might require a radically new way of doing science. That I myself am currently unable to supply this new paradigm is neither an embarrassment to me nor a refutation of my claim that it might be needed. I offer only an analogy, drawn from criminology. When a detective attempts to solve a crime, he not only searches for clues, he invents hypotheses. In this search and invention, the detective has this great advantage: He knows he is deciphering not some random occurrence, but tracking the work of a mind. Knowing this, the detective suitably modifies the character of his hypotheses and alters both the nature and focus of his search for clues, as well as his definition of what might or might not be relevant data. Human criminals, for example, unlike mindless and lifeless matter, have discernible motives and sometimes concoct false alibis in order to cover their tracks. In short, they leave clues of a very distinctive sort. The scientist, by the same token, if he were to entertain the God factor in his laboratory and decide to trace the workings of Infinite Mind rather than of mindless matter, might need to alter what he considers the boundaries of acceptable hypothesis, what he admits as relevant data, how he forms and executes his experiments, how he draws and articulates his conclusions, and what he imagines constitutes a convincing proof or refutation.

3   I am not saying that all physicists must or do have the same metaphysic, only that while they are doing their work they cannot avoid having one and applying it.

4 Michael Bauman, *Roundtable: Conversations with European Theologians* (Grand Rapids: Baker, 1990), p. 115.

EPILOGUE

"The central myth of the sixties was that [its] wretched excess was really a serious quest for new values."

GEORGE WILL

The Chronicle of an Undeception

I. The Tragic Vision of Life

I confess to believing at one time or another nearly all the pervasive and persistent fantasies of the sixties. In the words of Joni Mitchell's anthem for the Woodstock nation, I thought all I had to do was "get back to the land to set my soul free." I thought that flowers had power, that love could be free, and that the system was to blame. By 1968, I had the whole world figured out. I knew the cause of every evil — America — and I knew the solution to every problem — freedom and tolerance.

If truth be told, of course, I knew nothing, at least nothing worth knowing. I knew how to posture, but not how to stand. I knew how to protest, but not how to protect. I knew how to work up an impressive case of moral outrage, but I didn't know morality. I knew about peace, but I didn't know enough to fight for it. I knew about self-indulgence, self-preservation, self-esteem, and self-expression, but I didn't know about self-sacrifice and self-control.

Worse still, I didn't even know myself. I didn't know what Socrates knew about me — that I entered this world in a state of total and seamless ignorance, and that my ignorance could never be breached as long I remained blissfully unaware of it. I didn't know what St. Augustine knew about me — that the well of my soul was poisoned, and that whatever was down in the well would come up in the bucket. St. Augustine also knew this about my soul: No matter how hard it tried, no matter where it looked, it could never find its rest anywhere but in God. I didn't know what Edmund Burke knew about me — that no government could fix what ailed me, either by the things it did or by the things it did not. The most any state could do was to help protect me from myself and from others. Most importantly, however, I didn't know that I was Everyman. When I learned that, I stopped being a liberal.

Like almost all dissidents of my generation, I was a protestor without a plan and a visionary without a vision. I had not yet learned that you see only what you are able to see, and I was able to see only the egalitarian, relativistic, self-gratifying, superstitions of the secular, wayward, left. Please do not think that this was simply a case of prelapsarian innocence. It was not. It was ignorance and it was evil, although I would have denied it at the time.

Only slowly did I come to understand that my fellow dissidents and I had taken for ourselves the easiest and least productive of all tasks, that of denigrator. And only slowly did I come to understand that to destroy is easy, that to build is hard, and that to preserve is hardest of all.

But it was worse even than that, because my fellow dissidents and I were blind to the most obvious truths, especially to what Russell Kirk and others have called the tragic vision of life — the profound realization that evil is not something "out there," it is something "in here." The tragic vision of life arises from the fact that we are flawed — deeply, desperately, tragically flawed — and we cannot be trusted. We are broken at the heart; our defect is life wide and soul deep. Though we are capable of reason, because of our selfish passions and our moral weaknesses we are rarely reasonable. We ourselves are what is chiefly wrong with the world. We are this planet's most malignant and enduring ailment. We have our dignity, to be sure, but we have our horror as well. I can tell you this: I did not wake up until I met the enemy face to face. I met him in the mirror. We all do.

I had to learn to stare squarely into that face in the mirror, into the face of hard, fallen reality, and not to flinch. I did not, in fact I could not, comprehend the tragic vision of life until I learned that the problem of the human heart is at the heart of the human problem. Once I examined with care and honesty the habits of my own heart and those of my dissident friends, I learned that C. S. Lewis was right: to be one of the sons of Adam or the daughters of Eve is both glory enough to raise the head of the lowest beggar and shame enough to lower the head of the highest king. I am a human being. That is my wealth; that is my poverty.

Before that undeception, I was like all other cultural and political liberals. I had fallen prey to what Jeane Kirkpatrick identified as the error of misplaced malleability. I thought that human institutions could be reshaped at will to fit the plans already existing inside my head. It cannot be done. Human institutions arise from human action; human action arises from human nature; and human nature is notoriously intractable. Apart from the grace of God, human nature cannot be fixed, no matter how badly it needs fixing. I finally learned that my deepest need was not more freedom. I needed the grace and guidance of God. Until I understood that, I remained shamelessly superficial.

I had to put my insipid and airy romanticism where it belonged, on the burgeoning junk pile of the fatally flawed and conclusively overthrown fantasies to which the human mind seems continually to give rise. Not romanticism but religion, not Byron but the Bible, not poetry but Paul, not Voltaire but virtue, not trends but tradition, not idealism but ideas, not genius but grace, not freedom but faith could cure me. I had to exchange Wordsworth for the Word and revolution for repentance. Thus, while some of the things I valued were useful and good, they were not properly fundamental. I had to put first things first.

The tragic vision of life humbled me. From it I learned that it was not my prerogative to invent wisdom and virtue. That had already been done. My responsibility was to listen to the One who invented them and to those whom He taught. Wisdom and virtue, I had to learn, were not born with my generation, or with Rousseau's, or Matthew Arnold's, or even Eugene McCarthy's. I had to learn in the last half of the twentieth century what was already old news even in the days of Jeremiah, the ancient prophet, who wrote,

> Stand at the crossroads, and look,
>
> and ask for the ancient paths,

where the good way lies;

and walk in it, and find rest for your souls (Jer. 6: 16).

Wisdom is found by walking the "ancient paths." Those "ancient paths" led through the wilderness, through the sea, even through the valley of the shadow of death, and not through Berkeley, not Columbia, not the Village, not Watts, not Haight-Ashbury, not Altamont, and not Woodstock.

The tragic vision of life also taught me that order is the most fundamental of all political and social needs. Because it is, I learned that the police are not pigs. They never were, and are not now, an occupying army intent upon destroying my freedom. Quite the opposite; imperfect as they sometimes are, the police are the guardians of freedom and the paid protectors of life and property. In the line of duty, some of them even died for me, and for you. The tragic vision of life taught me that you cannot reject authority — whether civil, familial, cultural or divine — and yet live in an orderly world. When you "off the pigs," (of whatever sort) you give birth to an outlaw culture, not to freedom. To live outside the rules, to live outside authority, to live without the wisdom of the ages and of God, is to court slavery and death. Enforceable law and law enforcement are requirements of the first rank. Because human nature is what it is, without great volumes of enforceable law, freedom is impossible. As Dean Clarence Manion observed in the very last line he wrote before his death in 1979, "a society that is not held together by its teaching and observance of the laws of Almighty God is unfit for human habitation and doomed to destroy itself."

When is freedom not enough? Every time truth and righteousness are at stake. In a fallen world, that is almost always. Freedom must be exercised according to the dictates of truth and virtue, never the other way round. Freedom must be limited by the demands of justice, love, and revelation. The most important consideration regarding any action is not "Is it free?" but "Is it good?" When I learned that, I stopped being a libertarian. Freedom, furthermore, is an incomplete concept. Whenever someone insists upon freedom, you must ask "Freedom to do what?" You must ask that question because freedom, like tyranny, has its unintended and unforeseen consequences, some of which are colossally vile. In passing, I name but one — abortion.

From the tragic vision of life I learned that you have to do what is right whether it suits you or not. In the sixties, we hardly did anything that did not suit us. I also learned that the enemy is not the CIA, not the FBI, and not the GOP; it's the NEA, NOW, NBC, ABC, CBS, CNN, DNC, WCC and NPR, indeed the entire grab bag of alphabetized, leftist, subverters of culture, of tradition, and of revelation. I learned that those who deprive themselves of the wisdom of Western tradition are no more free than a baby left alone by its parents to do as it pleases. I learned that politics is not about equality, but justice; that personal action is not about freedom, but righteousness; and that sex is not about pleasure, but love and privilege and posterity.

Those things and more I learned from the tragic vision of life. I commend them to you. They taught me that in many ways the sixties were twisted and misshapen.

The sixties are over, and it's a good thing. The sixties were a bad idea, if for no other reason than because the sixties had no ideas, only selfish desires hiding behind the shallow slogans and freelance nihilism emblazoned on psychedelic bumper stickers, slogans like "I dissent, therefore I am." The only things about which we were intellectually modest in the sixties were the claims of objective truth. We seemed unable to wrap our minds around even the most obvious ideas. We seemed unable to realize, for example, that you cannot raise your consciousness until you have one. The sixties were perhaps the most unconscious decade in centuries. It was a time of suffocating intellectual mediocrity, from which our nation has not yet recovered.

II. Sixties Redivivus

I can imagine a student reading these remarks and wondering, "This all might be well and good, but what does it have to do with me? I wasn't even alive in the sixties."

My answer is simply this: While the sixties are over, they are not dead, not by a long shot. They live, indeed they thrive, not only in the White House juvenocracy (which is tragic enough), but in the faculty lounges and endowed chairs of nearly every college and university in the United States. Tenured faculty members everywhere have traded their tie-dyed T-shirts and their bell bottom jeans for a cap and gown, if not a cap and bells. Those faculty members are the entrenched purveyors of an unexamined and indefensible hand-me-down Marxism, and of what Allan Bloom called nihilism with a happy ending. They have become paid agents of the very colleges and universities they once tried to burn to the ground, and not because they gave up on the dreams of the sixties. What they failed to do as protesters they have succeeded in doing as professors. Quite possibly they have done it to you, because the entire teaching profession, from the pre-kindergarten level to the post-graduate, has become a political captive of the cultural left. Like roving street gangs prowling the halls of academe, power hungry bands of leftist professors everywhere have instigated countless institutional turf wars, most of which they won. They succeeded in burying the accumulated wisdom of the ages in the name of learning; in overthrowing academic freedom in the name of tolerance; in stifling debate in the name of openness; in exalting egalitarianism above all other ideas in the name of equality; and in segregating and tribalizing the university, the nation, and the culture by gender, by age, by religion, by race, and by sexual preference, all in the name of unity. The schools and colleges that hire and then tenure them commit academic treason. I simply remind you that any intellectual community that is unwilling or unable to identify its enemies cannot defend itself. David Horowitz was exactly right: Those who cherish free institutions, and the culture of wisdom and virtue that sustains them, must stand up boldly against the barbarians already inside the gates.

Because the sixties live, this decade has become irrational, ignorant, and morally illiterate. If the sixties were majestically self-indulgent, this decade is perhaps the most self-congratulatory decade our nation has ever seen, and not because we have succeeded where all other generations have failed, but in spite of the fact that we have failed where all other American generations have succeeded — in learning to learn, in learning to work, in learning to listen, and in learning to worship. This is a decade determined to ignore, if not belittle and malign, beauty, truth and goodness, three things most moderns foolishly believe are in the eye of the beholder. Our decade is the sworn enemy of revelation and of righteousness. If the threefold mantra of the sixties was "tune in, turn on, and drop out," that of today is comprised of that earlier mantra's four silly children, four sentences that no thinking man ever permits himself or herself to utter in the face of a moral challenge, sentences like: "Everything is relative," "There is no right or wrong," "There are no absolutes," and "Who's to say?"

If you cannot now figure out why belief in those four sentences is the death of learning and of virtue, then perhaps for that very reason you can understand why I spend nearly all my time and energy as a professor and as a writer defending the ancient liturgy of the enlightened mind — that right and wrong are matters of fact, not matters of feeling; that without God there is no good; that justice is not equality; that new is not necessarily better; and that relativism, secularism, and pragmatism are not the friends of truth and goodness. The denizens of modernity probably do not realize and probably do not care that they are the befuddled and bedeviled lackeys of designer truth, of made-to-order reality, and of *ad hoc* morals making. If you follow them, you walk into the night without a light and into the woods without a compass. I want to tell you as plainly as I can that their vision of academic tolerance lacks intellectual virtue. It dilutes the high cultural inheritance of the past with the petty and insupportable leftisms of the present.

A moment ago, I imagined a student that might be wondering about the relevance of my semi-autobiographical musings. I also can imagine someone thinking that all I've done since the sixties is simply to change sides in the culture war that rages around us. To think so, however, is to assume that flower power and Christianity are morally equivalent and that hippies rank equally with saints, two false assumptions that, if you make them, show just how much a child of the sixties you really are.

I have often wondered why today feels like a sixties renaissance. I discovered the answer to that question in a college cafeteria and in conversations with some of my students' parents.

First, the parents: I have often noticed my students saying and thinking the same sorts of things their parents say and think when I speak with them. Such things happen because the acorn seldom falls far from the oak tree. That fact is more than a little significant because the parents of today's college students were probably the young men and women of the sixties. Many of the responses my students learned to give to life are responses they learned from their parents. More often than not, those responses are the stock responses of the sixties. In one way, of course, that is good; I want my students to learn all the truth they can from their parents. But insofar as my students' responses mimic the responses of the sixties, they too must learn the lessons I had to learn. They must come to understand, with all the clarity and courage they can muster, the truth of the tragic vision of life: we are, every one of us, morally defective, ethically twisted, and spiritually broken. If my students fail to come to that realization and to act upon it, both they and their world shall suffer.

Second, the cafeteria: I often notice my students echoing some of the things they hear their teachers say. When talking with students in the cafeteria, for example, I sometimes have the eerie feeling that I'm not in the cafeteria at all; I'm in a faculty meeting. I say so because I frequently hear the clear and unmistakable intonations of my colleagues' voices, but coming from other people. Sometimes I even hear my own voice. Again, that's good; I want college students to learn all the truth they can from their professors. But here's the rub: like me, many of their teachers were children of the sixties; and like me, many of those professors have made only an incomplete break with the mistakes of that era. From their other professors and from me, my students have gotten many of their ideas. Like my students themselves, their ideas have parents. Worldviews and attitudes, just like the people who have them, show marked family resemblances. For that very reason, I often want to ask my students this question: From where do you imagine your rampant relativism and your not-very-carefully-hidden contempt for authority arise? In most cases, when I consider asking such a question, I already know the answer — from the sixties and from the people (like me) who reached their emotional and intellectual maturity at that time.

III. Undeception Redivivus?

Here's my point: If you believe in the sixties, or if you believe in today, you believe a lie. As I did, you need an undeception. In order to get it, you need to go back well beyond the sixties, back to a wisdom that is older than time. You need to go back to God and to the wisdom that spoke this universe into existence. You need to go back to the God who made you and redeemed you. Real answers are found nowhere else.

It should not surprise you when I tell you that, if you do what I suggest, you shall meet energetic and determined opposition, sometimes even from those who call themselves the friends of God and of tradition. As Socrates observed long centuries ago, most men do not take kindly to the preacher of moral reform, to the pursuer of the good. There is no telling, he said in the *Gorgias*, what might happen to such a man. But do not let that stop you. Do it anyway. Do it because you need it; do it because it is right; and do it because it ought to be done. Your task will be difficult. It's always easy to be a modernist; it's always easy to go with the spirit of the age. But in the face of the world's downward slide you must be vigilant, strong, perceptive, and courageous. The world needs people like that, people unafraid to turn around and walk back into the light. Our world needs people like that more now than perhaps it ever has because everywhere you look the adversary culture of the sixties has become the dominant culture of today.

Our cultural patrimony is being embezzled from under our very noses. If you think of yourself as a Christian, or as a conservative, or as both, the view from here is haunting: We don't own the public square; we don't own the media; we don't own the arts; we don't own the sciences; we don't own the arena; we don't own the marketplace; we don't own the academy; we don't own anything. We don't even own the Church. It's all owned by the sixties.

Therefore, if, as I did, you find yourself an unwilling or unwitting child of the sixties, I invite you, I exhort you, to turn with an open mind and an open heart to the prophets and apostles in Scripture and to the great poets and sages outside Scripture. They are your only liberation from modernist thralldom and from slavery to your own fallen desires. (Did you know that you can be a slave to your own will?) Put yourself on a quest for eternal truth, and never give up until you find Him.

While you are on this quest, you must always remember that most of the powers that be are of no help to you. Those who loved the sixties own today. The left still hates America, and it still hates what made America possible: faith in God, the sacredness and inviolability of the family and of life, individual responsibility, local and limited government, and traditional morality. The leftists of today are the enemies of heartland values. They want you to keep quiet. They want you to sit meekly in the corner of the room, hands folded, and mouth shut. They want you to be nice. They want the friends of beauty, truth, and goodness to speak only when spoken to and, when they do speak, to speak only those things that offend no one. That they have offended you seems not to matter. They want you to stick to the script. They want you to keep your views to yourself and to act as if your views were not true, indeed as if there were no truth. That's what political correctness — Or should I say political cleansing? — is all about.

Consider it for just a moment: What kind of man or woman would you be if you let yourself be controlled by the empty criticisms of the rootless left, and what kind of world would you be creating for those who came after you if you neglected to restore realism to human thought and turned your back on the only thing that can make you content even in dungeons, even in slums, even in the face of death?

My desire for you is that you throw off the vestiges of leftist cultural subversion, that you make yourself a devotee and guardian of the wisdom of the ages, that you become the sworn enemy of nonsense in all its forms, and, most importantly, that you become the faithful and ardent friend of God. Then, and only then, can you be free.

What has been given you as a heritage you must now accept as your quest. If you wish to be wise, you must learn to learn from your ancestors. You must learn to make peace with the wisdom of the ages and with those who gave it, regardless of their sex, their race, or their ethnic background. You must do so because wisdom and truth are not gender based, race based, or nation based. They are thought based, and thinking is very hard work. Knowledge is not parochial. It is not the private property of any race, any gender, any era, or any ethnic group. It belongs to those determined to get it, to those who seek it resolutely, and who will not be denied, no matter how difficult the circumstances arrayed against them.

In that light, I invite you today to make one of the most important choices of your entire life: Which will you have, truth or rest?

You cannot have both.

Selected Bibliography

Altick, Richard D. *The Art of Literary Research*. New York, NY: W. W. Norton & Company, Inc., 1963.

Augustine, St. *The Confessions of Augustine in Modern English*. Edited by Sherwood E. Wirt. Grand Rapids, MI: Zondervan, 1986.

Augustine, St. *The Enchiridion on Faith, Hope, and Love*. Chicago, IL: Regnery Gateway, 1961.

Bainton, Roland. *Erasmus of Christendom*. New York, NY: Charles Scribner's Sons, 1969.

Barfield, Owen. *Speaker's Meaning*. Middletown, CT: Wesleyan University Press, 1984.

Bauman, Michael. *Roundtable: Conversations with European Theologians*. New Orleans: Insight, 2005

Bauman, Michael (Ed.). *God and Man: Perspectives on Christianity in the 20th Century*. Hillsdale: Hillsdale College Press, 1995.

Bauman, Michael (Ed.). *Man and Creation: Perspectives on Science and Theology*. Hillsdale: Hillsdale College Press, 1993.

Bauman, Michael (Ed.). *Morality and the Marketplace*. Hillsdale: Hillsdale College Press, 1994.

Bauman, Michael; David Hall; and Robert Newman (Eds.). *Evangelical Apologetics*. Camp Hill, Christian Publications, 1996.

Bauman, Michael and David Hall (Eds.). *Evangelical Hermeneutics*. Camp Hill: Christian Publications, 1995

Bauman, Michael and David Hall (Eds.). *God and Caesar*. Camp Hill: Christian Publications, 1994.

Bauman, Michael and Martin I. Klauber (Eds.). *Historians of the Christian Tradition: Their Methodology and Influence on Western Thought*. Nashville: Broadman and Holman, 1995.

Beckwith, Francis J. and Gregory Koukl. *Relativism: Feet Firmly Planted in Mid-Air*. Grand Rapids, Baker, 1998.

Boyle, Marjorie O'Rourke. *Erasmus on Language and Method in Theology*. Toronto: University of Toronto Press, 1977.

Brown, Harold O.J. *The Protest of a Troubled Protestant*. Grand Rapids, MI: Zondervan, 1971.

Brown, Harold O. J. *Heresies: The Image of Christ in the Mirror of Heresy and Orthodoxy from the Apostles to the Present*. Garden City: Doubleday, 1984.

Brunner, Emil. *Our Faith*. New York, NY: Charles Scribner's Sons, 1949.

Brunner, Emil. *The Scandal of Christianity: The Gospel as a Stumbling Block to Modern Man*. Atlanta, GA: John Knox Press, 1978.

Chesterton, G. K. *The Everlasting Man*. Garden City, NY: Image Books, 1955.

Chesterton, G. K. *Orthodoxy*. Garden City, NY: Image Books, 1959.

Erasmus, Desiderius. "The Handbook of the Militant Christian," in *The Essential Erasmus*. New York, NY: New American Library, 1964.

Erasmus, Desiderius. "The Godly Feast," in *Ten Colloquies*. Indianapolis, IN: The Bobbs-Merrill Company, Inc., 1957.

Farmer, H. H. *Things Not Seen: Studies in the Christian Interpretation of Life*. London: Nisbet & Co. Ltd., 1927/1948.

Fischer, David H. *Historian's Fallacies: Toward a Logic of History*. New York, NY: Harper Torchbooks, 1970.

Gottschalk, Louis. *Understanding History: A Primer of Historical Method*. New York, NY: Alfred A. Knopf, 1969.

Guinness, Os. *The Dust of Death: A Critique of the Establishment and the Counter-Culture and a Proposal for a Third Way*. Downers Grove, IL: InterVarsity Press, 1973.

Hirsch, E. D., Jr. *Validity in Interpretation*. New Haven, CT: Yale University Press, 1967.

Lee, Philip J. *Against the Protestant Gnostics*. New York: Oxford, 1987.

Lewis, C. S. *An Experiment in Criticism*. Cambridge: Cambridge University Press, 1961.

Lewis, C. S. "Historicism," in *Christian Reflections*. Grand Rapids, MI: Wm. B. Eerdmans Pub. Co., 1967.

Lewis, C. S. *Mere Christianity*. New York, NY: Macmillan, 1952.

Lewis, C. S. "Modern Theology and Biblical Criticism," in *Christian Reflections*. Grand Rapids, MI: Wm. B. Eerdmans Pub. Co., 1967.

Luther, Martin. "The Freedom of a Christian," in *Three Treatises*. Philadelphia, PA: Fortress Press, 1970.

Mascall, E. L. *Grace and Glory*. New York: Morehouse-Barlow Co., 1961.

Mascall, E. L. *Theology and the Gospel of Christ: An Essay in Reorientation*. London: SPCK,1977.

Noebel, David A. *Understanding the Times*. Manitou Springs: Summit, 2007.

Oddie, William. *What Will Happen to God?: Feminism and the Reconstruction of Christian Belief*. San Francisco: Ignatius Press, 1988.

Pope, Alexander. "An Essay on Criticism," in *Poetry and Prose of Alexander Pope*. Edited by Aubrey Williams. Boston, MA: Houghton-Mifflin Company, 1969.

Schaff, Philip. "What is Church History?" in *Reformed and Catholic: Selected Historical and Theological Writings of Philip Schaff*. Edited by Charles Yrigoyan and George M. Bricker. Pittsburgh, PA: Pickwick Press, 1979.

Thielicke, Helmut. *A Little Exercise for Young Theologians*. Grand Rapids, MI: Wm. B. Eerdmans Pub. Co., 1962.

Thielicke, Helmut. *How Modern Should Theology Be?* Philadelphia, PA: Fortress Press, 1969.

Trueblood, Elton. *The Humor of Christ*. New York, NY: Harper & Row, 1964.

Wells, David F. *No Place for Truth, or Whatever Happened to Evangelical Theology?* Grand Rapids: Wm. B. Eerdmans, 1993.

Williams, Michael. *Far as the Curse is Found: The Covenant Story of Redemption*. Phillipsburg: Presbyterian and Reformed, 2005.

Wright, N. T. *The Resurrection of the Son of God*. Minneapolis: Fortress, 2003